I can tell the NAME OF AN ANCIENT AUTHOR, who pretends to show the WAY, how a man may come to walk about INVISIBLE, and I can tell the NAME OF ANOTHER ANCIENT AUTHOR, who pretends to EXPLODE that way. But I will not speak too plainly LEST I should unawares POISON some of my READERS. This much I will say; The notion of procuring INVISIBILITY, by any NATURAL EXPEDIENT yet known is I BELIEVE a meer PLINYISM; How far it may be obtained by MAGICAL SACRAMENT is best known to the DANGEROUS KNAVES that have try'd it.

— Cotton Mather, *The Wonders of the Invisible World* (1693)

Published by Semiotext(e)
PO BOX 629, South Pasadena, CA 91031
www.semiotexte.com

"Special thanks to Chris Kraus who saw the book before I did."
— David Rattray, 1992

Thanks to David Abel, Mary Geis, Georges Rivard and Cayal Unger.

Cover Photograph: Ira Cohen
© 1987 Ira Cohen Archives, LLC

Design: Hedi El Kholti
ISBN: 978-1-63590-072-9

Distributed by The MIT Press, Cambridge, Mass. and London, England
Printed in the United States of America

How I Became One of the Invisible

David Rattray

Edited by Chris Kraus

Expanded and with an Introduction by Robert Dewhurst
Afterword by Rachel Kushner

semiotext(e)

Contents

Introduction by Robert Dewhurst

A Philosophy of Surrender

"Love sees what is invisible."
—Simone Weil

What does it mean to *become invisible*? David Rattray, little known outside the poetic enclave of New York's Lower East Side when he died in 1993, might have quoted Novalis: "Poetry is the truly absolute real . . . All that is visible clings to the invisible."[1] An alchemy of life writing, poetics, scholarship, and short fiction, *How I Became One of the Invisible* is a sourcebook for Rattray's occult sense of poetry as nothing less than the catalyst or crucible of an otherwise imperceptible reality. *The world has been under an evil spell for centuries. Reality, I assured Van, had nothing to do with the real world.* Gliding from ancient arcana through the American epoch of "hydrogen doom" and back, *Invisible* traces Rattray's lifetime of wanderings into uncharted cultural waters in answer to poetry's siren song to transact with the unseen, its "call to a new, different way of seeing."[2] *Something is happening, Van says. Just tune in on it, you'll pick up.* This book is, as Jim Fletcher wrote of its first edition in 1992, "a pilgrimage to unlit flows."[3]

---

1. Novalis, "On Goethe," in *Philosophical Writings*, ed. and trans. Margaret Mahony Stoljar (Albany, NY: State University of New York Press, 1997), 117–18.
2. Unless otherwise noted, all quotations by David Rattray are cited from *How I Became One of the Invisible*.
3. "How I Became One of the Invisible," MIT Press (website), https://mitpress.mit.edu/books/how-i-became-one-invisible.

Born February 17, 1936, David Greig Rattray grew up in East Hampton, Long Island, where the year before his parents had purchased the local newspaper. "My father was a newspaperman," he later wrote plainly of his father, Arnold Elsmore Rattray, an Oakland native who served in France (during World War I) and Russia (for Hoover's American Relief Administration) before settling in East Hampton in 1925.[4] Rattray's mother, Jeannette Edwards Rattray, belonged to one of East Hampton's oldest families, with ancestry in the village dating back to 1650. In addition to publishing the *East Hampton Star* (which she helmed after Arnold died in '54), Jeannette Rattray wrote several volumes of Long Island history—books about shipwrecks and whaling and historic homes, with titles like *"Whale Off!": The Story of American Shore Whaling* (coauthored with her father, himself a shore whaler) and *Up and Down Main Street: An Informal History of East Hampton and Its Old Houses.*[5] Jeannette and her mother were members of the Ramblers, an East Hampton women's study group founded at the turn of the century. ("Whole winters were devoted to the history, people, literature, and physical conditions of any country you might name," recalled the club's oldest living member in 1985.)[6] When she died in 1974, an obituary in the *New York Times* described Jeannette Rattray as "A person of reginal bearing, proper manners and infinite curiosity . . . one of the best known and best informed women of [East Hampton], its unquestioned grande dame."[7] Though his own infinite curiosity would at times carry her youngest child far

4. "Arnold E. Rattray, Newspaper Editor," *Brooklyn Daily Eagle*, July 12, 1954.
5. "Jeanneatte Rattray, 80, Publisher of *East Hampton Star*, Is Dead," *New York Times*, May 21, 1974.
6. Ann Dodds Costello, *Smart Women: The Search for America's Historic All-Women Study Clubs* (self-pub., Lulu, 2015), EPUB, chap. 6.
7. "Jeannette Rattray."

away from East Hampton (and its middle-class mores), the village always remained a self-mythic touchstone for David: a place of deep history and family ties, a "country of the mind only," as he writes here in "The Darkened Chamber."

"My contemporaries in East Hampton call me Moon," Rattray relates in "The Angel," an epithet relating to the signal story of his childhood. "The nickname goes back to a day in 1944 when I electrified the schoolyard by pointing at the moon in the mid-afternoon sky and shrieking 'Moon! Moon!' I induced a crowd of other children to scream and point the same way. We pranced, screeching at the top of our lungs, back into the schoolhouse. This went on for weeks. Many who saw it never forgot." This event was somehow premonitory; shortly thereafter, he says, he started writing. An older Rattray would come to regard the moon as "a hieroglyph of exile," an emblem of wanderers, like himself, "who gyrated through both mundane and mystic spheres," were "citizens of a secret utopia." But other than this moment of lunar lunacy, Rattray's youth in East Hampton swung decidedly to the mundane end of the pendulum. He studied the piano from age six, specializing in classical and boogie-woogie, and gave regular recitals at the local Guild Hall. He finished a year early at East Hampton High School, graduating as valedictorian in 1953 and matriculating to Dartmouth College.[8]

In 1955, as a sophomore at Dartmouth, Rattray was a finalist in Mount Holyoke's Glascock Poetry Contest, a competition judged that year by Marianne Moore, John Ciardi, and Wallace Fowlie. A startling clipping from the *Christian Science Monitor* pictures the young Rattray—strait-laced in a suit and tie, typescript in hand, the very picture of a Rilkean "young poet"—alongside fellow finalist

8. "Senior Honor Students Named," *East Hampton Star*, May 14, 1953.

Sylvia Plath at the contest reading. Below their photographs, the article profiles Rattray thusly: "David Rattray, a competing Dartmouth sophomore from East Hampton, Long Island, attributes his love of writing to the fact 'I was brought up among books.' His father was a newspaper editor, his mother has written several books. 'I read a lot of poetry and I like to translate it.' He is majoring in Greek and says Homer is his favorite poet."[9] The contest was also covered nationally in the girls' lifestyle magazine *Mademoiselle*. Rattray told their reporter that he chose to live in "Wigwam," a "barracks-like" Dartmouth dormitory for "married students and social outcasts," because "a serious interest in writing is just not understood" on campus; after graduating, he planned "to live and write in Europe."[10] *Mademoiselle* also offers this image of the event, likely Rattray's first real reading, attended by some two hundred people: "[The finalists] read their work—some shyly, some hopefully, some dramatically—in an oak-paneled room crammed with Mount Holyoke students. There were girls jammed on the window seats,

---

9. Mary Handy, "'. . . Focus for Creative Work in College': Judges Hear Glascock Poetry Contestants," *Christian Science Monitor*, April 18, 1955.

10. Cris Christiaen, "Poet on College Time," *Mademoiselle* 41, no. 8 (August 1955): 49 and 52. Readers may recall that Plath briefly worked as a guest managing editor at *Mademoiselle* in the summer of 1953 (after winning the magazine's annual fiction contest the previous year), which experience inspired her novel *The Bell Jar*.

The very same weekend as the Glascock reading, Rattray penned a letter to school newspaper the *Dartmouth*, defending Wigwam, which was being eyed for demolition, and its misfit residents: "We have a community spirit—a natural one, that does not depend on pep rallies, brass bands, dormitory government, communal petting parties, the big ball, etc. We have no Dartmouth spirit, except insomuch as we like certain professors and certain courses, have a few student and faculty friends, appreciate the Library, and love the beautiful countryside around Hanover. The atmosphere of free thinking and free criticism pervades Wigwam, and there is unquestionably more intellectual ferment (which the administration says it wants to foster) here than in the dorms and fraternity houses." "Community Spirit," the *Dartmouth*, April 18, 1955.

girls on the floor, knitting quietly as they listened. There were girls taking notes and girls who had brought their dates. The room was hushed like a theater when the lights suddenly dim. From the auditorium below floated an occasional echo from the sound track of the *Glenn Miller Story*."[11] Plath, of course, won the contest.[12] But Rattray must have been absorbed by the judges' forum on translation the following morning. Fowlie's *Modern French Poets* anthology was published that year, featuring selections by Jean Cocteau, André Breton, and Paul Éluard—names which flicker like starlight in *Invisible*. A piece of Moore's advice also appears to have been providential for Rattray: before the reading, she counseled the finalists to "do something else for a living—something that doesn't grate on your nerves too much."[13]

Rattray's "Wigwam" roommate was Jerry Craddock, a studious companion from the steel-mill town of Pueblo, Colorado. "At Dartmouth we led a rather monkish existence, no girls, no frat parties, no skiing, but attended rather a lot of high-brow gatherings, concerts and poetry readings," Craddock recalls today. "Our main shared enthusiasm was Classical Greek, we were probably the only two Classics majors at the time. David had two essential interests, music and poetry, which his tone-deaf and prosaic roommate could only admire. He was an accomplished pianist and spent no end of

---

11. Christiaen, "Poet on College Time." The attendance figure of "about two hundred" is reported in Paul Alexander's Plath biography, *Rough Magic: A Biography of Sylvia Path* (Cambridge, MA: Da Capo Press, 2003), 155.
12. Plath shared the 1955 Glascock Poetry Prize with cowinner William Key Whitman, "a Wesleyan junior who eventually published a chapbook called *The Dancing Galactic Bear* but whose career as a poet did not get very far." Vivian R. Pollak, "Moore, Plath, Hughes, and 'The Literary Life,'" in *Our Emily Dickinsons: American Women Poets and the Intimacies of Difference* (Philadelphia: University of Pennsylvania Press, 2017), 156.
13. Alexander, *Rough Magic*, 155.

time practicing. . . . He was intensely interested in avant-garde poetry which pretty much went over my head, but I found his own poems quite comprehensible and moving."[14] The packet of poems the nineteen-year-old Rattray entered in the Glascock contest helps show what Craddock means. Wrought and pastoral, the poems evince Rattray's dueling interests in antiquity and modernism—one is a reverie on a Greek vase, another a translation of Rimbaud—and fail to set the world on fire. "Well observed," Moore wrote in a lukewarm judge's note, "but the manner is more rigid than the content seems to require."[15]

Over Christmas break during his senior year at Dartmouth, Rattray traveled to Washington, DC, where he visited Ezra Pound at St. Elizabeth's Hospital. Rattray found Pound in a querulous "Economic Mood," surrounded by a small cast of muses and sycophants, including painter Sheri Martinelli and publisher David Horton. On returning to Hanover, he wrote a narrative of his "Visit to St. Elizabeth's" and quietly filed it at the school library; the following summer, M. L. Rosenthal discovered it there and asked to publish it in the *Nation*, where it appeared in November 1957 under the title "Weekend with Ezra Pound."[16] A remarkable piece of writing by an undergraduate, Rattray's article paints an unvarnished portrait of Pound's makeshift literary salon (or "Ezuversity") at the federal mental hospital, while exercising judicious restraint. But for a few hints of Rattray's private perspective on the proceedings, readers are left to make their own judgments as Pound serves hot tea

---

14. Jerry Craddock, email to author, February 26, 2019.
15. Marianne Moore to Joseph Bottkol, April 18, 1955, Kathryn Irene Glascock Poetry Prize Records, Mount Holyoke College Archives and Special Collections, South Hadley, MA. Rattray's poems for the contest are archived in this collection.
16. This story about Rosenthal is related in "Local Writer in 'Nation,'" *East Hampton Star*, November 21, 1957.

in a recycled peanut-butter jar and urges his Ivy League caller to research twelfth-century Jewish "usurers."[17] Rattray neither arraigns nor apologizes for Pound, but simply bears witness to Pound and his mise en scène at the hospital, finding the whole thing a bit more like the Mad Hatter's tea party from *Alice in Wonderland* than anything else.[18]

"Weekend with Ezra Pound" had a ripple effect beyond what Rattray imagined. Richard Aldington read it in Sury-en-Vaux, France, and then sent it to Hilda Doolittle in Küsnacht, Switzerland. H.D. read and reread "Weekend" with rapt interest. The article unlocked something for her and directly inspired *End to Torment,* her memoir of Pound. "This 'Weekend with Ezra Pound' seems to me the first human personal presentation of Ezra that I have seen," she writes in that book's first pages; after reading it, "I laughed about Ezra, for the first time in the 12 years of his confinement."[19] Aldington agreed, writing her that "It is such a welcome change to have [Pound] reported as a human being, and not as a journalist's abstraction or political 'cause.'"[20] Throughout *End to*

---

17. For a biography of Pound's years at St. Elizabeth's and his "Ezuversity," Pound's own term for the court he held there, see Daniel Swift, *The Bughouse: The Poetry, Politics, and Madness of Ezra Pound* (New York: Farrar, Straus & Giroux, 2017).

18. This comparison to *Alice in Wonderland* is suggested by H.D. scholar Natalie Mahaffey, who writes of "Weekend with Ezra Pound": "At times, the narration is rather surreal, as if we are not reading of an actual encounter that took place between a scholar and a poet, but instead are reading about warped fictional characters who are pretending to live some semblance of normalcy in a world gone mad. . . . The sporadic madness of the scenes illustrated by Rattray can, perhaps, bring the Mad Hatter's tea party from *Alice in Wonderland* to mind." "Coming Down Out of the Tree: Exploring Memory and Identity in H.D.'s *End to Torment*" (master's thesis, Clemson University, 2010), 37–38, https://tigerprints.clemson.edu/all_theses/1008.

19. H.D., *End to Torment: A Memoir of Ezra Pound* (New York: New Directions, 1979), 19 and 34.

20. Ibid., 9.

Torment, the term "Weekend" (once, "my much-quoted 'Weekend'") is a magic word, an abracadabric portal to distant and vexed memories.[21] In 1959, Rattray's Pound portrait reached an even wider audience when it was reprinted in the critical compendium *A Casebook on Ezra Pound*. It is reprinted for the first time since then in the selection of newly collected texts here.

Initially, Rattray planned a two-year tour in the Navy following college, but after graduating from Dartmouth with numerous accolades—a Senior Fellowship, the Atherton Greek Prize, the Class of 1846 Latin Prize, the Grimes English Prize, the Edwin R. Perkins Literature Prize—he decided to stay the scholarly course.[22] From 1957–59, Rattray lived in France on a pair of consecutive Fulbright Fellowships at the University of Toulouse and the Sorbonne. In Paris, he spent time with his sister Mary (who had lived there since the late forties) while working at the Bibliothèque Nationale and absorbing the "received classics," as he later put it. Meanwhile he sharpened his travel-writing skills as a foreign correspondent for the family paper, dispatching about twenty perspicuous "Letters" from abroad for the *East Hampton Star* in the spring of '59 (highlights included reviews of the exhibition *Jackson Pollock and the New American Painting* at

---

21. Ibid., 42.
22. A note in Rattray's records from the Glascock competition reveals these "Future plans": "Writing—yes[.] Military—2 yrs away as enlisted man after graduation." Kathryn Irene Glascock Poetry Prize Records, Mount Holyoke College Archives and Special Collections, South Hadley, MA. During his first semester at Dartmouth, the *East Hampton Star* had reported Rattray's acceptance into the Naval Reserve Officers' Training program: see "Local News," October 1, 1953. For announcements of Rattray's undergraduate awards, see two additional *Star* articles: "E. H. Student Wins Honors," October 18, 1956; and "Dartmouth Graduate Will Have Year's Study Abroad," June 20, 1957. The subject of Rattray's Senior Fellowship at Dartmouth was "The Influence of Provençal Poetry on French Literature": see "Senior Wins Fulbright Prize; David Rattray Goes to France," the *Dartmouth*, March 22, 1957.

the Musee National d'Art Moderne, and of a Chopin workshop given by pianist Alfred Cortot.)[23] After passing the university's rigorous examinations that summer, Rattray left the Sorbonne with a Diplôme des Études Supérieures des Langues Classiques, a master's-level degree in classical languages.[24] A week after retuning to East Hampton in September, he decamped to Cambridge, Massachusetts, where he spent the next year pursuing a second master's degree—in comparative literature at Harvard University. Rattray's Harvard thesis was on "novelistic time" in Proust's *La Prisonnière*, composed in French.[25] As he was completing it in April 1960, Archibald MacLeish awarded him the Harvard Monthly Prize, given annually to "that student in the most advanced course in English composition who shows the greatest literary promise."[26]

---

23. Rattray's columns for the *East Hampton Star* may be found in the complete archives of the *Star*, digitized and searchable through the New York State Historic Newspapers project: http://nyshistoricnewspapers.org/lccn/sn83030960. For the Pollock column, see "Letter from France," February 19, 1959; for the Cortot column, see "Letter from France," April 30, 1959. Rattray mentions his work at the Bibliothèque Nationale in some of these columns: see, for example, "Letter from France," March 26, 1959. Rattray's sister Mary filed similar columns for the *Star* during this period.

24. Rattray wrote an entire column for the *East Hampton Star* (see previous note) about the rigor of the Sorbonne *diplôme* examinations and the dramatic public posting of students' scores: "Now that most of the crowd had managed to look at the posters," he wrote of the day scores were posted in the Sorbonne's Grande Galerie des Lettres, an annual rite, "the long gallery became a vale of tears, and a procession of unfortunates went away sobbing on the shoulders of best friends, fiancés, husbands and wives. The short space at the head of the gallery was occupied by the 'happy few,' chattering, embracing one another, talking about their summer vacation, etc. . . . I don't know if my reader can imagine the atmosphere of it from such a distance." See "Letter from France," June 11, 1959.

25. Rattray's hundred-page Harvard thesis is extant on microfilm at the Dartmouth College library. Curiously, the *Harvard Alumni Directory* records Rattray's enrollment in the Graduate School of Arts and Sciences in 1959–60 and 1964–65, but has no record of him receiving a graduate degree there.

26. "Local News," *East Hampton Star*, April 28, 1960.

At twenty-four, Rattray was well on his way toward a decorous life in academe, but that spring he would undergo an Ovidian metamorphosis.[27] Returning to Dartmouth for a "reading of works by Rilke and John Wieners" convened by Jack Hirschman, Rattray rekindled his friendship with poet Alden Van Buskirk and, in a lightning strike of illumination, discovered America's burgeoning poetic underground. A two-year appointee at Dartmouth who would later abandon academe to become an antiwar activist, street poet, and "Kabbala surrealist" on the West Coast, Hirschman was already an iconoclast.[28] "The Beats came to Dartmouth via Jack Hirschman," Rattray's friend Peter Kushner has recalled. "When Jack came to Dartmouth, the first thing he did was have a poetry reading. Jack read from Mayakovsky, he read one of his own poems, and then he read 'Howl,' the whole thing with the footnote. The college had never heard anything like this."[29] Hirschman's pairing of Rilke with Wieners's *The Hotel Wentley Poems* was equally potent. Only twenty-four when he had written the slim suite of heroin use and heartbreak two years earlier, Wieners was one of the youngest poets in the paradigm-shifting *New American Poetry* anthology that had just been published by Grove, and he was an outlier in that

---

27. Arnon Vered, a friend of Rattray's, recalls that "David once told me that reading Ovid's *Metamorphoses* was a turning point in his own metamorphosis." Email to author, March 6, 2019.
28. Hirschman left academia in 1966, when he was fired from an assistant professorship at the University of California, Los Angeles, for voicing his opposition, on campus and in local media, to the Vietnam War. For detailed biographies of Hirschman, see Marco Nieli, "Interview with Jack Hirschman," *Left Curve*, no. 25 (March 31, 2001): 33; and Jack Hirschman and Matt Gonzalez, "Jack Hirschman, Poet Laureate," *The Matt Gonzalez Reader* (blog), June 15, 2009, https://the mattgonzalezreader.wordpress.com/2009/06/15/chorosho. For Hirschman's poetics of "Kabbala surrealism," see his pamphlet *K. s.* (Venice, CA: Beyond Baroque Foundation, 1973).
29. Garrett Caples, "'Death Will Be My Final Lover': The Life of Alden Van Buskirk," in *Retrievals* (Seattle: Wave Books, 2014), 181.

book's constellation of emergent new poetries—less beatific bard than enigmatic *poète maudit*. ("Poems . . . are my salvation alone," Wieners had written in a poetics statement in the back of the anthology, before going invisible for a couple of years;[30] while Hirschman was teaching his poems to precocious undergrads at Dartmouth, Wieners himself was interned at a state mental asylum in Massachusetts, having mainlined Rimbaud's directives to "derange the senses" and "change life.")[31] This spring of intense reading was revelatory for Rattray, fusing his friendship with "Van" and opening his eyes to new literary vistas, from Wieners and the Beats backward to Malcolm Lowry, Jean Genet and, most crucially, Antonin Artaud. As Rattray would later say, "We'd never heard of these things. We got our initiation from Jack Hirschman . . . It was like living in the Book of Revelations."

Alden Van Buskirk was a middle-class kid from Rutland, Vermont. His ancestry was Danish, English, and Irish, though he leaned in to black subculture, à la Norman Mailer's "white negro," so much he could be mistaken for black—as he was by Kenneth Rexroth in the 1971 study *American Poetry in the Twentieth Century*.[32] Van's kindred spirit on the Dartmouth ski team was John Ceely, a fellow poet. In a eulogy later published in the Mexico City small magazine *El Corno Emplumado*, Ceely reminisced that at

---

30. John Wieners, "From a Journal," in *The New American Poetry*, ed. Donald Allen (New York: Grove Press, 1960), 425.
31. See Arthur Rimbaud, *Rimbaud: Complete Works, Selected Letters*, trans. Wallace Fowlie, rev. Seth Whidden (Chicago: University of Chicago Press, 2005), 376–77 and 281–82, as well as Whidden's foreword, xv and xxii.
32. Caples, "'Death Will Be My Final Lover,'" 178–80. For the mention of Van Buskirk by Rexroth, see *American Poetry in the Twentieth Century* (New York: Herder and Herder, 1971), 159. Rexroth includes Van Buskirk in a list of "young Black poets" whom he admires, naming him alongside the likes of Nikki Giovanni and Sun Ra.

Dartmouth Van "did about everything: English Lit., piano jazz combo, ski team, wrote much poetry which he threw away, got drunk." He was a showboat of a skier ("Team resented him because he'd go for broke & personal victory") and a jazz-piano prodigy.[33] Two years younger than Rattray, Van was David's more temerarious counterpart, but their friendship was mutually formative. Garrett Caples, in a thoughtful essay on Van Buskirk collected in his book *Retrievals*, writes that "The impact of [Van Buskirk's] encounters with Rattray and Hirschman can't be overestimated, as they put Van in touch with both the early European avant-garde and the most contemporary American poetry of the period." Incidentally, John Wieners became Van's favorite poet and a plaintive point of connection between him and Rattray—witness the scene in "Van" of David reading *Hotel Wentley* bedside after Van's emergency splenectomy.[34]

Rattray and Van Buskirk lingered on in Hanover that summer. In September they parted ways, Van headed to St. Louis on a scholarship for a PhD program at Washington University, and Rattray to Yaddo for two months of writing. Shortly after arriving in St. Louis, Van Buskirk would finally receive a diagnosis for the rare blood disorder that had afflicted him since his first winter in Hanover: paroxysmal nocturnal hemoglobinuria, then a fatal prognosis (today, this one-in-a-million disease is only curable by bone-marrow transplant). Understandably, the news rearranged his priorities. Ceely reports that Van "dropt out [of graduate school] after 2 months to move in with an underground group presided over by Johnny," the charismatic hustler portrayed in this book's

33. John Ceely, "A Personal View of Alden," *El Corno Emplumado*, no. 20 (October 1966): 58.
34. Caples, "'Death Will Be My Final Lover,'" 182.

"Harvest."[35] Johnny Sherrill, Caples reflects, "essentially became a Neal Cassady–like figure to Van's group of friends" in St. Louis, whose history Caples has usefully recorded.[36]

Meanwhile, at Yaddo, Rattray worked that fall on what he would later dismiss as "a series of long poems that were as bad as they were ambitious." One of these may have been "The White Poem," a necrophilic incantation that he would print privately as a chapbook in 1969. Beginning with a page-long epigraph from an account by Laurens van der Post, quoted in Jung's *Psychology and Religion*, of a Swazi witchcraft rite involving the ritualistic sacrifice of a young boy, "The White Poem" reads, in retrospect, as an oblique testimony to Van Buskirk's illness and imminent transubstantiation. Its language is wounded, primal:

> *Hurt child, you*
> *bleated in delirium, I*
> *heard deeper growls, waited for the*
> *roar.   Now*
> *broken child, in your*
> *unbroken cooing I*
> *hear the thunder rolling:*
>
> *thunder, voice of the dove.*[37]

In the Swazi rite, a tribal boy's flesh is "whitened" over the course of nine months as he is kept caged in a riverbed, before he is killed,

---

35. Ceely, "A Personal View of Alden," 59.
36. Caples, "'Death Will Be My Final Lover,'" 183.
37. David Rattray, *The White Poem* (self-pub., 1969), n.p. It is not clear how many copies of *The White Poem* were printed; the edition contains no publication

dismembered, and cooked; the tribe inhales the steam of his stewed facial appendages to strengthen its weak chief, while with the rest of his body the witchdoctor makes "a kind of bread for doctoring the tribe's crops."[38] "The White Poem" climaxes in a derivative scene of cannibalism, in which a pallid body is sacrificed and then "swallowed up and vomited . . . shit out and crammed in again . . . spit up and drunk again."[39] Rife with images of blood—hemorrhages, transfusions, clots—the poem exists in a wholly different dimension than Rattray's Glascock manuscripts of five years earlier, and feels like a purification ritual of its own: an act of white magic designed, like alchemy, to "redeem sick matter." Mysteriously, Rattray attributes the epigraph about the Swazi rite to *National Geographic* magazine, although it never appeared there. Below the passage in *Psychology and Religion*, Jung offers this commentary: "Laurens van der Post thinks that the purpose of the 'whitening' was to assimilate the mana of the white man, who has the political power. I agree with this view, and would add that painting with white clay often signifies transformation into ancestral spirits, in the same way as the neophytes are made invisible in the Nandi territory, in Kenya, where

information save Rattray's name. As for its date of composition, Rattray inscribed a copy of *The White Poem* given to Gerrit Lansing in 1981 with the date "1961," while he inscribed another copy, given to David Abel in 1991, with the statement "This 'White Poem' was written in the Fall of 1960 and printed in this present form in 1969." As this essay was going to press, I learned that Lansing's copy contains an additional inscription, in the place of a subtitle: "(Lament for Alden Van Buskirk)." Also of interest, a Rattray poem titled "from section before white poem" appeared in *Intrepid* magazine in March 1964, suggesting that the chapbook may have been excerpted from a longer work.

38. C. G. Jung, "Transformation Symbolism in the Mass," in *The Collected Works of C. G. Jung*, ed. William McGuire, vol. 11, *Psychology and Religion: West and East*, trans. R. F. C. Hull (Princeton, NJ: Princeton University Press, 1969), 243.

39. Rattray, *The White Poem*.

they walk about in portable, cone-shaped grass huts and demonstrate their invisibility to everyone."[40]

The summer of 1961 saw Rattray and Van Buskirk undertake the Mexican misadventure that Rattray would revisit decades later in *Invisible*'s elegiac early chapters "Van" and "The Angel." Late that spring, the pair rendezvoused in St. Louis and then headed for the southern border. Depositing Van's Buick in El Paso, they crossed into Mexico and caught a bus from Juarez to Oaxaca, and then another to the Pacific coast. When the two washed up in Puerto Angel in early July, blear-eyed from amphetamine and looking like a couple of "escapees from a reform school," they were following in the footsteps of Artaud and also enacting a kind of storybook fantasy of American letters—an adventure plot with a taproot reaching from Melville and Thoreau right up to Charles Olson, Jack Kerouac, and William Burroughs. "Every walk is a sort of crusade," Thoreau wrote in 1851, sketching the narrative arc of this myth:

> We go eastward to realize history and study the works of art and literature, retracing the steps of the race; we go westward as into the future, with a spirit of enterprise and adventure. The Atlantic is a Lethean stream, in our passage over which we have had an opportunity to forget the Old World and its institutions. If we do not succeed this time, there is perhaps one more chance for the race left before it arrives on the banks of the Styx; and that is in the Lethe of the Pacific, which is three times as wide.[41]

---

40. Jung, "Transformation Symbolism," 243.
41. Henry David Thoreau, *Walking* (Bedford, MA: Applewood Books, 1992), 6 and 22–23.

A century later, Olson would trumpet the same escapist allure of the Pacific Ocean in his monograph on *Moby-Dick*: "The Pacific is, for an American, the Plains repeated, a 20th century Great West."[42] This is the mythos Van is tapped into when he tells David, "coming here means arriving at the edge of America, the jumping-off place." But Rattray recognizes their trip as a kind of shared hallucination, while it is happening, undercutting the entire escapade as "a cliché in the collective fantasy life of the imperialist nation we hail from." While he indulges the era's already-worn trope of going "on the road," his self-reflexivity lends these stories a rare double vision, elevating them to a critical vantage that hovers over the American mythos of crossing the frontier to find an outside to the operations of the state or capital in an exotic locale. A cold sweat breaks in "The Angel" as Rattray realizes there *is* no outside, the Cold War shining on in the steady light of Sputnik overhead.

After wearing out their welcome in Oaxaca (and a scrapped attempt to hijack a cache of marijuana en route home), Rattray and Van Buskirk fled to San Francisco. Rattray briefly "settled in a Chinese boarding house on the edge of North Beach," inhabiting an adjacent urban underground to the one about which Wieners's *Hotel Wentley* had waxed lyrical. But as Van's health deteriorated, tensions between them rose and reached a breaking point. By late August Rattray had retreated to St. Louis, taking up momentarily with Johnny Sherrill and the rest of Van's crew there. *Invisible*'s "Harvest" offers an indelible snapshot of that scene. From St. Louis, Rattray hitchhiked to New York, where he connected with Martha Muhs, Van's girlfriend from St. Louis. Of the friction between David and

42. Charles Olson, "Call Me Ishmael," in *Collected Prose*, ed. Donald Allen and Benjamin Friedlander (Berkeley: University of California Press, 1997), 101.

Van in San Francisco, Muhs told Garrett Caples this: "Dave was a mentor, definitely, to Alden, but—not but, and, Dave was in love with him. Dave became a bit too much *there* when they were living together in San Francisco. It was overwhelming and Alden said, 'I can't do this; you're gonna have to go.' I met [Rattray] for the first time when he came back to New York and there was no question he was tormented."[43] David and Van corresponded throughout the fall of 1961—one peak was a long September letter from Van, written in the angelic afterglow of a psychedelic experience with morning glory seeds—as Van and Ceely made promises to rejoin Rattray and Muhs on the East Coast. "We were going to share a place in Hoboken. [Van] had heard from Dave Haselwood of Auerhahn Press that John Wieners was in New York, writing great things," Rattray writes at the close of "Van." But the two wouldn't see each other again. Alden Van Buskirk died on December 11, 1961, at the age of twenty-three.

Absent Van, Rattray stayed on in New York, loyal to the vision they had loosely sketched out. He rented an apartment at Twelfth Street and Avenue A on Manhattan's Lower East Side. Not yet rebranded the "East Village," and a half decade before the St. Mark's Poetry Project would open its doors there, at the time the Lower East Side was an outer edge of its own—an immigrant neighborhood with a "tradition of working-class radicalism and resistance" that was beginning to attract the "more adventurous or desperate" of the city's bohemians. Daniel Kane has written of the "frontier mentality" that characterized poets' initial migration into the neighborhood, who saw it as "a kind of no-man's land ready to be conquered."[44] Some of the newcomers to the Lower East Side even dressed like cowboys,

43. Caples, "'Death Will Be My Final Lover,'" 189.
44. Daniel Kane, *All Poets Welcome: The Lower East Side Poetry Scene in the 1960s* (Berkeley: University of California Press, 2003), 3, 18, and 17.

though Rattray's own uniform was more West Coast jazz than Wild West. In an interview with Ken Jordan three decades later, published when *Invisible* was released, he painted a vivid self-portrait: "I had this black suit and black wrap-around sunglasses, which I wore at all times. The breast pocket of the black suit was for my kit, which held all my drug paraphernalia . . . I was really quite a card, moving from one club to another listening to jazz, which was because of Van, who opened my ears to jazz. I embraced that romantic vision whole-heartedly." Besides jazz clubs like the 5 Spot, poetry cafés like Les Deux Mégots, and monthly rents as low as $25, Kane notes that the Lower East Side offered artists a certain invisibility compared to the more exposed scene in the West Village: "There artists temporarily avoided larger media scrutiny by keeping their 'scene' politically insular and socially marginal through their absence in community, academic, artistic, and literary establishment circles."[45] Rattray would live in this subcultural slice of Manhattan for the rest of his life, at some point moving within two blocks of his first apartment to a place on the west side of Avenue A, just below Eleventh Street.

Over the course of 1962–63, Rattray embarked on his first major work, translating the writings of Artaud for an anthology planned by City Lights. The assignment came from Jack Hirschman, the book's editor, and was needed on short notice. Twenty years later Rattray would describe his amphetamine-fueled working process in his "Talk on Translating Artaud," a lecture originally written and delivered for Chris Kraus's 1986 short film *Foolproof Illusion*. Rattray's translator's note offers an exemplary model for literary scholarship in any time: "I wanted to turn my friends on to Artaud and pass a message that had relevance to our

---

45. Ibid., 3.

lives. That's why I did it. Not to get a grant, or be hired by an English department." City Lights's *Artaud Anthology* appeared in 1965. Although fragments of Artaud's work had been trickling into American small magazines like *Origin* and the *Black Mountain Review* for years, the 250-page book was the first of its kind and an inflection point in Artaud's reception by the American postwar poetic avant-garde; scholar Stephen Barber has called the anthology "one of the most influential books published by City Lights Books in the 1960s."[46] Publisher Lawrence Ferlinghetti was thrilled by Rattray's renderings: "Reading the Artaud proofs, I realize what a big job of translation you did. The book is over half yours! Extraordinary + beautiful translations too," he wrote Rattray from Paris.[47] But the book had a cool reception among Artaud's circle in France, and Rattray would come to distance himself from it. In 1966, he wrote a letter to the editor of *Le Monde* explaining that his translations were never reviewed by Gallimard's Artaud specialist, as he had been promised, and that some were capriciously changed after he delivered them. The furor, however, had less to do with the book's translations than with the Beats's perceived appropriation of Artaud as an icon of insanity and transgression. "The book presents Artaud as drug obsessed, a sexually ambiguous crazy person and a precursor of 'pop art' whose oeuvre incarnates the obsessions of a certain America," Rattray fumed, siding with the French. "Those responsible for the anthology wanted to see Artaud as a 'nonconformist' in their vein: in no way did they attempt to uncover the

46. Quoted in "Artaud in performance: dissident surrealism and the postwar American literary avant-garde," by Joanna Pawlik, *Papers of Surrealism*, no. 8 (2010): 15. See Pawlik's article for a detailed reception history of Artaud within the New American Poetry.
47. Lawrence Ferlinghetti to David Rattray, May 1, 1965, David Rattray Collection, East Hampton Public Library, New York.

deep movement of an oeuvre that has nothing to do with what is commonly referred to as revolt."[48] Controversy aside, the *Artaud Anthology* established Rattray's reputation as a translator, and led to other projects (for one, Gérard Chaliand's *Armed Struggle in Africa*, which he would translate for Monthly Review Press in 1969). The anthology is in print to this day and may still be his most widely circulated work.

After Artaud, Rattray embarked on a second publication project in 1963–64, editing a collection of Van Buskirk's late poetry which would appear from Auerhahn Society in 1965. Titled *Lami* (a word he glossed as a "Negro sometimes Oriental demon of uncertain sex" in a prefatory editor's note), the book was not a casual undertaking. As Rattray's note explained, *Lami* was assembled from a stack of "[mostly] first drafts in nearly unintelligible scrawl."[49] Clive Matson, a young poet who was living a block away from David on Thirteenth Street and Avenue A, was the project's typist. "Rattray was going through all the papers and finding the poems," he recalls. "He did an incredible job . . . You know, you read *Lami* a couple times, you realize he's moved the order of them around. But it's really a fabulous presentation . . . The arrangement that Rattray did was really inspired. . . . And all I did was type the pieces of paper that Rattray would bring me, which were often handwritten, or they were often badly typed with marks on them. So I made clean copy, all the way from scratches on paper to relatively clean copy."[50] Rattray retained Allen Ginsberg (who never met Van Buskirk) to

48. David Rattray, "Une fausse image d'Artaud aux États-Unis" (A false image of Artaud in the United States), *Le Monde*, February 19, 1966 (trans. Noura Wedell).
49. David Rattray, "A note on the poems," in *Lami*, by Alden Van Buskirk (San Francisco: Auerhahn Society, 1965), n.p.
50. Clive Matson, interview by author, January 21, 2013.

write an introduction for the book, ensuring that the publication would draw sufficient notice. Appearing under the same imprint as Wieners's *Hotel Wentley*, *Lami* was an act of devotion as much as scholarship, garnering Van Buskirk a posthumous presence in the poetry world and a fitting literary legacy. "In the verse all sorts of weird electronic references, images of robot paranoia, city impulses of supersonic nerve thrill are recorded which parallel the sensibility of at least one reader, & probably everybody," Ginsberg wrote in his introduction. "This whole witty—somber—book . . . makes a complete statement of Person."[51]

Throughout the sixties, Rattray ensconced himself in the Lower East Side scene, publishing intermittently in mimeos like *Fuck You, a magazine of the arts* and *The Floating Bear*. He befriended Wieners, Stephen Jonas (vividly profiled in *Invisible*'s "Lightning over the Treasury"), Gerrit Lansing, and Rene Ricard, becoming something of an adjunct to Boston's so-called Occult School of poetry. He also flitted through the scene at Andy Warhol's Factory. A 1963 letter from Wieners to Charles Olson, scrawled in blue ballpoint, offers a tiny vignette of this time: "I was given this poem tonight and I liked it so much I wanted you to see it. . . . It is translated by David Rattray, a young man here in Manhattan, whose mother owns a newspaper in East Hampton, L. I. . . . I am sitting at a kitchen table with Herbert Huncke, and David and his girl, Lynn. We are smoking cigarettes and are very young and beautiful. You are with us." Enclosed was a translation of August von Platen (indeed, the same one that Rattray would years later quote in "Harvest," and again in his interview with Ken Jordan), inscribed "For my dear teacher & dearer friend John Wieners with love from

---

51. Allen Ginsberg, "A Note on *Lami*," in *Lami*, by Alden Van Buskirk, n.p.

David Rattray."[52] A tender friendship between Wieners and Rattray reached its apogee in Wieners's 1964 poem "For Huncke":

> *But if once you put your hand on my shoulders*
> *as David Rattray did last evening*
> *that would be enough . . .* [53]

But during this period Rattray also had a sharper edge, a sort of devilish intensity that was exacerbated by drink and drugs. "David was an odd character," Matson recalls. "He gave me a shot of heroin telling me it was cocaine. People get killed doing stuff like that! It was like, '*Come on*, David. Jesus.'" Poet John Godfrey suggests that friendship, drug use, and intellectual work were, for Rattray, entangled and almost athletic pursuits: "I think he was attracted to people who could come within a hair's breadth of losing all control, yet they could maintain control, and this could be because they had a sensitive and curious intelligence, a good memory and encyclopedic knowledge, or the willingness to use almost any drug or alcohol in combination. He liked people who could rave well."[54] Martha Muhs also speaks to the perks of Rattray's friendship, but remembers him as a complex and anguished person around this time: "David himself was an incredible personality. I think everyone who knew him, either didn't like him at all, or were ambivalent because

52. John Wieners to Charles Olson, May 31, 1963, Charles Olson Research Collection, University of Connecticut.
53. John Wieners, "For Huncke," in *Supplication: Selected Poems of John Wieners*, ed. Joshua Beckman, CAConrad, and Robert Dewhurst (Seattle: Wave Books, 2015), 78.
54. John Godfrey, remarks at *David Rattray: A Recognition*, St. Mark's Poetry Project, New York, April 6, 2013. Other remarks by speakers at this event follow in citations below. An audio recording of the entire April 6 program is held by the Poetry Project.

he had some wonderful qualities. He was truly altruistic. He wanted to help other people and wanted them to love what he loved. You became very interested in what David could tell you, because it was living. But his inner emotional life was rocky."[55]

In the fall of 1964, newly married to Carolyn Fisher, a writer, and with a newborn daughter named Mary, Rattray reenrolled at Harvard seeking a doctorate in comparative literature. The following year he secured a grant from Harvard and L'École Normale to research Artaud abroad, and took the whole family to Paris (where *Invisible's* "French Film Friends" picks up).[56] He never finished the degree, instead publishing his Artaud scholarship in a perfectly invisible form. In 1973, Rattray prepared a dossier titled *A. A.: A presentation of Antonin Artaud documents*, in an edition of ten. The small box contained a bootleg cassette recording of Artaud's banned 1947 radio play *To Have Done with the Judgment of God*, a transcript of the tape, and an unpublished photograph of Artaud from the period, as well as two long essays written during Rattray's year in France: "Antonin Artaud and the Cane of St. Patrick" (precursor to *Invisible's* "Artaud's Cane") and "Antonin Artaud and Lewis Carroll." Rattray explained the genesis of the project in an enclosed note:

POUR EN FINIR AVEC LE JUGEMENT DE DIEU has seldom been heard in America. My master tape from which the present cassette copies were made was given to me 10 years ago by a poet, who would probably prefer not to be named here. He was preparing to go in another direction and not come back. He thought I might be the best custodian for this tape. I have no

55. Caples, "'Death Will Be My Final Lover,'" 189.
56. "East Hampton," *East Hampton Star*, September 30, 1965.

idea whether he was right or not. It took me ten years to figure out what I must do. At last, I realized that I already knew a group of ten who needed these materials and would be happy to have them as an unconditional gift from me.[57]

For a time in the mid-to-late seventies, Rattray performed something of a live version of this box, in which he animated these documents with his inimitably fierce reading style. David Abel, who would later reencounter Rattray on the Lower East Side and publish his poetry, attended one of these performances in Rhinebeck, New York, in 1977, and recalls that Rattray "played the tape of the broadcast, showed slides of manuscripts and documents, and read translation and commentary in a histrionic fashion."[58] Today, at least two copies of *A. A.* remain extant, and virtually unseen, at Dartmouth's Special Collections Library and at the East Hampton Public Library.[59]

---

57. David Rattray, "N. B.," in *A. A.: A presentation of Antonin Artaud documents*, unpublished dossier, December 1973, n.p. The question of this tape's transmission into American poetry circles is still a point of interest among Artaud scholars: see Pawlik, "Artaud in performance," 12–13. According to Ginsberg biographer Barry Miles, Jean-Jacques Lebel stole an LP recording of Artaud's radio play from the studios of Radiodiffusion-Télévision Française in April 1961, dubbed it onto cassette, and then played it for Ginsberg, Peter Orlovsky, Gregory Corso, and Harold Norse at his apartment in Montmartre. Afterward, Ginsberg made copies for Julien Beck and Judith Malina, Michael McClure, and LeRoi Jones. Given this, LeRoi Jones—who changed his name to Amiri Baraka in 1965 and separated himself from the Beats to found the Black Arts Movement—may be the most likely candidate for Rattray's messenger. See *The Beat Hotel: Ginsberg, Burroughs, and Corso in Paris, 1958–1963* (New York: Grove Press, 2001), 247–49.
58. David Abel, email to author, April 10, 2019.
59. Rattray appears to have donated Dartmouth's copy of *A. A.* himself; the copy held by the East Hampton Public Library was donated there by his sister Mary, and appears to have been her personal copy. Nowhere in *A. A.* does Rattray name the project's other recipients, and their identities remain a mystery.

Having "stepped out" of academe, as he would put it to Ken Jordan, Rattray gradually found work in lexicography and editing. After returning from France, he was hired as a senior editor on the *American Heritage Dictionary of the English Language.*[60] "I enjoyed that a lot," he told Jordan. "Writing a dictionary was like studying the language and it sort of paid to be a student of language forever." When that gig ended, he started freelancing for the General Books division of Reader's Digest, after writing an exhaustive chapter on the Maccabees for their 1974 volume *Great People of the Bible and How They Lived.* Eventually, this led to a full-time position. Rattray would keep this job for the rest of his life, developing projects such as *Success with Words: A Guide to the American Language* (1983), a writer's manual, and *The Magic and Medicine of Plants* (1986), an herbal. The work suited him, and he had no compunctions about forgoing an academic career. "Reader's Digest respects my autonomy as a person and my dignity and independence a hell of a lot more than Princeton University or Yale or Harvard would do," he told Jordan. "It may seem strange—people turn up their nose at Reader's Digest—but I find that I get more respect and friendliness and concern, and less meddling—they don't meddle with me at all! They've never done anything to make me feel that they were breathing down my neck or messing with me, and if I went to work for an Ivy League college, I can guarantee you there would be all kinds of shit like that."[61] Rattray's projects for Reader's Digest are another invisible

---

60. "East Hampton," *East Hampton Star*, September 29, 1966.
61. This portion of Rattray's interview with Jordan does not appear in the published version newly collected here, which was abridged for publication in the *Poetry Project Newsletter*, but is found in the interview's unedited transcript, extant in the Semiotext(e) archive: see Ken Jordan, "Speaking with David Rattray," unpublished manuscript, 1992, Sylvère Lotringer Papers and Semiotext(e) Archive, 1960–2004, Fales Library and Special Collections, New York University, 29.

aspect of his oeuvre, where his specific contributions—typically substantial—are unattributed and incognito.

The texts in *Invisible* first appeared in small magazines throughout the eighties and early nineties, the era of Rattray's emergence as a more focused writer. People who discover this collection "are always knocked out that there was such a guy, this literary scholar and adventurer, who found his own poetic voice at what seemed like the late middle of his life,"[62] Eileen Myles has written. Rattray's midlife prolificacy corresponded to him joining AA and getting sober in 1983. (The last round of his drinking fell around the time of the vituperative "Yoga of Anger," newly collected here, which he "preached" at the Pyramid Club that summer.)[63] In 1983 Rattray's first book of poetry, *A Red-Framed Print of the Summer Palace*, was published by Vincent Fitzgerald & Co., in a fine-press edition with drawings by Peter Thomson. Over the next decade he would publish two further fine-press books with Vincent Fitzgerald, each containing a single poem: *To the Consciousness of a Shooting Star*, with paintings by Gérard Charrière, in 1986; and *To the Blue Wall*, with etchings by T. Kurahara, in 1993. At the same time, he took on passion projects as a translator, publishing René Crevel's *Difficult Death* in 1986 and Roger Gilbert-Lecomte's *Black Mirror* in 1991—the occasions for his essays on those writers in *Invisible*—as well as Alain Daniélou's *Fools of God* in 1988, for Raymond Foye's beloved Hanuman Books. A lifelong student of the ancient, obscure, and unlikely, with sobriety Rattray also developed other pursuits—he

---

62. Eileen Myles, "Views of David," in *Themes & Variations: The Publications of Vincent Fitzgerald & Company 1980–2000* (New York: Columbia University, 2000), 51.
63. Chris Kraus, introduction to "Yoga of Anger," by David Rattray, in *A Queer Anthology of Rage* (London: Pilot Press, 2018), n.p.

studied Sanskrit, researched and interpreted the sixteenth-century "In Nomine" musical idiom that he writes about here (giving a piano recital at the Kendall Gallery in 1989), and obtained a black belt in judo. Painter Basil King, a friend from the sixties, remembers Rattray's transformation fondly: "When David sobered up, Martha [King] convinced him to do a reading, and it was really something because everybody knew David from his drinking, and as a coke head, and God knows what else, and he gave this reading at this little library on Tompkins Square, and he gave this marvelous reading. He did a performance. He told me, 'I practiced a lot.' And then he started playing the piano again."[64]

At the end of 1990, Rattray published his only full-length collection of poetry, *Opening the Eyelid*, with David Abel and Katherine Kuehn's diwan press. Abel, a poet with a store on the Lower East Side called the Bridge Bookshop, had arranged for Rattray to read at the Ear Inn in the mideighties. The other reader that night was a no-show, so Rattray read for a full hour, commanding the audience. "Everyone was floored," Abel says. "I had known about his work before that, but that really converted me." A few years later, Abel essentially created diwan to publish a trade paperback of Rattray's poems. As he tells it: "After that extraordinary reading at the Ear . . . I went to try to find more of [Rattray's] work and discovered that the only collection of his own poems—not the translations for which he was renowned, but the only collection of his own poems—that was available was a fine-press, limited edition of nine poems . . . which was inaccessible to most people. I just thought, 'This is crazy. This work is so compelling.' So I said, 'Why don't we publish a book of your poems?' And that

---

64. Basil King, interview by author, January 2, 2012.

was the beginning of a three-year process."[65] Rattray initially planned for the collection to be composed of half original poems, half translations, but, Abel says, "once we looked at a version with the poems alone, it was clear to both of us that the result would make a stronger book."[66] The poems of *Opening the Eyelid* are spiraling and cerebral, written in a Creeley-esque short line that moves through a procession of mystical sources, modernist allusions, flashes of personal memory, and moments of grief. The book's most poignant poems have the quality of prayers, invocations. One begins and ends like this: "Make the feast season forever / rites of passage know no end," and "there is no remedy / in the stately calendula / no peace / beneath Cassiopeia / life never heals."[67] Another contains these lines, which seem haunted by Van Buskirk: "Pain is always young. / You get your wings / When you can be there for others / At distances of an order / Only birds maybe have a feel for."[68] *Opening the Eyelid* had a quiet reception in the poetry world, though some received the transmission. "In a nation of a million poets, poetasters, and potentates who do not read each others' books of poems, our cultural ptosis is the third epidemic," wrote Richard Blevins in *Rolling Stock*. "We need the radical surgery of David Rattray's *Opening the Eyelid*."[69] The book begins with "West from Napeague," the diary of East Hampton beachcombing that reappears in *Invisible*. Some of *Opening the*

65. "David Abel in Conversation," interview by Al Filreis, PennSound Podcasts, *Jacket2*, March 28, 2014, https://jacket2.org/podcasts/david-abel-conversation.

66. David Abel, email to author, April 16, 2019.

67. David Rattray, "Feast Season," in *Opening the Eyelid* (Brooklyn, NY: diwan, 1990), 36.

68. David Rattray, "To the Blue Wall," in *Opening the Eyelid*, 10.

69. Richard Blevins, "Blind Sunlight," review of *Opening the Eyelid*, by David Rattray, *Rolling Stock*, no. 19–20 (1991): 30.

Eyelid's lost translations—of Hölderlin, Émile Nelligan—spurred other texts in *Invisible*.[70]

As Rattray's publishing output became steadier, so did his friendships. Eileen Myles, one of Rattray's closest friends during this time, has written about the generative, generous quality of his friendship: "David had a quality of mind that met one's own interests dead on and then energetically enhanced them. If you became friends with David you soon became the recipient of a lot of correspondence—letters and faxes, phone-calls, sudden pointed digressions in the course of talking with him that expanded your own understanding of exactly the things you cared about. It was as if his intelligence began downloading into your intelligence once you struck up a friendship with him."[71] Other close writer friends included Chris Kraus and Lynne Tillman. "Rattray's presence—tall, lean, with an angular and haunted face—was electrifying and formidable," Kraus recalls.[72] Tillman writes that "David was a vital and vivid presence to many of us, and to many, a best friend, an intimate, a wise man, a mentor. . . . He was an anomaly among anomalies, a teacher who never professed but who taught, and did it unlike any teacher most of us had ever known."[73] Betsy Sussler, cofounder of *BOMB* magazine, where Rattray published often and served as contributing editor, also paints the late Rattray as preternaturally kind: "As a contributing editor, David was the most generous of writers, palming his choices in beautiful descriptions as if they were birds: He believed people were gems, precious, and he treated them accordingly. . . . David was

70. Abel, email to author, April 16, 2019.
71. Myles, "Views of David," 50.
72. Kraus, introduction to "Yoga of Anger," n.p.
73. Lynne Tillman, Anney Bonney, and Betsy Sussler, "David Rattray: A Recognition," *BOMB*, May 7, 2013, https://bombmagazine.org/articles/david-rattray-a-recognition.

one of the most eloquent, accomplished and iconoclastic."[74] Many of Rattray's friends from around the St. Mark's Poetry Project—John Godfrey, Kim Lyons, Simon Pettet, Susie Timmons, and others—express similar sentiments. "He had this very theatrical but not quite easy-to-pin-down presence . . . He was the artiest person I think I've ever met," says Timmons.[75] Lyons lived down the street from Rattray and recalls, as do others, that chance run-ins with him would become impromptu soliloquies:

> Pretty frequently I would bump into him on the way to work, on the film noir set of Avenue A at 8:15 in the morning. I would be trotting along and there would be David Rattray . . . He was a looming presence with the apocalyptic shadows on Avenue A at that time in the morning, and ever the Midwesterner I would say something like 'Hi, David Rattray, how are you?' And he would look at me and set down his briefcase and say, 'I am very well, thank you. I am immersed right now in the study of Sanskrit motets.' And he would really discourse. How lucky was I, to stand there and listen to him talk about his recent studies? For all I know he had been up all night long, and he was a patient and kind person to just lay that on me.[76]

During these years Rattray also maintained a robust friendship and correspondence with Gerrit Lansing, in Gloucester, perhaps the only poet who could equal his erudition in matters esoteric and occult.

74. Betsy Sussler, "David Greig Rattray: 1936–1993," *BOMB*, no. 44 (Summer 1993): 2.
75. Susie Timmons, remarks at *David Rattray: A Recognition*, St. Mark's Poetry Project, New York, April 6, 2013.
76. Kim Lyons, remarks at *David Rattray: A Recognition*, St. Mark's Poetry Project, New York, April 6, 2013.

Conceived and edited by Kraus in 1992, *Invisible* presciently gathered Rattray's loose ends of this late, productive period. "I always felt . . . with David that I was just in the presence of culture and history embodied," Kraus has said. She recalls the genesis of the project this way:

> [Sylvère Lotringer and I] had just started the Native Agents series with Semiotext(e) . . . And it was supposed to be mostly first-person, mostly women, and while David certainly wasn't a woman, he was writing in the first-person; he often talked and spoke in the first-person, in this very high first-person that was a witness of culture, a very kind of personal witness of culture. . . . [It] was really serendipitous because he at that point had begun digging into his old diaries that he kept from his twenties, when he and his friend Van Buskirk traveled, like, you know, for actually three weeks that felt like three years, in southern Mexico, in Oaxaca, and those stories became the basis of the book, as well as these other wonderful essays.

The prose pieces she and Rattray collected for *Invisible* document the people and pet obsessions that had preoccupied David his whole life, forming an intellectual self-portrait that coheres despite their many genres.[77] Though Rattray would acknowledge that Kraus "saw the book before I did," he would come to understand *Invisible* as a "poetic autobiography." In his conversation about the

---

77. Chris Kraus, remarks at *David Rattray: A Recognition*, St. Mark's Poetry Project, New York, April 6, 2013. Rattray had begun revisiting the diaries of his time with Van Buskirk in mind of editing a collection of their correspondence: *Invisible*'s "Van" was originally written as an introduction to that project, which was never completed. See Jordan, "Speaking with David Rattray," 13–14.

book with Ken Jordan, recorded in December 1992, he expanded on this at length:

> Whether it's stories of what happened in my life, as a young man and then later, or essays about books and writers that I considered or translated, the book always has to do with whatever it is that poetry is trying to find and communicate. I think that idea of finding and communicating is very important. Somebody recently asked me to define poetry, and I think it can be defined—people say that it can't, but I believe that it can. I think a simple one-phrase definition of poetry is: the invention of life or reality through language. To invent reality through words, this is what poetry does. . . . I think that poetry has a real kind of . . . I wouldn't say preachy kind of a function, but it definitely is there to support and encourage people to realize that there's a worthwhile life out there to be lived. A way of living that is there—that all you have to do is invent it. It's available to all of us.

Rattray's concept of "poetic autobiography" suggests a vision of poetry as "creative writing" in only the purest sense. Though written in prose, it is this vision that *Invisible* ultimately puts forth, a vision of poetry as a literal creator of new possibilities for life—and as a conduit to life's unseen possibilities. Above all, Rattray derived this vision from Artaud, who claimed that "Art is not an imitation of life, but life is an imitation of a transcendental principle with which art restores communication."[78] (It was also Artaud who

---

78. Antonin Artaud, "Documents relating to *The Theater and Its Double*," in *Collected Works*, vol. 4, trans. Victor Corti (London: John Calder, 1999), 180.

inspired Gilles Deleuze's similar concept of literature as a change agent for life: "Writing is inseparable from becoming . . . to the point of becoming imperceptible.")[79] Like the literal facts of Rattray's biography, *Invisible* is an abundant reminder that the poetic life—that is, the different life—is "available to all of us," if we can find the courage to commit to the process of its unfoldment. Doing so means opening oneself to the unknown, living by a Sufistic "philosophy of surrender rather than one of conquest." Artaud also wrote that "The finest art is one which brings us closest to chaos," and Rattray understood real living, like real poetry, as a series of serious risks—as "throwing oneself in the arms of god," to quote the first sentence of *Invisible*'s title chapter.[80] In a poem, he once put it this way: "But there is no such thing as obscure / poetry. The objects of a poem / are as bright and clear as can be. / The boast that its words come from the heart / is true of each real poem, each / word written in blood. / Who wants to look at a color / so bright it hurts the eyes?"[81]

In the first days of 1993, Rattray gave a reading at a dive bar called Mona's on Avenue B. In the middle of reading "Mr. Peacock," a new long poem, he momentarily spaced out. Afterwards, walking home with some friends, he spaced out again and walked into a lamppost; a few minutes later, he did the same thing again. He saw his doctor the following Monday and a CAT scan revealed a brain tumor. Within a week, he received a surgery to remove the tumor, but was told he had three months to live.

---

79. Gilles Deleuze, "Literature and Life," in *Essays Critical and Clinical*, trans. Daniel W. Smith and Michael A. Greco (Minneapolis: University of Minnesota Press, 1997), 1.
80. Artaud, "Documents," 167.
81. David Rattray, "A Division of Water," in *Opening the Eyelid*, 23.

"The whole thing—from the publication of the book, to the interview in the *Poetry Project Newsletter*, to him getting diagnosed with cancer—was like a matter of weeks," Kraus recalls. Rattray had just finished having a summer house built in Amagansett—a "poet's house," he told her, his dream house—and he moved there with his wife Lin. Kraus visited and remembers the place as pristine, nautical. "It was like a seashell," she says.[82] Eileen Myles also spent a lot of time at the Amagansett house. "There is no place better in the world than the bedside of a friend who's dying," Myles wrote of David's last days there, where in winter the sand dunes looked "like the desert" outside "this little house which he accidentally built in which to die." Successively, Rattray lost his physical faculties. "First he couldn't type and then his pen dragged across the paper awkwardly, losing control," Myles writes. "After a while he walked crooked on the beach, and then could only ride by the ocean in cars . . . The doctors basically said the last thing that happened was the lights would go out."[83] Through his illness Rattray tried to remain industrious, and began assembling a book of "collected poetry and prose," titled in manuscript *The Curve*, that he would never complete.[84] He wrote for as long as he could, keeping a fragmented journal whose last entries fall the week of his fifty-seventh birthday, February 17. "Smiling calm installs itself in my soul," he wrote on that day. A month later, on March 15, he died in Amagansett. A memorial service was held at St. Marks Church-in-the-Bowery, among the poets.

82. Chris Kraus, interview by author, March 13, 2019.
83. Myles, "Views of David," 49.
84. David Abel, email to author, April 15, 2019.

In my own early twenties, after reading *How I Became One of the Invisible* for the first time, I made a pilgrimage to Puerto Angel. I was relieved to find it, almost a half century later, much like Rattray described it in 1961. There was one hotel, and a handful of hostel-like *posadas*. Winter is whale-watching season, so in June the place was all but vacant. My *Blue Guide: Mexico* devoted a mere sentence to this "still unspoiled resort, discreetly grown from a fishing village."[85] Méx. 175, the highway to the coast from Oaxaca, has long been paved, but was otherwise a living image of Rattray's "ribbon of mud strung between curtains of silver fog and sleet." Just before my bus dropped into the jungle, I thought I saw a woman selling magic mushrooms roadside—with an artful hand-painted sign, like the strawberry vendors along Pacific Coast Highway—but this could have been a mirage. Pedro, a rangy ex-pat I met my first night in Puerto Angel, was disappointed when I told him about David and Van; he arrived in '67, and always thought he'd been first. Up the road at Zipolite, another ex-pat would tell me that Americans only found these towns in 1970, when a total solar eclipse, best viewed from the southern Mexican coast, drew a huge flock of hippies. When I asked Pedro what Puerto Angel was like in the sixties, he only said, "In 1961, *coming* here was different. It was an adventure. It was serious. You could die."

For nearly thirty years now, *Invisible* has steadily found an audience, moving through the poetry and larger worlds with a capillary action that's defied prevailing currents. In 2001, Robert Creeley sang its praises for a book titled *Lost Classics*, comparing

85. John Collis and David M. Jones, *Blue Guide: Mexico* (New York: W. W. Norton, 1997), 706.

Rattray's narrative voice to those of Montaigne and Robert Louis Stevenson in that he "can say anything, go anywhere, and be there so specifically in its own compelling interest that all, the reader included, then follows."[86] Many have followed. A 2013 symposium in New York, *David Rattray: A Recognition*, packed rooms at the Poetry Project and the Leo Koenig gallery for two days, bringing together writers, readers, artists, and others in celebration and study.[87] *Invisible* has quietly influenced some of my generation's best poets, such as Ariana Reines and Dana Ward. It has certainly changed the course of my own life, inspiring scholarship and other choices that I will reckon with for years. With this new and expanded edition, I hope *Invisible* will be more visible than ever.

Back then in Puerto Angel, I looked for landmarks like the casino and Café Estrella and "the Angel," but couldn't find them. The cemetery that David and Van lived beside is obvious—and beautiful, crowded with brightly tiled, joyful tombs. A local painter named Mateo, whose family was one of the oldest in the town, told me that before it had been built, they simply buried their dead on the beach; he still remembered playing with bones on Playa Pantheon as a child. Rereading *Invisible* there, and again this winter, I thought of Whitman:

> *When you read these I that was visible am become invisible,*
> *Now it is you, compact, visible, realizing my poems, seeking me,*
> *Fancying how happy you were if I could be with you and become*
> *your comrade;*

---

86. Robert Creeley, "*How I Became One of the Invisible*—David Rattray," in *Lost Classics*, ed. Michael Ondaatje, Michael Redhill, Esta Spalding, and Linda Spalding (New York: Anchor Books, 2001), 41.
87. *David Rattray: A Recognition* was held on April 5–6, 2013.

Be it as if I were with you. (Be not too certain but I am now with you.)[88]

Puerto Angel was named by pirates, Mateo told me. They came ashore in the seventeenth century to bury a treasure that has never been found. As the legend goes, they looked back at the beach as they left the bay. They saw two angels rising from the water.

Robert Dewhurst would like to acknowledge the following: Rattray's friends David Abel, Kevin Cooney, Jerry Craddock, George Green, Basil and Martha King, Chris Kraus, Gerrit Lansing, Kim Lyons, Clive Matson, Eileen Myles, Simon Pettet, and Arnon Vered, for dialogue recently and over the years; Allison Chomet, Fales Library and Special Collections, New York University; James Maynard and Alison Fraser, curator and assistant curator of the Poetry Collection, University at Buffalo (SUNY); Gina Piastuck, department head of the Long Island Collection, East Hampton Public Library; Morgan Swan, special collections education and outreach librarian, Rauner Special Collections Library, Dartmouth College; and Nicole Wallace, managing director of the St. Mark's Poetry Project.

88. Walt Whitman, "Full of Life Now," in *Complete Poetry and Collected Prose* (New York: Library of America, 1982), 287.

How I Became One of the Invisible

Lightning over the Treasury

Early one morning in the summer of 1963, I joined a couple of Lower East Side friends in pooling our money to be split two ways, the lion's share to get high and the remainder to be entrusted to Steve, a poet friend visiting from Boston, who was on his own track with dexedrine and wanted for nothing in the getting-high department. Steve would take the $5.50 we gave him and go grocery shopping. Then in the evening he would make eggplant parmigiana, we made him promise, to be washed down with a gallon of Chianti, which we would be ready for, as the effect of the drugs should have worn off by that time

Everything went off according to plan, at first. Then around six p.m., just as we were all coming down and starting to hunger and thirst, Steve returned. He brought no food and drink, however, only a plain brown wrapper with a dog-eared pamphlet of mid-1930s vintage inside. On its cover, beneath the title *Lightning over the Treasury*, was a clawlike hand, its long nails and hairy wrist dripping with blood, closing over the porch of the U.S. Treasury building in Washington, D.C., a façade collapsing under a sky black with thunderheads, which Steve (quoting Shelley) called "the cloud of mind discharging its collected lightnings." All this added up to an allegory of the international conspiracy to wreck America's monetary system and seize her wealth, a conspiracy well known to readers of Henry Ford among others. Steve had used our money to buy this tract, and forgotten all about the Italian dinner he had promised. We realized that we were about to go hungry, but there was no point in even saying anything to Steve. He was a certified lunatic.

No one was surprised a few days afterward to learn that he was back in a V.A. psychiatric ward in Boston. Nor was I surprised a quarter-century later, in 1991 when Steve Jonas's works were reprinted and honored in a series of public readings on both Coasts, to hear that that particular pamphlet had remained a prized possession until the poet's death by a heart attack in 1970. I have just acquired a pamphlet myself, one that is considerably more attractive to me than *Lightning over the Treasury* was. Reading this presentation of three hitherto unpublished works by Steve printed by Rose Books, Berkeley, in a cream-colored cover under the title *3 Poems*, I realize that I am actually hearing his voice for the first time in nearly thirty years, and a wonderfully curious voice it is. At their best the poems have an intensely oral, I would like to call it glossolalic, freedom, as if they captured the essence of what one might like to express in a moment of rapture. His most important poems were in fact titled the Orgasm Sequence. For him the reference was by no means glib. An actual orgasm experienced early in life still burned in him like an open wound. A schoolteacher had taken him to her home one day when he was barely past puberty and seduced him. At the moment of orgasm—he had entered her only seconds earlier and she was already coming too—such terror filled him that he pulled out while ejaculating and rushed from the house stark naked, running all the way home to his mother through the fields of the Georgia farming community where this took place. It was Steve's only sexual encounter with a woman.

To backtrack a bit, I had first met Steve Jonas during an unseasonably warm spell in the last week of February 1963. He was in New York from Boston for a few days with John Wieners at 154

Avenue C. It was at my own place on Twelfth Street and Avenue A that we became friends in the course of one of those marathon conversations friendships are often founded upon. Steve was maybe four inches shorter than me, powerfully built, with broad shoulders and a narrow waist. Although he claimed in that first conversation to detest all forms of exercise save long walks and solitary dancing to radio music in the privacy of his own apartment, I could see that he moved with the grace of a gymnast. His face, handsomely modeled in olive and sepia with big dark eyes and crowned with a luxuriance of wavy black hair, was disquietingly vivid and mobile; it could move, through a succession of masks reflecting hilarity, sympathetic interest, disdain, indignation, murderous rage, or screaming terror, all with an intensity and speed that very few could keep up with, since many of these masks were but outward signs of the chemical upheaval with which his body and mind were continually afflicted.

As long as I knew him, he loved to strut up and down when feeling good. At the time of our first meeting, he boasted about his 30-inch waistline. Although he did look quite trim in the cream-colored suit he was wearing, it was a visibly tight fit, and I never saw it again after that first visit. The suit gave Steve the look of a man from far across the sea, someplace like Brazil.

I made a remark to this effect as we were heading for Bellevue Hospital where I was taking him the day after we met, to get treatment for an abscessed wisdom tooth. He gave me a quick sharp look but apparently decided that I was paying him a compliment, and the suit became the pretext of a hoax we played five minutes later at the emergency ward, Steve having explained that he had spent half his life waiting in hospitals but today just wasn't one of those days. So when we presented ourselves to the nurse in charge, the waiting room was treated to a floorshow—Steve holding his swollen cheek, wailing, grimacing, and babbling in fake Portuguese, as I explained that my Brazilian friend was in agonizing pain, had fainted twice getting there, and required immediate attention. Within a couple of minutes Steve was installed on a bed in one of the examining cubicles, with me along as interpreter. He was quickly looked at and given a prescription for an antibiotic to be filled at the Hospital's free pharmacy. This only provoked a new and more insistent onset of groanings, at which the doctor yawned and got out a handful of codeine tablets, which he gave to Steve in a small paper box. Steve looked them over suspiciously and then said, in clearly enunciated English, I don't suppose these things can be cooked up to shoot. Without betraying the faintest surprise at the patient's sudden switch from 'Portuguese' to plain English, the doctor assured Steve that they would turn to a useless mush if cooked, and then, without waiting for a reply, walked out of the room. A bit rattled, I suggested that we get the hell out of there. Steve laughed all the way back down to the Lower East Side.

He did not need to worry about what Gurdjieff used to call "the material question." Since the end of the Second World War he had lived on a veteran's pension. He spoke of the Army with loyal warmth and said he would have gladly served as a career soldier. His poems, like Stefan George's, often seemed to reflect what to us children of the Sixties was an archaic military and imperial stance. It was a put-on. Steve's connection with the service had ended under some sort of a cloud, the details of which I never learned. In retrospect, I can't imagine anything about the service that could have been attractive to Steve except the servicemen. As he put it in one poem, proclaiming his tastes:

Yes,
it is delightful looking at a
beautiful boy . . .

At the same time, Steve told other friends that it was the Army that had driven him crazy. However, a big part of the craziness was a distorted reflection of the American racism he had grown up with. Steve was born a mulatto in post–World War One rural Georgia, a world where lynchings and fiery crosses and gunshots fired from passing cars in the night were a commonplace. His original name was Rufus Jones. For all the years that he lived in Boston, Steve passed as a white of mixed, let us say Mediterranean, background verging upon what is called on Cape Cod a Portuguee. His own expressed views on race were always vehemently old-time cracker populist, with the Jews looming large, as in the fulminations of Ezra Pound, whom we both admired boundlessly. Like most of my poetic contemporaries, I took Pound's racism and his Jefferson/Mussolini angle with a grain of salt, without altogether dismissing it—after all, some of his greatest work, for instance, the Usura Canto, came straight out of that. But Steve had swallowed it whole. In spite of this difference, we found common ground in the E.P. universe, not just that part of it, but the whole business from Provençal troubadours to Imagism, and from there to the jump-cut discourse of the *Cantos.*

When I think of Steve's poems, however, and of himself as I knew him, the one image that stands for both in my mind's eye is that cream-colored suit, for me an emblem of the far-flung, quasi-Lusitanian realms of Steve's imagination, ranging from the Gold Coast to Brazil, with islands scattered under azure skies the whole way to India and Cathay, taking in the realms of Melville, Pound, Jack Spicer, and Olson as a matter of course.

Steve was forty-two when we met but looked a somewhat weathered twenty-nine. He spent most of his time at home. Strangers were never turned away. He liked to feed people, and welcomed runaways with open arms: "If I'm not here, come in the window—everybody does." The place was crammed with books, manuscripts, movie magazines, diet pills, and wrinkle cream; a stuffy kitchen full of mainly youthful refugees from hospitals, jails, and delinquent homes, awaiting his return with half the Italian market stashed in a string bag. I often had meals with Steve and his houseguests. My visits sometimes stretched to overnight. I remember a long spell lying half passed-out on his floor, unable to move but watching the dust motes in a shaft of sunlight migrate across the room to an accompaniment of laughter, Poundian bombast, and the familiar ring and crash of Steve's typewriter.

Van

In the spring of 1957 some cronies and I had a supper club in the dining room of the Green Lantern, an inn on the edge of Hanover, New Hampshire, where I was a student in my senior year at Dartmouth. One evening I had drunk a lot of wine over my meal when someone began telling about a new member of the ski team who was presently holed up in a sleeping bag on a mattress, sick with flu, in the team's sleeping quarters on the top floor of College Hall. It would seem that this 19-year-old NROTC scholarship jock was actually a poet.

I got up and went straight over to College Hall.

The object of my curiosity was dead to the world when I arrived. I turned on the light, a bare bulb in the ceiling, and shook him, asking what he had done with the church key.

I opened a couple of aged-in-the-wood India Pale Ales, which in those days came in a tall, thin, green bottle, and assured my new acquaintance, Alden Van Buskirk, or Van for short—he was still blinking and rubbing his eyes in bewilderment—that the strong ale was bound to bring relief. I was only sorry not to have been able to mull it for him, with cinnamon, nutmeg, peppercorns, sugar, rum—the sovereign grippe remedy.

I noticed Van was reading Whitman, Eliot, Hart Crane. Also Dylan Thomas. Had he read Pound, or Rilke, or Mallarmé? He shook his head. Nope. Homer? Yeah. Virgil? Mmm . . . A mellifluous bore. One ancient that he really dug was Ovid. Talk about a Book of Changes, we have one: Ovid's *Metamorphoses.*

Van sat up cross-legged on the floor, shedding the sleeping bag, and lit a Camel. I noticed his fingertips like my own were both tobacco and ink stained. He had nothing on his pale, skinny, hairless body but a pair of also ink-stained jockey shorts. Although the room was warm, there were goose pimples on his arms. He tried to blow a smoke ring, but sneezed. "Bless you," I intoned.

"Fountain pens leak," he informed me.

That summer I went abroad, and for the next three years we did not communicate. Early in the spring of 1960, when Van was about to graduate, I returned to Dartmouth, and we met again, this time thanks to a reading of works by Rilke and John Wieners that had been organized by Jack Hirschman, then an instructor in the English Department, whose first book of poems, *A Correspondence of Americans*, was at the printer's when we met. From him Van had first learned of the new poets who were springing up in Boston, New York, and San Francisco, outside Academe and in opposition to all that Eisenhower America stood for.

The almost slight teenager that Van had been when we first met had filled out to a not quite stocky yet powerfully built man. There was a jaundiced pallor to his face whose formerly prominent cheekbones were lost in an unhealthy puffiness, a moon-faced look quite out of character. His pale blue eyes were bloodshot. He made a crack about drinking. Drinking had nothing to do with it. He had been sick for about a year. His mother had had leukemia. When she died, he had a dream that he would go next and, soon after, the first in a series of spells in which the urine darkened from mahogany to black, or "Coca Cola," as he put it, while he suffered paroxysms of vomiting till there was nothing left to bring up but bile. After a day or two in the hospital, with transfusions and I.V. feeding, he would return to normal. It had happened several times. The black urine contained blood that had broken down and passed through the kidneys. His doctors had put him on high doses of cortisone steroids, which seemed to hold off the crises and speed recovery from them, but, he told me, the side effects were rugged. At one point the "little green pills" had made him see spaghetti-like worms coming out of walls. They lowered the dosage after that. Now he was okay, but the doctors still had no idea what was wrong. Although unable to confirm any of their speculations, they still inclined to a "preleukemia" hypothesis. He shrugged. Maybe some weirdly toxic ski wax had gotten onto the sheath knife he had been using to cut salami.

This conversation took place on a warm afternoon in early spring, as Van and I were climbing from the still-frozen River at the foot of West Wheelock Street, along sidewalks rutted with thawing mud and slush, to a stone tower at the top of which, in a corner out of the wind, we paused in a sudden dazzle of raw sunlight. In his wrap-around sunglasses my companion looked like a racing car driver. The world has been under an evil spell for centuries, I explained. It was a revelation that I owed to a recent discovery of Antonin Artaud, who had died only a dozen years earlier. Reality, I assured Van, had nothing to do with the real world, which was in any case about to go up in flames. It turned out that he shared my apocalyptic expectations, except to him it seemed the world was already on fire. The Book of Revelation, Blake, Artaud, Jean Genet had all come down the chimney and were dancing in our heads.

The illness had caused Van to drop out of the NROTC. Great, I said. That made both of us draft-exempt. A year before in Paris, I confided, the daylight hours at the winter solstice had seemed to dwindle to no more than a couple in every twenty-four. It was a delusion, but I thought I was witnessing a final blackout. The sun would never return. Life would cease.

"*When night doth meet with noon,*" Van interrupted, "*in dark conspiracy . . .*"

Huh?

"Keats," he informed me.

Right. I went on. Night after night, I awoke choking with asthma in the wee hours and burned mounds of Vesuvius Powder, a nostrum purchased from the pharmacy two doors away, inhaling the smoke through a paper funnel, which set off fits of sneezing and cleared the bronchial tubes. Then I would drink a cup of brandy and lie there waiting for the world to end. Early one morning I awoke on the floor with the feeling I had died. I had had a grand mal seizure. They put me on anti-convulsant medications. My draft status would have to be changed from 1-A to 4-F.

"Well, they won't be giving us any grief as draft dodgers," Van rejoined. "I was just about getting ready to leave the NROTC anyhow. No one in their right mind would be willing to fire shots in anger to defend this." With a sweeping gesture he took in the surrounding treetops and nearby clocktower of Baker Library gleaming golden in the late afternoon sun. To a casual observer we might at that moment have looked like nothing more than a couple of college boys sharing a cigarette.

We were fit for only one thing on the job market: teaching. Yet we recoiled from the prospect of joining a profession that seemed no better than a guild for the transmission of established values. The poetic vocation was a horse of another color. It was the call to a new, different way of seeing, of being, the call of Rilke's "Archaic Torso of Apollo": *You must change your life . . .*

Meanwhile, Van had accepted a fellowship at Washington U in Saint Louis as a means of postponing his entry onto the job market. I also was stalling. I had decided to spend a few months with my piano teacher at Dartmouth and immerse myself in a work that I believed held a key to the universe tucked away inside its dense and enigmatic fabric, Beethoven's Hammerklavier Sonata.

I was able to do this thanks to my mother, who had agreed to give me $100 a month until I became self-supporting. Although unhappy with the arrangement, she had acquiesced to it when I pointed out that her father had helped her when she was beginning as a writer in the early 1920s. He had paid her bills all the way to Outer Mongolia and back.

Nonetheless I told people that I was living on an income inherited from whaling ancestors. The latter were real enough; only the inheritance was imaginary. To Van, however, I admitted the truth. It came as no surprise. His own situation vis-à-vis Robert Van Buskirk, Sr. was similar. Both recently bereaved, our respective parents were terrified lest we end up as burdens to them, disgraceful failures. We resented their Philistine views and decided to ignore the old folks' existence except when it became necessary to block their oppressive, if well-meant schemes.

After graduation Van stayed on in Hanover so as to be within reach of the hospital. The home of a mutual friend happened to be vacant, and Van was invited to house-sit. I had a similar arrangement across the River in Norwich, where I had installed a piano. From his home in Rutland Van fetched an old car, a 1941 Buick convertible. He started dropping by in mid-afternoon, to improvise at the keyboard. He was a good musician. At the time I didn't give a hoot about jazz. He pretended to think I loved it.

On nice days we went to a swimming hole. Sunbathing on its margin, we read *Nightwood* out loud. We talked about drugs, which neither of us had ever taken.

I took a furlough from Beethoven. We went hiking in the White Mountains, wandering along ridges high above treeline from peak to peak for several days. One afternoon Van plunged into an icy pond from which one could see all the way from Maine in one direction to Lake Champlain in the other. He jumped up and down, shouting to me to come in. I shouted back that I'd rather stay dry.

Almost next door to where I was staying in Norwich was the 20-year-old Lisa Yeomans' house. Van and Lisa had met as teenagers while skiing at Pico and had been seeing each other on and off ever since. Tall, fine-featured, blond, awkward, yet radiating adolescent grace, Lisa had a soft voice, observant eyes, sudden laughter. Van loved her and was always giving her advice.

One night he and I drove over to the Rutland State Fair. I was still young enough to see something like poetry in blue-collar America at play of a summer evening. Swarms of insects circled the arc lights. Van's dark-goggled face took on an eerie glow. His hair became the helmet of a humanoid alien. From his full, pale lips came a stream of sarcastic invective against the wasteful, exploitive, murderously hypocritical, witless, *Leave-It-to-Beaver*, Dairy Queen–slurping American way of life.

A week later Van lent me the Buick, and I went down to East Hampton for a few days at the beach. While I was there, he got deathly sick. Lisa phoned to tell me that he had been operated on to remove his spleen and might not live.

Van had just been moved from the recovery room to a private room when I arrived. Barely conscious, he asked me to read from John Wieners' *Hotel Wentley Poems*—the book was on the bedside table. His fingers a waxy yellowish gray, he fiddled with an ice sliver, touching it to his lips. The sky outside the window was bright blue. I paused. "Don't stop," he urged.

A few days later Van was out of the hospital. Soon the only memento of the operation was a scar over his solar plexus. He groused some about an inability to concentrate or think clearly enough to write. I did not sympathize but told how Sinclair Lewis had once been invited to look in on a creative writing workshop. He was smashed, and boiled his exhortation down to one sentence. It went something like this: "You folks want to write, get out there and WRITE."

One morning early in September we took off in the Buick. We buttoned the canvas top down and played the radio into the wind. Crossing the mountains, Van told of trout fishing with his dad when very young.

Over in New York State I dropped him off at a Thruway entrance and turned back to Saratoga Springs, where I was to spend the next two months at Yaddo, hard at work on a series of long poems that were as bad as they were ambitious.

Arriving in Saint Louis, Van found himself a furnished room on Waterman Street and registered for school. The student body consisted of several thousand airline stewardesses and crewcut types in shirts and ties. Van sauntered in in ink-stained khakis, a teeshirt full of holes, and bare feet in the filthiest tennis sneakers west of the Bowery. Some were drawn to him; others found him disturbing. He started writing me letters. (There was never a phone, so we never had a long-distance conversation.)

Checking in at the university clinic on September 20th, Van met a medical student named Jim Gaither, who was to solve the mystery of his disease. Gaither was about the same age as Van, and the two hit it off. Like their colleagues back East, the specialists at Washington University School of Medicine had posited an idiosyncratic preleukemia. Gaither was assigned to analyze test data and research the literature. Lacking background in hematology, he quailed at the prospect of the sophisticated blood work involved and decided to start with the urine, a simpler, more old-fashioned point of departure. The approach paid off. A finding of numerous fine, dark granules that stained blue in a potassium ferrocyanide solution sent Gaither to a recently devised diagnostic test for paroxysmal nocturnal hemoglobinuria, a blood disorder that had been observed in fewer than 200 cases since it was first described by the German hematologist Paul Strübing in 1882. The test turned out positive. A second acid hemolysis test using a normal person's serum was also positive. The diagnosis was established. From Gaither, Van learned that his prospects were not too good. One patient had survived with the disease for 20 years, however.

A few days after learning his diagnosis, Van wrote saying he was glad to know what he was up against inside himself, in the place where, as he put it, "all pursuits end . . ."

A letter written soon after hints at a feeling that something extraordinary would happen on Hallowe'en. Van had been staying up all night writing for several days. On the evening of October 31st, he went out for a drink and met a 30-year-old ex-convict named Johnny Sherrill, who was on parole and earning his living as a worker in a machine shop. The son of migrant fruitpickers—his part–American Indian mother also worked for a time as an artist for Disney Studios—Van's new acquaintance had spent the years since his teens drifting from state to state, scamming, jamming, pimping, gambling, doing time both for things he had done and things he hadn't. Johnny got along with the black guys in jail better than the whites. He identified with everything that had soul—gospel music, the blues, jazz, the rhythms of black speech, the witty verbal style, the subtleties and flourishes generally lacking in the language of their putative superiors on Tobacco Road.

Van had read Mezz Mezzrow, yet nothing could have prepared him for Johnny. The previous summer Van had reveled in Jean Genet's *Thief's Journal*. Now he was meeting someone who could have stepped straight out of its pages.

Van and Johnny left the bar and drove across the Mississippi to East Saint Louis, where at 4 a.m. in the riverbottom enclave of Brooklyn, Illinois, they stepped into a labyrinth of pink and blue neon, the Harlem Club, a palace of iniquity that might as well have sprung full-armed (indeed, bristling with weaponry) from the brow of Chester Himes.

The kid from Rutland had never seen anything like it. Here was a crowd of well-dressed, well-heeled, mainly black pleasure-seekers belonging to a culture having few points of contact with Middle America outside the used-car lot, the police station, and the hospital. Everywhere was a smell of strong spirits, perfume, marijuana, and tobacco, the strident beat of rhythm 'n' blues numbers such as "Quicksand" and "Soul Food."

Inside were several bars where you got your set-up by the half-pint bottle, with the mixer in a paper cup, and rooms where various legal and illegal games were in progress, as well as a little striptease theater, and yet another room with dancing. It was to this room that Johnny led the way through the crowd of drug dealers, pimps, hookers, and drag queens prowling the floor. Shortly before daybreak they were joined at their table by a red-haired transvestite who flirted shyly with Van.

By this time, Van was quite stoned. The idea of having sex with a boy was out of the question. However, what blew Van's mind was that he could not only sit still for such a flirtation, but open his heart to it and be deeply moved by what he saw and felt in the stranger's eyes, a love that to his amazement he found himself wholeheartedly accepting.

"I have seen a God," he wrote me the next day. Johnny had invited the transvestite to come with them but was softly rebuffed. She kissed Van goodbye, her lips barely touching his.

Upon reading his letter, I was put in mind of the lines from "Hermaphroditus" by Swinburne:

> *Whosoever hath seen thee, being so fair,*
> *Two things turn all his life and blood to fire:*
> *A strong desire begot on great despair,*
> *A great despair cast out by strong desire . . .*

It seemed as though fearing for his life had opened Van to love, any love, and maybe at this point the most impossible could be felt as the highest, and, because accepted though never consummated, as the love that casts out fear. The god he had glimpsed was none other than Eros, I supposed.

Van made plans to move in with Johnny, to buy a motorcycle. Christmas came. He spent part of the holidays with me in New York City, staying in an artist's loft on Second Avenue. One night I left him alone in the loft smoking some strong weed. I came back to find him all shook up. He had been crying, he wouldn't say why. Months later, the experience was evoked in a poem:

> *Last will and*

> *If I die in sleep it will be in a convulsion whose "terror"*
> *and "beauty" proved irresistible at last. I rise, the*
> *quivering bud afraid to blossom.*
> *It comes out of dreams where music,*
> *color and objects interchange*

but for their continual flame. It is within this flame-
flower I am drawn up sweating half awake and
horizontal. Spine arches in short
spasms. I see nothing above.
Darkness everywhere or are my eyes gone out?
Before now: I gave in to life and awoke
trembling—a coward.
But every time more rigid,
every time more pull, I
hurt with desire to
explode and vow no more retreats.
God wants to fuck me too,
and death will be my final lover.
I give her all.

With the New Year, Van returned to Saint Louis and the apartment he intended to share with Johnny. There was a newcomer in Johnny's life, a 19-year-old prostitute named Carol. Carol and Van fell for each other, and the two moved out, to a vast and decrepit biracial hotel on Cabanne Street.

Here for a short time Carol's way of moving, talking, dancing, making love became Van's. Carol referred to him as the professor she was married to. One day they were chased by a gang of black teenagers. This fit in with our mystique of the coming bloodbath. To me he wrote:

Young Negroes could purge the city here by bloodshed. That I was almost victim I applaud no less. Let all of it explode.

From my room in Hanover I also applauded, quoting to Van from my translation of Stefan George's *Heliogabalus*:

I chance while descending a marble stair
Upon a headless corpse just halfway down—
Oh my—my brother's blood congealing there.
I merely lift my trailing purple gown . . .

Carol was eager to support him, Van said. He didn't want that, he just wanted her to quit turning tricks:

I hurt to see her in black tights and leather jacket dancing out. I feel as if she is lost in some world of shining sewage, silver and gold, in a night I cannot enter or see . . .

Carol became in his words "the hieroglyph of my suffering." Then he was back in the hospital, this time with a hemolytic crisis precipitated by a bad dose of the clap. Upon leaving the hospital, he moved back to the white rooming house on Waterman Street where he had been in the fall. Carol begged him to come home to Cabanne Street. He refused.

While all this was going on, John F. Kennedy had been elected President and inaugurated, a development that meant nothing to any of us. Writing me soon after JFK's New Frontier speech, Van quoted a verse from the recently discovered *Gospel of Thomas*:

Jesus said: I have cast fire upon the world . . .

His old room on Waterman Street was occupied by a young woman student. A Florence Nightingale type, she took to waiting on Van. They were soon sleeping together, although he didn't really like her. He was now intensely aware of his deteriorating health. At times it filled him with rage, and he projected his nightmares onto the new housemate. Eventually she decamped.

Far from these upheavals in Hanover, I continued to prepare my Beethoven recital. We made a plan. In June, after the recital, I would drive out to Saint Louis in the Buick. We would proceed from there to Mexico.

While our letters discussed the coming trip, Van fell in love again. This time it was neither a transcendent vision as the divine stranger in the Harlem Club had been, nor a pink-heeled figment of the light fantastic, nor a nightmare phantom, but a reserved, extremely intelligent, ethereally pale, and entirely willing 19-year-old woman, Martha Muhs, a student at Washington U. Their love coincided with the coming of spring and was to continue for the rest of Van's life.

From a mail-order nursery in Texas I had obtained a boxful of peyote buttons and sent some to Van. A hilarious and touching letter reports on the rainy April day Van, Martha, and Johnny communed over the peyote.

On June 16 I drove west. Saint Louis was laid out flat in a heat wave when I got there. Van had moved into a huge new apartment with Johnny. Inside, Martha and her friend Jim Bryan were sitting fully clothed in a cold bath for relief from the heat, reading out loud from a story by Edgar Allan Poe. A horn honking in the street outside announced the coming of Johnny, who within moments was sharing a six-pack with Van and me. I was impressed. I found Johnny every bit as electrifying as Van had cracked him up to be.

My big moment came the next day, when someone wangled access to the university chapel organ. Pulling out all the stops for Van and his friends, I played the Hammerklavier finale.

Soon after that, Martha went home to Chicago. The two lovers took leave, promising to meet up in the fall. Van and I sat up all night reading Kerouac's *Doctor Sax* out loud. We began to prepare for Mexico.

Worried about the effect the trip was likely to have on Van's health, Johnny urged him not to go abroad. I paraphrased Beckett: "It's suicide to be abroad. But what is it to be at home? A lingering dissolution."

One morning toward the end of June we stepped over the border, having left the Buick in an El Paso parking lot. As we ground our teeth from the speed we had been ingesting ever since Saint Louis, the bus rattled over the sierras of Chihuahua heading south. Little did we know that we were passing through the very same region where a quarter-century earlier Antonin Artaud had witnessed the peyote dance.

A week later, we found ourselves facing the Pacific just north of the Guatemala frontier, outside a fishing port Van had chosen for its name: *Puerto Angel*. He had seen it on a map and said,

"Let's go to Angel Port, man."

We had rented two open-air huts made of palm leaves on a hillside over the beach. From here Van wrote to Martha:

In the trees overhead vultures alight & sail off on black wings; jungle insects make electronic sounds and tiny lizards run around everywhere. The sea itself is the blue center of all this; its transparent azure shows thousands of strange fish drifting about— bright blue tiny fish, bigger black ones, gold-tailed fish, barracuda; and even, 10 yards from shore, we saw an enormous shark once about 10 feet long. The water is slightly cooler than body temperature, the most delightful for swimming I've ever found . . .

Our landlord was the police commander. The commander had a safe full of narcotics given him in part payment for allowing the CIA to use the port for mysterious operations a few months earlier, during the Bay of Pigs adventure, according to a local schoolteacher, a Castro sympathizer. I had no idea whether there was any truth in the story, but did think the teacher somewhat nuts to be saying such things to me, a stranger, and a gringo to boot, in spite of my indiscreetly expressed opinion that Mao and Fidel were the great men of the century. I had also chatted up the postmaster on our arrival, telling him of our desire to stay for a time at Puerto Angel and write; he had taken us to call on the commander. Van's letter to Martha describes the scene:

> *El Señor Commandante (highest functionary in the town, who is sheriff, etc., but, most important, the Rent Collector) lives in the best house & has a moth-like servant or lackey who hovers at his shoulder. He looks like a William Burroughs figure—old, grey-haired, with those transparent green glasses, a pistol in his belt, high on junk all the time, very formal, reserved, but junky-like in silences & gaze. The postmaster explains that we are writers "with a great poetic mission to fulfill here" and want a house at a precio modesto. The Commander nods gravely at the former statement as if he were accustomed to meeting such personages, and brightens at the latter statement. Dave & I look serious & poetical.*

Actually, our tanned, beat appearance had led one new acquaintance to ask if we were merchant sailors. We hoped to make some kind of a drug deal that would permit us to live off the proceeds for a year or so. We were also hoping to write wonderful stuff right there in Puerto Angel.

One evening we saw what looked like a bright star moving in a steady straight line across the twilit sky over the ocean. Van pointed it out and informed me it was Sputnik. He went on to say that he liked the idea of metamorphosis because change is the law of life, whereas permanence suggests spiritual as well as physical death, both of which are also strongly suggested by the idea of closeness with another person.

Bored and peevish, we got new clothes and took to visiting a bordello owned by the commander. Van had been warned by his doctors not to get the clap, so he outfitted himself with condoms, setting off a minor stir.

The commander had a treasure that fascinated us, an ancient Mixtec jade statuette of a seated figure with a human face surmounted by a jaguar mask. This, the commander said, related to the teaching that each person's soul splits off amoeba-like into two souls at a key moment during the as-yet-unborn individual's earthward descent from the stars, and that the duplicate thus produced comes in the shape of an animal, bird, insect, or plant spirit that accompanies one throughout life like a twin. Van remarked on the similarity between this teaching and a certain Gnostic doctrine.

"With my eyes of light, I see my Twin," the commander quoted.

"The last words of Mani," Van exclaimed.

"Indeed," the commander answered. "Spoken while he was being flayed alive by the King of Persia."

I became fearful. According to an entry in my notebook:

Van gets skinnier and skinnier, yet it's impossible to think of him as being sick with a fatal illness. I doubt that any of the locals suspect. As we stepped out of the commander's doorway earlier today, I got a glimpse of him framed in pale afternoon sky, the

rainbow-striped blazer loose about his shoulders, arms out because
of the heat, his brown neck and thin shoulders forming an
improbably jaunty angle, an effect completed by pegged slacks of
olive-colored silk and a brand-new pair of dark brown ankle-
strapped Argentino boots.

One day we helped the commander perform an experiment on his mozo, the "mothlike" retainer Van had spoken of to Martha. The commander had found out that we had brought a few tabs of acid with us. He had two girls from the casino pin the little fellow while I dropped a tab in his mouth and poured in some tequila to wash it down. The commander was eager to observe the effects of lysergic acid first-hand. Later that afternoon he made a speech to us about Heaven and its impossibly desirable blue body, the sky.

Van began to wonder what sort of experiments might be in store for us, if we were lucky enough not to get ambushed by the mozo with a machete.

At length we bought a handgun from the Commander and embarked on a hare-brained scheme to hijack a small cache of high-grade bricks that I had gotten a line on in Nochistlán, a pueblo fifty miles north of Oaxaca, where there had been an earthquake weeks before, and people were crossing the still-open fissures on planks thrown casually across.

Here we hit a snag. In Van's words to Martha: "We broke into the biggest narcotics ring in Mexico by mistake and were nearly murdered."

We managed to escape in a rented truck we had left near the highway outside Nochistlán. One week later we smuggled a pound and a half of marijuana into the United States taped to our torsos and legs.

We recovered the Buick and started for California. En route Van got sick. We just made it to San Francisco General Emergency. After a few days he was better, but I had become terrified he would die, and wanted to hang onto him so he wouldn't vanish. This infuriated him. "Dave's suddenly following me everywhere in San Francisco, feeling put down every time I go out alone, adopting my ideas," he wrote to Martha. I began to imagine that an act of concentrated willpower might bring him back. My presence became insufferable.

Bad things kept happening. One day we were out driving in the Buick with the top down. Van's college friend John Ceely, who had just moved to the Bay area, was at the wheel. We'd been smoking some of the Mexican grass back at the apartment where Larry, another college friend of Van's, was putting him up temporarily. (I'd just settled in a Chinese boarding house on the edge of North Beach and was stoned all the time on paregoric I had gotten a doctor to prescribe for the dysentery that had followed me back from Mexico.) Van was in the front seat, next to John. I was alone in the back. As we swung onto the approach to a bridge, I hunched over and lit a joint I had brought with me. After a deep drag which I held in as long as possible before letting it out in a paroxysm of coughing, I stood up in the wind, toking at the joint held between my thumb and forefinger, flaunting it. Then I started screaming at the top of my lungs.

"Be cool! Sit down!" Van shouted, glaring angrily, adding in a stage whisper loud enough not to be lost in the airstream: "I'm holding!" I kept on yelling. I can't remember what the words were, if any. After a few seconds I sat back down, my face covered with tears. When I woke up I was alone in the car, its canvas top up, parked outside Larry's house. I had passed out and slept I had no idea how long. I wanted to go straight back to my Chinese boarding house, but instead trudged to the door and rang the bell to be let in. Climbing the stairs, I realized I hated Van.

A week later, walking through North Beach, we encountered posters reproducing a painting of a little girl ragamuffin with huge eyes, in a gloomy landscape like a bad children's book illustration. There was something irritating about those big dark eyes. You just knew the emotion they were supposed to convey was fake. There was a gratuitous perversity as well that repelled me.

"What on earth are they?" I exclaimed as we passed a cluster of them around a boarded-up doorway.

"They're Keanes," Van replied in an acid drawl.

"Oh no!" I said.

"Oh yes!" he replied

"No," I insisted. "There's nothing keen about it, it's kitsch . . . "

This led to another bad moment. Van told me he welcomed Keanes as one more ingredient, like Dairy Queens and Montovani records, of the coming in fact already arriving Garbage Apocalypse. He said my European esthetic standards simply didn't apply to the reality of America. As he droned on about Apocalypse and American reality, another sad-eyed-waif loomed up at arm's length. I reached out to rip it down.

"For Christ's sake," he interjected "Let it alone!" We walked on in silence.

A few days after that we exchanged some more bitter words. I decided to leave.

I hitchhiked to Saint Louis and moved in with Johnny. Johnny now had a steady named Freddie Quinn. Freddie's girlfriend Nackie and I got together briefly. Van's letters to me resumed. Freddie was pregnant. (Six months later, when the baby was born, it was a boy; they named him Alden, after Van.)

In September, during the Cuban missile crisis, we read about ourselves in the *Saint Louis Post-Dispatch* as unidentified "marijuana operators" on whose trail the police were in hot pursuit. Eventually I grew uneasy and hitchhiked back to New York.

In between ever-lengthening hospital stays, now at the U Cal Medical Center, Van took an apartment in Oakland with John Ceely. Here he wrote poems representing in his words "the last vision, the last light & my last body consumed."

Toward the end of November, after Van had been in the hospital for a month or more, John informed me that Van was running dangerously high fevers and because of clots in the extremities his toes were gray and there were red splotches on his arms, neck, and face. "Probably you've wondered," John wrote, "if you ought to come out and see him. What good would it do?"

I took peyote and had a vision of Van with tubes in him on a hospital bed, yet somehow also outside time in a heightened, eternal here-and-now state that the peyote made me feel was one in which everything in the universe past, present, and future is alive and simultaneous. From the experience I made a poem and sent it to Van. It now seemed to me that every word we exchanged had a special weight, and the power to cross immeasurable distance.

Postcards from him came every few days. He was going to be out soon. We were going to share a place in Hoboken. He had heard from Dave Haselwood of Auerhahn Press that John Wieners was in New York, writing great things. He was reading Melville's *Pierre*. He had a reservation for a flight arriving December 18th at Newark Airport.

On the morning of December 11th, my sister knocked at the door where I was staying to tell me someone had phoned with the news that Van had died the night before.

The Angel

July 2, 1961, en route from Oaxaca to Pochutla. It's now more than a week since we drove from Saint Louis out to Texas. We left the Buick in El Paso, with arrangements for its eventual recovery, crossed the border and caught a southbound bus out of Juárez. We have been up on amphetamine much of the time. We look like escapees from a reform school.

In Oaxaca we examined a map with elevation lines like spider webs. I noticed quite a few peaks above 3,000—in other words, 9,000 feet. Looking at the Pacific coast, we had to choose between Puerto Escondido (Hidden Port) and Puerto Angel (Angel Port). I liked Hidden Port where you vanish. Van insisted on Angel Port: "We'll get our wings."

The mountains between Oaxaca and the coast are cold and steep. The one-lane highway never stops climbing, a ribbon of mud strung between curtains of silver fog and sleet. An hour ago, hail was beating against the rusty frame of this bus. We huddled together, sweating and shivering and grinding our teeth from too much dexedrine. A handful of our fellow-passengers are Indians; the rest are Spanish, a dozen in all. There are also a goat and several crates of chickens. The storm passed, and the inside of the bus flooded with moonlight. I could see the driver's face in the rear-view mirror, black-mustached under a quasi-military cap.

Van's mind is like an all-night movie house. I sleep, then wake up, the bus standing still. Van tells me there was a couple fucking in the back seat. The driver and his Cuban assistant joked about the floor show. We just reached the head of the pass. From here on, until we reach the coast tomorrow morning, it's downhill. We step out into a cold wet cloud, Van humming Round About Midnight.

The cloud flowing round us, we piss. Lit up by the bus headlights on the rockface, there is a shrine the size of a bird house with a statue of the Virgin Mary: Ntra. Sra. de la Soledad. The floor of the inside of the shrine is bright red, its walls cobalt blue, suggesting a point where Heaven touches a blood-soaked hilltop.

The mountain is sopping wet and makes the same sound all mountains make when the sounds of forests, streams, and waterfalls are far below.

The cloud parted. We plunged in brightest moonlight, covered with mist droplets as if with tiny diamonds. We could see fifty miles of mountains stretching westward from the glistening sheet of mud at our feet.

We went to the refreshment shack at the roadside and bought some mezcal. Does it contain peyote? We cracked jokes about gruesome accidents on mountain roads.

At dawn we reached Candelárias, on a plateau at the head of the foothills leading down to the coastal plain, a village of mudbrick houses with palmleaf roofs. It is the relay station for the last leg of the journey to Pochutla. The relief driver who should have been waiting was not there. Our driver announced there would be a stop of several hours in Candelárias. We could sleep for free on the terrace outside the cafe.

The sun rose through the treetops, a warm red disk. The cafe owner offered straw mats for those who bought food and drink. Hung-over and shaky, we got glazed donuts and some cafe con leche, then went for a walk in the still-cool morning.

On either side, the dirt path was overspread with lush vegetation, leaftops powdered with dust. Van estimated we were looking at no less than fifty different narcotic plants. We peered at them, trying vainly to guess which were the ones.

Little Rootie Tootie is also a favorite of Van's. He once tinkered with it for hours on my piano, expanding it into a cadenza from a Romantic concerto, then rendering it à la Satie, and at last filling it out Cecil Taylor fashion. He assured me the history of music was in that one tune. There was a bar with a piano in Saint Louis where Van was improvising one afternoon last winter. A black musician came in and laughingly told him he had "a deep streak of coon."

July 4, on the beach outside Puerto Angel, in a shack rented from the local police commander. Steaming under the sun, the jungle that starts just behind this place is full of birds, yellow, orange, green, singing, screaming, screeching mostly, sailing among the floppy leaves of nameless trees, tearing through holes in the treetops and out into the sky. Victory rolls, Immelmanns, loop the loops. That's some crazy flying, Van comments.

From his verandah in Pochutla when we made the rental agreement for the shack, the commander was taking pot shots at small crocodiles in the adjacent ravine. He collects pistols and has a library of Spanish classics, as well as Greek and Latin authors, Church fathers, and many books on philosophy and the history of religions, magic, and the occult.

The Pacific: a warm bathtub filled with an infinity of parasitic and carnivorous beings. One does not feel like stout Cortez. The barracuda are too close. I wade in in the underpants I've had on for the past few days. This will wash them out. Tepid water disgusts me. Van plunges in, wearing nothing but his sunglasses. He says he loves water like this. After splashing about for a few moments we emerge, unrefreshed, in steaming sun. In this light Van's hair looks burnt-gold, curling like Alexander the Great's. There could be a hint of Africa in his cheekbones. His lips contribute to this impression; his body is lean to the point of emaciation, with a thin, vertical scar over the solar plexus, from the operation last year.

Paroxysmal nocturnal hemoglobinuria is a chronic, invariably fatal disease. The splenectomy was a shot in the dark before they knew what he had. Now the diagnosis of P.N.H. has been established, it turns out the operation was a serious error. He is likely to die any time now. On the other hand, he might hang on for years.

July 5. Puerto Angel is such a small place, one meets the aliens immediately. Outsiders are not particularly unwelcome here, but not all that welcome, either. Yesterday we made friends with Chino, a Colombian sailor, age twenty-nine. His English is perfect. He lived in the States. Van says it's obvious Chino is on the lam.

July 6. Leslie Fiedler has an essay in which he pulls together a half dozen instances in American literature of men swimming together and demonstrates that it is really a homoerotic fantasy more or less unconsciously sublimated. This flashed into my mind yesterday, as Van and I paddled in the lukewarm Pacific between stingrays and a bright miasma abuzz with horseflies and mosquitoes. There I was, swimming in an ocean I'd never seen until that day, with my best friend, the two of us like an updated Thomas Eakins. Are we men or boys? I don't know. We do swim a lot.

Last summer, shortly after he recovered from the splenectomy, Van and I made a trip to the White Mountains. We hiked over summits and ridges above timberline, slept in lean-to shelters and cabins. In my mind's eye I remember seeing him jumping up and down in an icy pool in the heat of the midday sun, bathing.

Van talks of blood. Having a blood disease makes him think about it all the time. He quotes Artaud: "To be somebody, you need blood . . . "

By the time a person turns into "somebody" via a method of analysis whereby one is reduced step by step to a submolecular level, the process is complete. Like a viable work of art, this life continues to evolve in the minds of those touched by it. At an unforeseeable moment, the person living it vanishes.

We have rigged up tents of mosquito netting inside this shack. "Shack" is a grandiose term. It has a roof of palmleaves supported by four posts with a couple of hammocks slung between. There is one wall. The floor is pounded dirt. We have a couple of kerosene lamps borrowed from the commander. I wonder if we will leave here alive.

My mother's friends in East Hampton shop around for a doctor with the perfect bedside manner. Don Giovanni ran through his thousand and three. As a child I was forever daydreaming about Atlantis. According to Van, the kingdom of heaven is here and now, no place else. He quotes the *Gospel of Thomas*. I on the other hand always want to be elsewhere, someplace like Mu.

Van is concerned about my drinking. It's a strange thing for him to be worrying about, considering the company he kept in Saint Louis. My eyebrows shot up the other day on the mountain pass, when I saw the serape-draped roadside vendor in a round-crowned Indian hat pouring mezcal into empty Coca Cola bottles through a funnel and found out the price was about a dime for a pint. Van noticed my reaction. I expected some kind of comment. Instead he got drunk with me.

July 7. We made friends with the prisoners in the Pochutla market-place. We went in from here on the dawn bus and found them in front of the jail, playing basketball. They get out twice a day, morning and afternoon. We shot a few baskets with them. Soon it will be a habit. Yesterday afternoon we swam out to a rock in the bay near our beach. Sitting on the rock, we saw a barracuda swim past a couple of times. We raced each other ashore.

Whenever we order something to eat at the cafe on the beach, a little Indian girl waits on us. Van says he would like to take her back to the States.

Van has a blazer from Saint Louis that shimmers like a rainbow. He wore it to Pochutla one day and the commander, joking, called it his coat of many colors. Around here Van wears his torn chinos and, when going to the port, puts on an old black teeshirt and tennis sneakers.

We got shaves and haircuts in Pochutla. In the barber shop I read a picture magazine article on Willi, the yodeling parrot. His first owner was a Hitler Youth leader. They are shown skiing in the Tyrol in the summer of 1938. They taught him to scream, "Sieg Heil!" In 1941 he was part of a revue given for Hitler at Berchtesgaden. Today, Willi belongs to a flea circus on tour in the Middle East.

Our general plan is to live here and write books. Puerto Angel's relation to Pochutla is that of Piraeus relative to Athens. Every now and then, the government announces a plan to transform Pochutla and Puerto Angel into something big, because a lot of coffee and other produce move out of here, in spite of the fact that loading is all done by rafts, in the absence of any docks. This year they resurrected the project. The only evidence of anything actually happening is the presence of a German engineer, engaged to survey the possibilities for a real port. No one has any idea what they may be.

Evenings, the cafe on the beach can have its charm. Watching the shadows of the hammocks slung next to the door jump back and forth to the flickering of a kerosene lamp, I recreate the scene as an engraving in a *Harper's Monthly Magazine* of the 1870s. In my mind's eye I picture a title like "Tramping in the By-Ways of Oaxaca." In this light the engineer sitting alone at his table on the other side of the cafe has a pre-Raphaelite bohemian look. Van grows ever more enthralled with the little Indian girl. She is the owner's niece.

As I pause from writing, I can look straight up into the Milky Way. When I climb into the hammock, my feet will point west, toward the Pacific. Van says poetic license is freedom to do exactly what you feel like doing from one minute to the next.

Some things repeat themselves and have to be turned off. Lost continents. A belle époque. I'm twenty-five. This is my belle époque. I am losing out on it. The idea of loss keeps bobbing up to the surface. I don't like putting it in words, even mentally, much less on paper, because saying it makes it come true. I concentrate on the idea of finding, or invention. I draw a blank on that, too. I asked Van if invention wasn't an illusion.

In reply, he said something about alchemy and the concept of the philosopher's stone as a scorned, or unnoticed, beautiful thing that is there in the dust by the roadside, free for the taking. "Just something like a dime you find on the sidewalk, when a dime is what you need."

He said he liked the idea of metamorphosis because change is the law of life and permanence suggests spiritual if not physical death, both of which are also strongly suggested by the idea of closeness with another person: "No one can ever come close to touching another person. Heaven help them if they try."

We saw what looked like a bright star moving across the twilit sky. Van informed me it was Sputnik.

July 8. Van gets skinnier and skinnier, yet it's impossible to think of him as being sick with a fatal illness. I doubt that any of the locals suspect. As we stepped out of the commander's doorway earlier today, I got a glimpse of him framed in pale afternoon sky, the rainbow-striped blazer hung loose about his shoulders, arms out because of the heat, his brown neck and thin shoulders forming an improbably jaunty angle, an effect completed by pegged slacks of olive-colored silk and a brand-new pair of dark brown ankle-strapped Argentino boots.

July 10. Last night Van and I were on the beach looking at a couple of racked-up fishing dugouts that had been parked in the sand. Men, women, and children were coming and going. At sunset, with mealtime impending, there is always much activity on the beach. People here eat seafood caught by themselves or their relatives every day of the week and sell the rest in Pochutla.

You don't need to be an expert to recognize what part of the world this racial type came from. I picture their ancestors trekking from Asia.

One of the dugouts has captured Van's fancy. He thinks it seaworthy. We want to find out whose it is, and whether we could rent it.

Van got diarrhea yesterday. I'm a little off myself. It may be getting time to start taking the Enteroviaform. Dysentery is supposedly endemic here.

I hate the cafe because they play the radio so loud, mostly commercials, a half-hour at a time, and then one ear-splitting love song after another, in which the key word is *corazón*. We can hear the songs deep into the night all the way over here at the shack, half a mile away across the water.

There was a movie on the beach last night. They stretched a bedsheet between two poles. A schoolteacher from Pochutla who has been chatting with me about Lumumba and Fidel manned the projector. For the equivalent of a nickel apiece we rented folding seats from the cafe. It was a double feature. First, a film starring Cantinflas, who looks like many of the guys around here. It was pretty much incomprehensible to us, save for the commedia dell'arte hamming that by itself was worth the price of admission. The second show was an Alan Ladd war movie I had never seen, with flickering Spanish subtitles and a damaged soundtrack. Small boys were crawling in the sand at our feet.

Pochutla Casino bar, Wednesday, July 12. Yesterday we fasted. The shits have gone away for the time being. Van went fishing with Chino today, in a boat Chino has the use of. Later they picked me up at Chino's place en route to Pochutla in a pickup truck belonging to the cafe owner, loaded with fish. I just came downstairs from fucking a half-Indian, half-Spanish prostitute named Chica in one of the rooms here. Van is still upstairs with the other one, Anita. Chica appears to be in her mid-twenties, my age. Her face is that of an intelligent but perverse child. This was my first experience with a prostitute in America. Van and Anita were still giggling in the next room when Chica and I came down to the bar a few minutes ago. Chino is visiting a woman somewhere else and supposed to come back here in an hour. I am sitting alone with a mezcal and a Carta Blanca. This expedition is costing us somewhere between $5 and $10 (U.S.) apiece. It was Chino's idea. We had no inkling of this place's existence, but when Chino told us about it, we were eager to make the scene. I don't believe Van has ever been inside a bordello in his life, but he sauntered in as if he owned the place. There was no sign of any pimps or bouncers. A crone with bleached hair in a bolero outfit who tends the bar here was the one who collected our money. Chino advised us to tip each of the women $5 (Mexican).

When Van and Chino went out fishing this morning, Chino gave me the keys and told me to go into his storeroom where I would find a bag of marijuana. He asked me to make up a few joints. He says smoking makes driving an adventure; you see more interesting things along the way.

Chino's house is at the other end of Puerto Angel from our shack, next to the Pochutla road, which is the only road leading out of Puerto Angel. The house is built into the side of a small cliff. Its front porch, or sleeping balcony, stands up on stilts. From it one sees the beach and ocean at a distance of maybe 150 yards. Several coconut palms shade the porch and a small front yard. The cliff is overgrown with vines, and there are plenty of birds in the trees overhead. Today they were sitting quietly, because it was raining.

There is a screen of netting round the porch. The house was unlocked. Going in alone, I felt like an intruder. I would make a poor burglar. Both the *Gita* and Bessie Smith advise: Do Your Duty. Another's duty, the *Gita* adds, no matter how well you may do it, will make you insane.

The first thing I saw was a hammock and a Sterno stove on the floor in one corner. The wall was decorated with religious pictures. Candles were set up in front of them on tin cans. These in turn were placed on a red silk cloth, next to a dream book with Art Nouveau lettering on the cover.

In the other corner there was a little alcove with mirror and washstand, a bar of soap and a straight razor.

I unlocked the storeroom door. The room is built into the hillside. It's cool and dark. I lit the kerosene lamp hanging in the doorway. Chino's cat was there, crouching in front of a cracked spot at the angle of the wall and the floor, seemingly poised to spring.

I located the marijuana. There was a table and chair. I set the lamp on the table and poured out some of the grass to roll. The cat remained motionless. I noticed, on the floor at my feet, a dead rat, or rather, half a dead rat. The cat had eaten the head and shoulders and part of the legs, but left the rest. Now he was waiting for another, perhaps one that would taste better.

The rat's viscera had begun to dry, taking on the look of a piece of old kidney. I was struck by the absence of flies. The netting works. But the room was a mess, with empty Carta Blanca and Coke bottles and stubbed-out cigarettes on the floor.

The cat sprang. There wasn't even a flurry. He might as well have blown the rat's head off with a gun.

I rolled four, five joints. The cat looked up at me, the prey dangling wetly from his mouth.

I heard steps in the front door and recognized Van's light-footed stride. "Everything under control?" He pushed the door open and took in the scene: me, the marijuana, the cat, the two rats.

"A stricken field," he commented, making a face. The cat slipped by him with a little bound, the rat still dangling. We stepped into a drizzly fog, the same fog and drizzle we have had since yesterday.

I got in the truck next to Chino, giving Van the window place, and showed Chino the jays I had rolled. "Perfecto." As the truck jolted forward, I glimpsed the cat staring at us, its eyes green jewels.

Puerto Angel, July 13. Although Van never mentions P.N.H., he fears he may get a relapse of the "disgusting condition" here. The phrase is a reference to Burroughs: "I am not innarested in your disgusting condition." When someone questioned Van about it, he said it was too disgusting to discuss, and "since I'm not innarested, why should *you* care?"

We consider the difference between *neether* and *nyther*. Both of us *neether* people, we despise twits that say *nyther*. My grandpa used to say *envellup* for "envelope." Noah Webster probably said it that way, too. I hate linguistic change. Van welcomes it. In an *American Legion Magazine* found in a hospital waiting room he once read the following poem:

> *Whence all these new faces?*
> *Whither are they going?*
> *Indiscriminate mixing of alien races*
> *May yet prove America's undoing.*

"Who's the poet talking about?" he asked, poker-faced.

I said I couldn't begin to guess. "He's talking about us," Van laughed. "The man is an American Indian."

It has been two weeks since we got here. The commander has grown steadily more familiar. Something is happening, Van says. Just tune in on it, you'll pick up.

It began one afternoon when the commander, in a fit of bonhomie, got out a prize possession he keeps in his safe, a jade statuette of a seated jaguar-masked figure that he informed us was a representation of its original owner, an ancient Mixtec prince, or, rather, his heavenly double.

"It's mirrors that are recent," Van pointed out. "Twins have always been around."

"Have you seen the mirrors here?" the commander rejoined. "The black ones? Thomas was Christ's twin."

"Every time I see double," Van replied, "I get the feeling I am peeling off layers."

"*With my eyes of light I see my Twin,*" the commander quoted.

"The last words of Mani," Van put in.

"Spoken while being flayed alive by the King of Persia," the commander added.

As the two of them volleyed back and forth, I sat at a stereopticon viewer that the commander had affably insisted on getting out for me. Replacing the cards one by one in the device's sliding frame, I inspected a series of 3-D images of trussed-up persons being dismembered inch by inch with machetes during the repression of a turn-of-the-century uprising not far from here.

"My father's time," the commander explained.

As I gazed, fascinated, the commander invited us to join him later for dinner at the Casino.

Taking leave of the commander for the time being, Van and I issued forth. A letter awaited at the post office, from my mother. She sails next month for Southampton on the *France*. After sleepless nights worrying that I might come to harm in the wilds of southern Mexico, those deck chairs will be heaven, unless they get torpedoed by a Russian submarine. She is dieting to prepare for shipboard dinners. The wicked French make it easy for one to break all the rules without a moment of regret.

Arriving at the Casino, we noticed that Chica and Anita were not present. It turns out the commander owns the place.

The color scheme is red and yellow. Yellow bar, barstools, chairs, tables. Red walls, ceilings, floors, ashtrays. Tibetan colors, Van pointed out. We found the commander enthroned amid half a dozen girls, in an alcove surrounded with potted palms, drinking beer. In the middle of the table was a blood-red bowl filled with flowers. Bullfight music blared from a jukebox. Chatting with the madam-cum-bartender in her bolero outfit, the commander had the air of a queer Oriental potentate. Did Solomon in all his splendor know glories such as these? Addressing us with courtly formality in the presence of his satellites, the commander wanted to know if we were happy out there in Puerto Angel, did we need anything, would we mind if he came calling some day soon? So he is definitely going to be coming over here this afternoon, or possibly tomorrow. He will bring Chica and Anita, Van tells me.

The dysentery is coming on, no way to stop it. Van jokes about running down the beach and shitting green. There is a low fever and a feeling of tiredness, whether hung over or not. Three tablets of LSD sit in my knapsack like a time bomb. There is a small cemetery a hundred yards east of the shack. People were standing around in there with lit candles yesterday morning when both of us were too sick to move. An Englishman who lived for a time on the beach here a few years ago is buried nearby, whether inside the cemetery or outside of it was not made clear.

July 15. Van envies Beckford for writing *Vathek* at one sitting. In 1782, when Beckford did that, facility was at a premium. To be any good, a work of art had to be "easy." Beckford took piano from that paragon of ease, Mozart, and was twenty when he composed *Vathek.*

I have been up for the past couple of days on speed, outlining a story based on our coming here. I wrote a bit, then drew a blank. To finish it would be too easy. Van says coming here means arriving at the edge of America, the jumping-off place. I don't want to jump in the ocean, thank you. One of my ancestors did just that. She walked into the water at Amagansett beach one night in the 1840s. All they ever found was footprints down to the surf line. For me, coming here was more like jumping through an invisible hoop that is in the air, and if you go through just right, you are on the other side. Also, there is something special about the mountains and the wilderness to the south of here.

For instance, 120 years ago a Danish botanist named Liebman was in that very wilderness collecting specimens and came upon a village of blond Indians speaking old-fashioned Danish. He later looked into records at Pochutla and learned that a Danish pirate ship was wrecked off Huatulco in 1600, or thereabouts. Survivors made their way up the coast. Their descendants were still speaking Danish in the vicinity of Pochutla within living memory, Mexico's secret Vikings. The commander's father was on friendly terms with them.

My contemporaries in East Hampton call me Moon. How are they hangin', Moon? The nickname goes back to a day in 1944 when I electrified the schoolyard by pointing at the moon in the mid-afternoon sky and shrieking "Moon! Moon!" I induced a crowd of other children to scream and point the same way. We pranced, screeching at the top of our lungs, back into the schoolhouse. This went on for weeks. Many who saw it never forgot.

Soon after, I began my first writing project. A chum named Frankie showed me a children's book, *Many Moons*, from the local library. We did a stage adaptation. I wrote the script, and Frankie directed. My whole reason for doing it was to play the role of the black-caped, elegantly Luciferian villain.

Frankie and I squabbled over the parts in a version to be played by just the two of us. Frankie said I wanted all the best ones. He called me a show-off.

Our thoughts were diverted from the theater when we found a huge Victorian baby carriage in the barn, a natural for the nacelle and landing carriage of an 1899 model Clément Ader "Avion." All it needed to become airborne was an engine hooked up to an aerial screw, I explained, plus a pair of batlike wings and a tail. This could all be easily put together at the garage, Halsey's, where Frankie's dad was a mechanic.

"David," Frankie said (he never called me Moon), "that carriage is a stagecoach."

Years later, I learned the moon was a hieroglyph of exile, separation, separateness, a way-station for souls descending from the stars into the bodies of "all creatures here below" (in the words of a hymn we sang in church Sunday mornings). Ultimately, it stood for the presence of the Deity withdrawn from the world.

I called the hermits in my story "girovagos" because they were wanderers (vagos) who gyrated through both mundane and mystic spheres. They were also citizens of a secret utopia.

July 16, the commander's visit. Today was a turning-point. I think we are going to have to leave soon.

There is a crummy shell of a building, on a bluff over the water midway between our shack and the port, belonging to the commander. He is reviving a plan to fix it up and open a casino here in Puerto Angel. Wait till they start building the new port, he exclaims. In his enthusiasm the commander refers to the old concrete ruin as The Angel. You fellows have got to come out to The Angel with me this afternoon. It's fascinating. The path is overgrown. My mozo is going up right now with a machete.

The commander's valet was off and running. Van gazed after him from behind horn-rimmed wraparounds. The commander had brought Chica and Anita from the Pochutla Casino, as well as a bottle of tequila. We had been shitting our guts out of late. I hoped the strong drink would give some relief. We stood round the jeep, clinking glasses. "To The Angel!" The tequila burned going down. My head swam. We gazed at the lagoon shimmering in wet heat half a mile out over the bay.

"Yesterday an Indian was half killed by a barracuda over there," the commander mused. "Incidentally, I read an article about an experimental product, LSD. Are you familiar with it? Writers I would expect to keep up with such things. You must have looked into it. I wouldn't be surprised it you had brought some with you here. If so, could I ask you as a favor to part with some of it? I have an experiment in mind. A single dose would do."

"As a matter of fact," Van answered, and I didn't believe I was hearing him say this, "we are able to oblige. It is a tiny amount, but that is all that's necessary."

The commander enacted a pantomime of delight, his hands and eyes upturned as though thanking Heaven.

Had someone gone through our things? Did Van tell him? I was scared. I spoke, for the first time since we had toasted The Angel, "I'll get it out for you before you go back to Pochutla."

"Oh, no, thank you," said the commander. "I'd prefer to look at it immediately, if you wouldn't mind. I was asking the doctor only yesterday. He knows very little but thinks it may be related to some of the substances Indians use. He has noticed people in the marketplace at times when they come down from the hills, places you wouldn't imagine exist in this day and age, with something very odd about their eyes and the way they move. He'd like to check. I was thinking, as a favor, don't you know, why not provide a subject?"

The valet was returning, trotting along the road, his shouldered machete gleaming in the sun.

Van went into the shack and returned with one of the tablets, setting it on the red oilcloth in front of the commander. The commander filled a glass, then rolled up his sleeves. I noticed marks that had to be needlemarks on the veins of his forearms.

"Should it be dissolved or just washed down?" the commander asked.

'Washed down is okay,' Van replied.

"All right, my boy," said the commander, "here's your drink and here is a special vitamin for your head."

He patted the mozo on the head, then shouted, "Yes, your head, your head," slapping it from side to side, "*tu cabeza*, your pretty little head, *tu cabecita, chico!*"

Like a Bedouin storyteller unfolding a tale in which the hero is carried by a bird to a city of greater than material splendors, the commander raised one hand to point to the clouds over the mountains thirty miles to the east: "You will walk on those clouds over there."

The commander's lower lip was edged with a hint of froth at one corner of his mouth. The skin over his cheekbones stretched smooth and taut, his eyes were pinned. The mozo knelt at his feet, hands clasped, eyes imploring, gasping as the commander continued. The machete was out of reach, in the back of the jeep. The mozo stood up with a shriek. The commander knocked him down and pinned him in the sand, whooping delightedly. The mozo was unable to move. Chica pried his jaws apart, jamming his cheeks between the molars. The mozo was stubborn. Anita held his head still, whispering endearments. Chica located a gap in his teeth and pushed.

Van stood there looking imperturbable behind his dark glasses. The commander gazed up at me. I knew what I was supposed to do.

I picked up the tablet and dropped it into the mozo's bleeding mouth. He tried to spit it out, an impossibility because his mouth was being held open. The commander looked up again. The glass of tequila. I stared at the orange tablet. It was stuck to his tongue, which for the moment had stopped lolling around inside his mouth. The tablet was dissolving. His tongue was coated white. The tablet formed a little patch, magenta on white, slashed with a vivid streak extending from it like a comet's tail. I could count each individual taste bud on the tongue's pink-and-white stippled surface. The bright orange reached me out of the midst of it like the fiery wheels Ezekiel saw bursting out of the cloud. The tongue started moving. Amazing how much the human tongue resembles the tongue of any other animal.

The commander was gazing insistently into my eyes. The drink. Get the drink and pour it down his throat. I'd forgotten about that. I turned to Van. He hadn't moved. Behind the dark glasses he was staring, too. The valet was struggling now. I reached for the glass and poured its contents in his mouth. The mouth was bleeding quite a lot by this time. What was left of the tablet vanished down his gullet. They clapped his mouth shut and held it tight. He gulped, trying to vomit. After a while he lay still. Chica ran to the jeep and returned with two lengths of rope. We tied the mozo and carried him to the back of the jeep. Anita wiped his face, licking a corner of her handkerchief and dabbing the cut on his lip. She wiped the tears from his cheeks, kissing him, "We love you, honey, we wouldn't do you any harm."

"*Maulhalten!*" said the commander. He turned to me, "That's what the German fellow says when he has heard enough girl-talk."

"*Maulhalten!*" he repeated, imitating the engineer. Anita looked down at the still-tearful valet. She kissed his eyes and patted him.

We all went down to the water's edge and washed the blood off our hands. Women are sentimental, the commander said. Yes, Van agreed, they are. The commander poured a final round before setting out for The Angel. He said he intended to turn our friend over to the doctor as soon as they returned. As we filed through the path hacked out of the thick undergrowth by the mozo an hour earlier, the commander questioned Van about symptoms, duration of intoxication, and possible after-effects.

Anita and Chica followed the two of them; I brought up the rear, cradling the tequila bottle in my arm. I wondered how I could ever have been attracted to Chica. Her cream-colored jacket sagged to one side from the salt cellar and lemon she had picked up from the back of the jeep when we stowed the mozo. She wasn't wearing it when she helped subdue him. The commander paused to roll down his sleeves. As always, he was wearing a white shirt. Van and I were in teeshirts, slapping bugs. We climbed round another little bend in the path, then after a quick scramble past some freshly mutilated undergrowth, we were there, on top. The commander stretched his arm in a seigneurial gesture. We seemed to have moved outside the mosquito zone. Gulls were going crazy in the sky between us and the bay.

Since the advent of concrete, one abandoned semi-finished resort hotel is more or less identical with another, making due allowances for size. I've seen them in several parts of the world, and they're all alike. The Angel was no exception, only it was smaller and tackier than most.

The sudden change in perspective, together with the first breath of somewhat cooler air in days, brought about a sudden, if only momentary, clearing of the mind. In this interval of lucidity, it occurred to me that our journey to the edge of the world was just a copy of something we had been reading and seeing movies about ever since childhood. The white adventurer who goes to an exotic land, usually some tropical hellhole with dark-skinned people and a cast of characters evolving from G. A. Henty and the Tom Swift books through Bowles, B. Traven, and on to Burroughs, in search of buried treasure, gold, diamonds, drugs, the secret of life, what have you. After many adventures, the hero grabs the goods and hightails it home. Many fail (*The Treasure of Sierra Madre*, for instance, or Rimbaud's attempt to get rich off gun-running and the slave trade), but others make a go of it. Would we want to be among the successful ones? I rather doubt it. Van actually sympathizes with the locals. I don't all that much myself, in spite of an admiration for Castro and others like him, but that kind of reading predisposes me to look on our whole enterprise, Van's and mine, as a cliché in the collective fantasy life of the imperialist nation we hail from. Only a couple of years ago in Paris, I even toyed with the idea of renouncing my nationality in order to become a naturalized French citizen. This was when my fellow-students and I actually believed it possible to turn the struggle against De Gaulle and his generals into a revolutionary civil war, and what a joke that was! This is an even bigger one. Thanks to our books, Van and I have gravitated toward the kind of people and situations we read about, and now we are in the middle of the same sort of mess in real life, only there is no story-line, no coherence to it, it's just a mess. The commander is a lunatic. I am quite sure he could kill us on a whim and never give a thought to the consequences; but I think behind all his funny ways he's too conventional, too much of a mediocrity to dream of doing such a thing. In real life the commander is more like a figment of a Hollywood imagination than he would be if we saw him in one of the thrillers they project on a bedsheet on the beach here Sunday nights.

These thoughts were erased when I took a swig from the tequila bottle. This cleared the palate and emptied the mind.

A moment later, arriving at a bare patch of gravel in front of The Angel, Chica did a little dance. I joined in. Soon we were skipping about, raising dust. Van started scatting, clapping, strutting to the beat, singing in a squeaky falsetto, bopping along, as we moved in a little procession toward the entranceway. The ever-obliging commander clapped to applaud, with a chuckle and a little bow. Even Anita was smiling for the first time since the excitement at the shack. I had handed her the tequila when we started dancing, and now she took a quick sip from the bottle. The commander led the way up a short flight of steps onto the front porch.

"This is a palace!" Van exclaimed. "Why aren't we living here? Dig the view. Mountains, seabreeze, it's got everything."

"It is indeed a palace," said the commander. "Have you noticed the walls and ceiling in my Pochutla Casino? That meat red, and the eggyolk yellow of the bar itself and other furniture, save for the ashtrays, which are the same red, so it's rather like putting out one's cigarettes on a steak?"

"Whereas upstairs," Van rejoined, "the color scheme is reversed—walls and ceiling egg-yellow, and window shutters, chairs, bed, washstand all the color of meat in the marketplace. I recognized a choice . . . "

"Well," the commander interrupted, "there is no mystery about any of that, or, rather, it does exemplify a mystery I am quite fond of. But here at The Angel we are considering something belonging to a wholly other realm. This front door represents the entrance to a house that will be all in grays, blues, and whites, ever so subtly interwoven. Look at this room. Do you see how clean it is? Let's sit on the floor. Right here. Look out the window. Picture snow on those mountains. Sometimes I make believe this room is a walled garden on a high rooftop. If there was ever anything blue and empty, it's the sky here, even in the minutest spaces between the leaves of the one source of shade, which is an orange tree. There's a special scent in the air. The day itself is like an immense golden rind sectioned again and again, until there is nothing left except for the tears in our eyes and a smell of orange peel and the sky all around, blue and unchanging, because we can look at heaven any way we like, but it's always the same. No scream of terror or despair or hate or the imploring eyes of sixty million saints and innocent children ever moved it. It is forever the same, igual, pareil, egal, repeat it in six thousand languages, there is nothing that can change the sky or make anything even approaching a wrinkle in its skin, that impossibly desirable perfect ideal smooth blue body that is the outward shape of Heaven. How can you desire a thing like that? How could anyone not? You know what I mean. I'm talking about GOD."

"Wow!" said Van

"I could supply details," the commander went on, "about the river running beneath these walls as long as the summer snows up there go on melting. The air in this room is water-cooled but dry, so dry it would be delightful to immerse one's entire body in oil. Think of it. When I sit still and give it a chance, everything here is transparent, colorless. The vibrations of one's own self are lost in an infinitely receding lacework of spirals, which in turn reduce to an essence like that of a rose whose shape continues in the mind."

The commander's arabesque sent me into a reverie from which I had no desire to be roused. As the others got up to continue the house tour, I remained seated on the floor, waving vaguely when asked if I was all right. They disappeared through a doorway, permitting me to follow out my own thoughts where the commander had left off.

My mind went back to two summers ago, when I was in Granada to see the Alhambra palace and explore the Sierra Nevada that separates Granada from the sea.

Forming the northern Pillar of Hercules (the Atlas range in Morocco is the southern Pillar), the Sierra Nevada rises more than eleven thousand feet to the Mulhacén, highest mountain in Spain. From the summit, Morocco is visible on a clear day. I wanted to see Africa. It's said to be the cradle of the human race. But my immediate ancestry is European. To approach Africa, I wanted to have at least one foot on native ground. At the same time, I realized the geographic displacement was hardly necessary, considering that the whole of Africa and her prodigious history were in me, too, and, for me, not elsewhere.

Why the Alhambra? Because it was the residence of an African monarch in Europe, near the gap separating the two continents. Also because its architecture, in common with that of hundreds of similar buildings from Morocco to India, represents a philosophy of surrender rather than one of conquest and redemption. My favorite subject at school was geometry. I took Greek to read Euclid in the original. But the geometry of the Greeks clings to the obvious like seaweed to a rock. I wanted another geometry, one that would follow the contours of pure space.

In the rambling, seemingly disjointed suites of rooms and halls, gardens and levels that make up the Alhambra, I found a linear translation of that dream. All the patterns: a story of hidden treasure; of an upside-down tree whose roots are in the zenith, an image of reality pulsing forth out of the nothingness at the core of things; of a garden with a fountain at its center, of expansion and contraction, of movement centrifugal and centripetal, of endlessly repeated rhythmic patternings flowing on and on, eluding the trap of time. I bribed guards to let me in early in the morning, to watch sunrise in the throne room with its ceiling embodying the seven heavens in red and green bands rippling outward from a colorless center to a nut-colored periphery. Round the arched doorways were calligraphic verses in which the palace described itself to the beholder: "Within me is a shining dome of enchantments tangible and recondite . . . "

One afternoon found me writing in my notebook on a bench in the Generalife gardens above the Alhambra, in midday heat under a cloudless sky. From where I sat, the snowy ridges of the Sierra twenty miles to the southeast were clearly visible. That night I rode an electric tram ten miles up from Granada to a terminus high in the mountains.

Four days later I stood on the summit of the Mulhacén. It was late morning, on a clear day with no wind. Stamping up and down in the snow, I could see in all directions. Now for Africa. There it was, a squiggle on the curving lip of the sky. Breathing quietly again, I smoked.

It was a Camel from one of the last packs out of the three cartons Van and I brought with us to Puerto Angel. I was sitting cross-legged on the floor of the commander's special room, trembling with excitement at the memory of standing atop the Mulhacén, looking at Africa. I wondered where the others were and at the same moment heard them on the stairs, the Commander's voice rolling on:

"I suppose it could be said that what I am planning here amounts to a monstrosity. Those of us unfortunate enough to have been posted to the frontier of a declining empire are condemned, I fear, to a life of caricature. As you get older, you'll see. Dreams are the only reason to continue."

They entered. Van was interrupting the commander:

"I've no idea how long I will be staying on."

"Oh but you mustn't disappoint us," the commander protested. "I had been planning for you and your friend to have the best apartment here, rent-free. You told me only the other day you were thinking of staying several years, with an occasional foray into the hinterland, explorations, investigations, experiments. You're writers. You'll be writing your books. If that's what you want, your troubles are over. You're my guests. No more rent. Rooms at The Angel. It's up to you, of course."

The girls looked angry. I surmised that Chica had registered disapproval of the experiment. Anita would have told her to shut up. She counts on the commander hiring her as manager of The Angel. Van told me later that it was this expectation of hers that motivated everything Anita did. When he became aware of it, Van went on, he decided Anita had to be a nit.

"The Angel is never going to exist outside the commander's head," he concluded. "I wouldn't lay too much money on his head, either, at this point."

Van himself looked pretty bad, standing there with the commander, much paler than before, his eyes bloodshot. He gave me a dirty look. I wondered if that was for sitting by myself during the inspection of The Angel. I stood up, my head spinning.

"You don't look at all well," the commander remarked. "Let's have a drink, we need one."

He was right, the tequila did wonders.

When we hit the level ground below, next to the beach, the commander strode ahead, brisk and chipper, eager to look in on the mozo. Reaching the jeep, he recoiled with the look of one who has just come upon a horribly mutilated corpse. Now he was in a hurry to get back to Pochutla. I glanced at the mozo. He lay on his back, with eyes fixed and lips compressed. I couldn't understand the

commander's reaction. The mozo looked perfectly normal for someone on acid. Chica went to kiss him. Van touched her arm, "Don't
mess with him now—he's radioactive."

Van asked the commander if he could ride back to Pochutla
with him. Of course, my friend, you're always welcome. Van
brushed past me, his face averted, and went behind the screen in our
shack to spruce up. The rest of us finished the bottle. I realized that
I was more than slightly drunk. I wondered what Van was going to
do but knew there was no point in asking. He came down to the
road and swung himself into the jeep. The rest had already climbed
aboard. He turned and said, "Don't expect me before tomorrow."
Then I saw his profile and the commander's, both looking straight
ahead, side by side on the front seat of the jeep, moving out into
the sunset.

July 17. Last night, as I watched the commander's jeep bounce away
into the trees at the turn-off onto the Pochutla road, the thought of
Van's impending death grew on me. He has been reading Clement
of Alexandria. The book was lying open on his table yesterday
morning. I noticed a passage marked in ballpoint: "Have no fear of
devastating illnesses. Even illness stops when we put our entire soul
into the purpose of doing God's will."

Opening a beer, I went in the shack and slipped into my usual
late-afternoon routine of talking to the objects in the room. Behind
the screen, where Van had been combing his hair twenty minutes
earlier, I made faces in the mirror. On the stand beneath, in between
the big comb that we share and a tube of hair grease bought in
Oaxaca, was the little matchbox we have been using as our LSD
stash. I opened it. There was only one tab left. So that was what he
was planning to do in Pochutla. I supposed he thought I would

share this one with him at some future time. I decided to take it immediately.

Soon I began to imagine I could see the two sides of the human personality, female and male, rotating in circles first tangential, then intersecting, until in superimposition they formed a single circle, which at first lay perfectly flat, an even, unbroken surface like that of the pool on the granite shelf where Van and I stopped to drink last summer, beneath the summit of Mount Clay. It began to waver in concentric ripples, as if a stone had been dropped into it, and then in a whirlpool motion which increased until it opened into a tremulous, glistening cone like the one in Poe's *Descent into the Maelström*. This vortex then split into two furiously spinning tops like eddies seen in rapids from above. Suddenly they turned inside out and flew upwards like waterspouts. I saw them swaying in a slow, strong dance. Both were snow-covered mountains. Billions of grassblades along the shoreline were waving in the wind. Atop one of the mountains was a transparent dome enclosing a bush of white roses and a beehive.

Next day. Van returned this afternoon, blazing with amphetamine. He brought with him a box containing a pistol purchased from the commander. He had spent the night at the Casino with Anita and another woman I never saw, "but she is too much, man!" He launched into a description of the circumstances that led to the three of them ending up in bed together.

"How was it?" I interrupted.

He screwed up his face in a funny little look that I have come to loathe: "A lesson in humility."

"How so?"

"Well, in present state of mind," Van replied in mock-Chinaman style, "speck of dust weigh heavy like year in jail."

He took a long drag on the joint he had been rolling, and broke into a fit of coughing, then with a deadpan look shook his finger at me and whispered:

"A hair could be the trigger."

"Sure could," I said to myself, picking up one of the commander's empty shellcases and blowing on it to make it whistle.

At that moment Chino arrived. I asked him how long he had known the Commander was a junkie. Chino said he had found that out while dropping by to pay the commander what he owed him. The doctor was almost always there.

Van remarked that the commander must have been high the first time we met. The doctor was leaving when we got there, and the commander was out on the porch shooting at baby crocodiles in the ravine.

"He probably got his taste just a few minutes earlier. The glow was still on."

"Right," Chino agreed. "I was never down with that many junkies, so it wasn't until I dug the doctor a few times that I got hip to it. Lately the commander has been letting the doctor shoot him up in front of me. He doesn't give a fuck about anything. He has plenty of bread, owns most of what's around for rent. Postmaster calls him a black sheep. I doubt that. He often mentions his father. I don't know, though, he's too casual. It's not normal to put everything you do up front like that. Let's face it, man, we're all strangers here. I think he's into something else, deeper, something we don't know about. Maybe he's just crazy. What do you make of the fact he collects money from me, which he doesn't need, obviously, and at the same time tells you cats you don't have to pay rent. Doesn't fit. What worries me is, he's no fool. I ever tell you how he got hold of the safe full of heroin? That's recent. When I first came here, the doctor was bringing the taste. Now he gets it out of the safe. I was here when it arrived. The whole transaction lasted several days. Everyone here witnessed it."

Nochistlán, July 21. We left Pochutla day before yesterday and are now 200 miles inland on a high plateau. I can't believe what we are about to do. I was never in a place like this before.

I just heard music. I may be dead within a few hours. The mere possibility makes me horny. I was already feeling horny this afternoon when I went out to the end of the last street at the edge of this town. Huge cracks ran along the ground from a recent earthquake. Horniness came up in waves that filled my chest and rose into my throat. Everything looked changed. It was exactly like being high. Things appeared sharper and somehow magnified. Maybe this is how Van feels all the time.

Today was a bright, cloudless day. I felt as though I could see the stars and they were talking to me. A field across the road from where I was walking seemed to be swaying, like a sea in slow motion, its baked floor glistening, every pebble polished and alive. The sun was hot enough to knock the breath out of anyone. I wondered if the atmosphere these impulses were traveling in wasn't too rarefied to breathe.

The adobe house was shimmering in midair ahead of me like an island I was swimming toward. A curtain of turquoise and coral red beads covered the door like a Moroccan entranceway.

Puebla, July 22. We returned the truck in Oaxaca. The whole thing was unbelievably dumb. We got rid of the gun. We're running.

Harvest

4338 Enright Avenue, Saint Louis, August 26, 1961. Johnny and I made an expedition to the riverbottom near Kansas City over the weekend and harvested twenty pounds of marijuana growing wild on a levee. He had spotted it from a rented boat while fishing on the river some weeks ago. We posed as fishermen, because of a previous run-in not far from there with a deputy sheriff whom Johnny had bluffed into not reaching for the carbine on the front seat of his pickup. They'd had an ostensibly amiable but in fact deadly little exchange of pleasantries, and then Johnny had gotten out of there. He'd had his buddy Ken with him. This is where I came in. Johnny thought the fisherman pose would work better with a new face. So early Saturday afternoon found us driving down an unpaved county road near the Missouri River, some thirty miles north of Kansas City.

Having parked the "short" (Johnny's word for car) in the woods next to a cornfield, we got out our 29-cent golf caps, together with Johnny's fishing pole, a camera, and a plastic-lined cardboard box with a butcher's knife inside. Carrying these, we walked down the gravel highway, unnoticed by anyone save for a faraway twelve-year-old on a bicycle. After a couple of hundred yards, Johnny went into the bushes by the roadside. I followed. We plunged through a jungle of what looked like poison oak and deadly nightshade, then emerged in a dried-out marsh at the foot of an arroyo, which led to a railroad embankment with an opening through which we passed beneath the tracks and came out on a pond divided by a barbed-wire fence, in which we saw a number of dying pike and catfish.

Using a forked stick, Johnny managed to flip out one of the fish. He picked him up in such a way as to avoid the barbed horns and spine. Then grinning at the fish, 'Old Fat Jaw, aren't you a deep goodie,' he lobbed him back in.

On the levee facing us was a stand of female marijuana plants, deep green, waving languorously in the warm breeze. Johnny pointed out the yellowish male plants, which were shorter, drier, sparser, the fertilization cycle complete, and the females lusher, greener than ever. I wonder if going on thirty bothers Johnny as much as twenty-five upsets me.

Johnny selected the best stalks and with easy, swinging slices cut and cast them like ritual spears into the sun. I caught and stacked. Soon soaked in sweat, we drank a couple of short bottles of 7-Up each, then went into the shade beneath the railroad trestle to strip the stalks, taking only leaves and flowers, until we had filled the box. We had cut many more stalks than would fit. These Johnny stripped and left in heaps between rows of cornstalks. He has a theory that the plant's "jolly," in other words, its toxic principle, is generated by a self-defense mechanism. We had noticed the plants were all perfect; not one showed any signs of having been attacked by insects, birds, or animals. What drives them away attracts us. Johnny also believes that a good part of the toxicity stored in the leaves will drain back into the stems after cutting, so it is best to strip the leaves immediately.

I closed the box and stashed it in a bush next to the embankment, while Johnny went back to the pool and flipped out a half-dozen of the moribund fish. The tail of what had been a huge pike remained with part of its spine protruding from the mud next to the pool.

Johnny pointed out the tracks of the raccoon that had caught the pike some hours before.

We took some lucky fisherman snapshots: Johnny sitting under the railroad trestle, a cigar-sized reefer in one hand and a catfish in the other, me holding out several fish on a string in front of a stand of seven-foot-tall marijuana plants silhouetted against the late-afternoon sky.

We climbed back out on the highway just in time to be spotted by a passing family of deeply tanned, tow-headed Okie types who waved and shouted boisterously, pointing at the fishing pole. We flagged them down and gave them the fish—an encounter straight out of Steinbeck.

An hour later we had checked in at the Kansas City Salvation Army Mission and were showering.

"It's lights out at ten o'clock, Dave, but that's cool because we need to get back there early."

Johnny shook me awake at dawn. I could hear thunder crashing outside. We hurried out to the car and took off.

By the time we got there, our second batch was awash between the corn rows. Amazingly, the heaps were still intact. Lightning was flashing all around as Johnny ran into the corn to sack the leaves. I arrived panting and terrified at the embankment where lightning was actually striking the trestle only a few feet overhead, and I found myself swimming towards it through the tall weeds of the arroyo to where I found my box safely floating in its bush. I put my hand inside. The compressed leaves were dry and warm, almost hot. Minutes later, in bushes next to the road, with the lightning still flashing on every side, I waited until Johnny came along in the car. A terrific thunderclap accompanied the flipping open of his trunk and hasty toppling of my box inside. A second later, we were speeding toward Saint Louis. I undressed and changed from my drenched Levi's and teeshirt into dry chinos and a jersey. We raced along Highway 61, rubbing each other's backs, singing, taking hits from a pint of Granddad, doing 85 in the rain.

August 27. Out in the kitchen when I got up to make coffee was a note on the table from Johnny's fiancee Freddie.

"J.—Bar-B-Q today at 5. Bring D. Love, F. Quinn. P.S. Also 1 case Miller Beer (in blanket). Thanks."

Freddie had gone to help her mom prepare. The barbecue would be held in the big side yard next to the Quinn family house. This being Sunday, Freddie's mom would be in church. Maybe Freddie and Nackie had gone with her.

Freddie occasionally teased Nackie about how once as a teenager at that church she had been filled with the Spirit and started "thrashing her arms and spinning like a top."

Freddie's mom, a stalwart woman in her fifties with gray hair and a good-natured voice, advised her daughter not to joke about religion: "Don't play with the Lord."

I found it impossible to imagine the sullen, phlegmatic Nackie filled with the Spirit. She and I first slept together the night I got here last June, before Van and I took off for Mexico. Nackie was still around when I returned here after my blow-out with Van in San Francisco, where we had fetched up after nearly getting ourselves done in south of the border. Now Nackie and I share a bed and occasional sex in the apartment Johnny and Freddie have taken at the "mixed" end of Enright. Nackie has amazingly smooth, clear skin. She has a way of posing the most disagreeably candid questions. I keep changing my mind as to whether she is smart or dumb. My mother's diagnosis (if she survived the shock of seeing me with "a Negro") would doubtless be "not quite bright." But matters are never that simple. For years I've been trying to dismiss Mom as a "Hokinson lady," although there is obviously a good deal more to her than that. However, it's a great relief she's gone to England until October 17th. Her antics, using East Hampton connections to reach high into the State Department while I was supposedly missing in Mexico, were a sore embarrassment when a Federal officer actually ran me to ground in San Francisco and ordered me to get on the horn with Mother, pronto. Sweet creeping Jesus, as my brother, who has been working for her at *The East Hampton Star*, says several times a day.

"Dave!" Johnny shouted. "This here crop is going to be ruint if it don't get cured."

"The automatic laundry on Delmar," I shouted back. "Put her through the drier."

"Where did you think of that?" Johnny asked.

"Van suggested it when we got to San Francisco. Some of our Mexican shipment got rained on coming through the mountains in the Buick. We had the top down. Went to a laundromat in North Beach. Dried right out."

"You boys are the greatest practical inventors of all time," Johnny assured me.

We put the sacks in for two hours. The first male customers began arriving, silk bandanas tied over process hairdos. The same police car kept slowing down each time it passed. We got out of there.

Back at the apartment we tried baking small quantities in the oven. This raised a strong and unmistakable smell.

The deli sold us a case of Miller's, as requested by Freddie, but made us come round back because of the blue law.

At the barbecue, Mr. Quinn and a couple of friends from his job at the Union Electric plant stood on the sidelines drinking lemonade, talking about a strike that might be called soon by the auto workers. These gray-haired men represent a first generation of black union members. We ate quantities of ribs folded sandwich-fashion between slices of Wonder Bread.

Freddie cautioned me not to let her dad see my beer. "You better keep it away from my mom and the church people too. And, mind, no reefer! Absolutely N-O!"

The most respected person present was Freddie's 97-year-old great-grandmother. Nicknamed "Grammear" after her grand-daughter, Freddie's mother, whom everybody calls "M'Dear," the tiny white-haired woman occupies a couple of rooms in the attic of the Quinn house.

Born in 1864 in the Deep South, Grammear could still remember the era of Federal occupation after the Civil War. When she was twenty, her husband traveled north to Saint Louis and sent for her after he had found work and a place to live. She has been here ever since.

Grammear told me I could come upstairs and visit whenever I liked. This will be a treat. I would rather hear a story told by a 100-year-old person than read any book on earth.

As we were leaving Freddie went inside and fetched a letter from Van that arrived yesterday.

He toys with the idea of visiting Hirschman in L.A. From there he might move on to Santa Fe with Ceely: "I know I could live with him easily, write in the same room with him, in fact." This referred to a bone of contention between Van and me in Mexico, where he said my presence was too strong to write in the same room with. The letter concluded: "I miss you but am glad you're gone. You know all that, feel the same, I guess."

August 28. A couple of seedy-looking youths—white—were at the door this morning, talking hip, looking for "smoke," wanting to buy "a heater." Johnny assured them they were in the wrong place. Then they said they had noticed a lot of cash in a drawer at the deli down the road: "a cigar box full of thins like that, yeah, man." Would Johnny like to help knock it over?

Johnny put them out the door with a suggestion they go to the Foundling Home and bust open the piggy bank. He said it like a joke, clapping one of them on the back, as their eyes widened at the sight of Freddie and Nackie walking around in their pants and bras in the living room to the sound of Ornette Coleman.

Closing the door and locking it, Johnny crooned, "I'll see you sissies in my dreams."

He went on: "They'll be from the joint, Dave. A heater! Did you dig that? Seeing as these punks are going back to the shithouse directly, I hate to think of them trying to save their silly skins by snitching on us. We have to get that weed out. I knowed it'd be time to move about now."

August 29. We rented a new place yesterday and moved the weed last night. None too soon. A car was waiting and tried to force us over, Johnny, Freddie, and me. There were three of them. All strangers. We raced ahead. They gained on us and fired twice but missed. We may have been saved by the cops. They were coming the other way and did a U-turn. Johnny, running without lights, hung a hard right and spun us off into an alleyway, where we tore along in the dark, then came out directly behind our new building.

"God damn it," Johnny said as we hauled the sacks in through a rear entrance, "there has got to be a way."

August 30. This morning Johnny said he suspected Nackie of ratting on us: "Where was she at last night?"

Freddie didn't believe it. Neither did I. Johnny kept saying, "I don't want that cunt knowing my business. Don't you be telling her nothing, Dave. Hear?"

Johnny left us sitting over our coffee to take a long shower. Like Archimedes he immerses himself to weigh ideas.

"Got it'" he shouted and danced dripping into the middle of the kitchen. "There's a spot where it's going to cure real nice, plenty of sun, and it can't get rained on."

Several hours later found us at an overpass near Chesterfield, Missouri, where the highway crossed the railroad.

The still-damp weed we spread on a cement slab that (just as Johnny had promised) was sheltered from wind and rain but open to sunlight and, most importantly, altogether invisible unless you were right on top of it, a most unlikely event.

The cured portion we had already put up in a dozen waterproof packets. These we hid in a bush next to the tracks.

We stopped for coffee at a nearby diner on Highway 40. It had a throbbing red neon arrow pointed skyward at an angle we thought comical. We named it The Pulsing Cock.

Johnny began chatting up the waitress, a blond woman with red hands named Lucy Mae who called me "kid." The jukebox was so loud they had to shout. It was suppertime, and trailers were pulling up. For a fleeting moment, it occurred to me to ask myself why we were taking so much trouble and risk over this marijuana. We've smoked some and must admit it's pretty weak. It relates to the cannabis grown in Mexico as 3.2 beer to real booze. You can get a buzz if you try hard. However, I wonder if even that isn't more a state of mind.

August 31. Johnny has a nickname, which he used to sign a note to Van telling of our adventures since I got here: Zambito. The nickname was bestowed by Mexican fellow-prisoners when Johnny was doing time for bashing a man's head in with a fencepost in a fight. Properly spelled San Vito ("Saint Vitus"), it refers to Johnny's inability to sit still.

Everyone in this neighborhood knows I am here. This is a part of Saint Louis where no white face apart from Johnny's is ever seen. People are either friendly or just look through me. They all know who I am, who I'm staying with. The cops must know, too. I feel like a suitcase in a baggage room, waiting to be picked up. Not that they come round here with less than a dog and a shotgun.

The black community of Saint Louis has its own scandal sheet, a cheaply printed four-page weekly, *The Evening Whirl.* A few months ago, Freddie, Nackie, and a couple of other young women pulled a series of stunts that culminated in their arrest. The paper related the alleged misdeeds in glowing terms, alongside a popular nightclub owner's approving crack about the "Big Four," as the writer facetiously styled them, under a photograph of the girls at a recent party. *The Evening Whirl* is on sale at the corner grocery on West Labadie. I picked it up with a *Post-Dispatch* and went back into Freddie's folks' house, where Freddie, Johnny, Nackie, and Freddie's brother Willie were sitting in the front room.

"DOG'S EDUCATED NOSE SNIFFS OUT HIDDEN MARIJUANA," I read out loud from page one of the *Post-Dispatch*: "Acting on a tip, Sergeant Harold Bloss and members of the police narcotics squad waited at the Cates Avenue apartment of Quintella Thurman . . . "

"Cates Avenue, man," Freddie interrupted, "that's only ten blocks away from here."

"I know that bitch," Nackie put in scornfully.

I went on reading: "Opening a closet, searchers turned up a locked metal box, which Duke pawed vigorously. Duke has also picked up packets of the weed hidden in open fields . . . "

At this, Freddie's brother whistled and exclaimed,

"Johnny, you dudes are playing with fire, man, you being on parole and all, shit."

"I'm glad I don't live around here," Nackie said.

Willie passed me a joint he had just lit and a pint of white lightning in a paper bag to help drown the smoke.

"Just make sure my dad don't see it. He'll be home from work in a couple hours. He hates this shit. Something I have been meaning to ask you, brother, do you have kin in Saint Louis?"

"You and your family and Johnny are my only kin here," I replied.

Just then the two-year-old Valerie came over to my knee.

"Are you kissing kin?" I asked.

The baby answered in a clear voice, "Kiss my chin!"

Willie turned on the TV. Franz Fanon calls television the shop window to which the Third World's nose is pressed. It's no good to dismiss soap opera as a distortion. Our lives (I mean, the lives of us middle-class white people) are indeed, as Huessy used to say in his philosophy lectures at Dartmouth, turning into picture-motions of motion pictures. I can't tell if my friends here despise what they see of us on the tube, or envy us, or simply think we're crazy. They call it the gray box. This screen couldn't be had for money the way it is. Helen Trent looks like an El Greco Christ, Dr. Malone like Gertrude Stein in the funhouse. There is something wrong with the sound, too. They talk in deep, fruity tones like Wurlitzers.

Freddie got up, leaving Johnny, Nackie, Willie, and me to the gray box, to take Valerie back to her mother in the kitchen, a graceful figure in a loose-fitting green skirt that fluttered as she moved, scooping her up before the child had time to protest. Willie followed. I wondered how many months pregnant Freddie might be. Four, I speculated. It's only just noticeable. That means the baby is due in February.

Yesterday Johnny and I put on suits and went downtown to see his parole officer. I was introduced as an instructor at Harvard. Johnny told him we were sharing a place. The man shook his head and, when they spoke behind closed doors, told Johnny I looked mighty strange and was probably a bad influence. Then he repeated his strictures about Johnny living with Freddie and hanging out in colored neighborhoods. Johnny hasn't told him Freddie is pregnant. As we left, the man walked us to the street door where he clapped me on the back and winked, squeezing my shoulder:

"Remind Johnny-boy here he's got some time to make a few changes, 'cause, come October . . . Well . . . You tell him, Johnny. October's your Good Behavior Month, old buddy."

My mystification lasted no longer than it took Johnny, all smiles at the man still standing in the doorway, to ease the car out of the parking slot without burning rubber. Once we were in traffic the expletives went off. Johnny told me he was up for discharge at the beginning of November, but that depended on the report his officer gave the review board in the last week of October, "that blackmailing motherfucker."

Were Johnny to marry Freddie without permission while on parole they could send him back to jail. That's what happened to Ray Bremser in New Jersey last year. He and Bonnie hadn't been married very long when Van and I stayed with them on Newark Street, Hoboken. Shortly after that, Ray was back in the can. Freddie sometimes refers to Johnny as her husband but neither of them ever talks marriage. If the man knew, he might make some kind of crack that would cause Johnny to fly off the handle, or he might just congratulate him and point out that it was high time to think about life's responsibilities. How the information might affect his parole was impossible to know. Johnny thought it would do no good.

Freddie remains imperturbable. There are several young adults in and out here. Some are siblings, some girlfriends and boyfriends, and others just friends. In the course of their everyday comings and goings, an outsider could never sort out the relationships from appearances alone. They behave like brothers and sisters, without any hint of romance. They are as skilled at masking their feelings as were the heroes and heroines of the old Viking sagas.

Freddie took the paper from me and read that a carnival with a freak show will be opening in Chesterfield on Saturday night.

"Let's go to it," she said. "The freaks are out of sight." At that moment M'Dear, Freddie's mother, was passing through the room.

"What's that about freaks?" M'Dear asked.

Freddie repeated it to her mother.

"That's good," M'Dear said "We've been getting this weather long enough. The garden's drying up. Freaks bring rain, you know."

"Well," I said as soon as M'Dear had left the room, "freaks can be a bad omen, too. Maybe we should watch it."

"Right," said Nackie, without taking her eyes off Dr. Malone.

Johnny turned on her. "What do you want to look at that shit for, girl? Why don't you go home and get your ass ready to hit the street?" Nackie swore, rose, walked out.

Johnny and I agreed to inspect our marijuana soon, tomorrow night maybe.

"You better watch yourself," Freddie said.

"Don't you be fretting about us," Johnny replied.

Freddie switched off the sound on the TV and put on a rhythm 'n' blues side, a forty-five. I picked up the newspaper so as not to be looking at them as they started grinding, cheek to cheek, with Johnny whispering, trying to sweet-talk her upstairs, while Freddie kept repeating she had to help M'Dear out in the kitchen.

According to the *Post-Dispatch*, police in East Berlin have been using tear gas, water cannons, and firecrackers on crowds of protesters. If such crowds gathered here, they would be termed "rioting mobs."

Little Valerie came toddling into the room. Sucking her thumb, she stared up at the grownups as they moved to the music, the hard-on in Johnny's bluejeans bumping up against Freddie's thigh. Suddenly M'Dear was in the doorway:

"Don't shame this baby!"

Freddie stopped dancing and laughingly lifted Valerie up in her arms, hugging her, then carried the pleased baby into the kitchen with M'Dear.

Johnny and I stepped outdoors into blinding sunlight. In a spot next to Mr. Quinn's vegetable patch where we were concealed from the street, we lay down on the grass, our shirts off, and shared a quart of ale. I recited: *Come, let us sit upon the ground, and tell sad stories of the death of kings . . .*

Johnny snored. Lying back, I looked up at the apricot-colored light inside my closed eyelids and realized he was only feigning sleep. The sky continued cloudless, temperature high and dry, a perfect day.

September 5. We didn't make it to the carnival in Chesterfield till last night. The weekend was rained out. We worried that our stash would get blown away in the thunderstorm Sunday. M'Dear was right, the freaks brought rain.

I didn't want to go in the freak show. There was a school for spastics in East Hampton when I was young. They brought the "crippled kids," as we called them, to the Sunday School and tried to make us behave as though we were not horrified.

Lao-tse held that odd exceptions, or sports, were a key to the understanding of nature, whereas Confucius dismissed them as trivial and insisted that nature would yield its secrets only to the study of normal, endlessly reiterated patterns.

I'm officially on the Taoist side but secretly can't stand freaks. So I didn't go in with Johnny and Freddie, but dawdled on the midway till they emerged from the painted tent. From there we went to the railroad crossing and tiptoed through the dark to check our stash. It was intact.

We had no sooner gotten settled at The Pulsing Cock than a colorful group arrived to occupy the booth next to ours. It was the Seal Lady and her barker, both still in costume. With them were an old Irishman who ran the Ferris wheel and his wife, a red-cheeked woman with white hair and hard, square hands.

"We caught you an hour ago, ma'am. You're the greatest," Johnny enthused.

"Flattery will get you nowhere, sonny," the Seal Lady replied. "Give me a light."

With the flipper emerging from a gilt-trimmed right shoulder, the Seal Lady flipped a Pall Mall up to her heavily rouged lips and leaned forward, winking at me and nodding to Freddie, as Johnny held out his lighter.

There were five tiny pointed nails at the end of each flipper. These were neatly trimmed and lacquered pink.

The Seal Lady's warm contralto kept going off into a squeaky falsetto. Forgetting my terror of freaks, I marveled at Johnny's ability to fall in with the carny talk and point of view. Soon we were hearing the Seal Lady's story, from youth in Sweden during the Second World War—"I was a mere child," she said, again winking at me—to arrival in America sometime in the late 1940s. Houston: "I lived in the Turning Basin with a big Hawaiian named Pineapple, gone now, died in jail."

September 7. Today I sunbathed in the Quinns' back yard. We are having a sudden heat wave. The yard is completely enclosed in a high board fence. Mr. Quinn has nailed up little lath crosses here and there. He grows tomatoes, squash, and sunflowers. By himself he talks to Jesus and mutters something about "half-peoples." No one is supposed to notice.

An unused corner of the yard holds Nackie's pink and white Pontiac, jacked up amid piles of broken furniture. We are going to put the car on the road next week. Yesterday I made an unwise promise to give Nackie driving lessons.

September 8. We drove out to Chesterfield last night to check the stash. A sixth sense led Johnny to stop first at The Pulsing Cock. Who should we meet but the Seal Lady and her friends finishing their supper. Over coffee the Seal Lady remarked that they had just seen a big police stakeout back where the highway crossed the railroad.

"Somebody," the Seal Lady reflected, "is going to jail. I'm glad it's not me."

September 11. Shaken by the Seal Lady's disclosure, I have ventured forth every morning for a *Post-Dispatch.* At last in today's paper the following item appeared on page 3:

Marijuana Cache Discovered

Marijuana with a "retail" value of around $10,000 was found near Chesterfield alongside a railroad track where someone was curing the weed, police disclosed Monday. About five pounds, cured and ground for use in making cigarettes, was found in a sack. Another 15 pounds of whole leaves were found curing on a slab beneath the Highway 40 overpass at the Rock Island Railroad tracks. A worker found the processed weed, 12 packets of it, in a gunny sack, in growth along the tracks last Thursday. Searching the area Detective Robert Schupp found the drying leaves. Detectives substituted alfalfa and set a watch for the harvesters. But by Monday they decided the marijuana operators had been scared off and weren't coming back. Detective Capt. H.C. Birmes estimated there was sufficient weed for 20,000 cigarettes for which pedlars usually get 50 cents apiece.

Back in the kitchen, I read this out loud, to Johnny and the girls. He and I did a little skit on police procedures, clowning for Freddie and Nackie. We howled, then (in a sudden fit of shared paranoia) put everything in the apartment down the toilet and got ready to move.

By afternoon we had found a new place in a more upscale, still mixed, neighborhood, our third home in a month. Freddie went back to spend time with her folks on West Labadie; and Nackie left for an undisclosed destination, turning tricks, according to Johnny.

At Freddie's parents' was a message that Van's Washington U classmates Kitty and Bill would be arriving from San Diego on Friday and wanted to crash with us.

We decided on a party in their honor. What better housewarming for the narrowly escaped marijuana operators? Kitty is a fine looking bitch, Johnny observed of the graduate student. Our guest list included Freddie's brothers and their girlfriends, along with an assortment of drug dealers, car thieves, department store boosters, hookers, and a handful of Washington U students, all white, plus Jim the Desert Rat, a tanned, quiet, mean, tall, skinny Texan with a cretinous drawl, one of Johnny's coworkers at the machine shop.

I had had no grass in days. One toke sufficed. Everybody was drunk but no one feeling their nuts, so there was no fighting. The record player (Coltrane) was so loud nobody could have heard an insult. Johnny had rigged up a revolving pedestal boosted from a store display with Christmas tree lights in the living room. The lights flickered across Kitty's tawny locks and high freckled cheekbones. She glanced at me. I shouted something inane to the effect that she was looking "quite leonine." Her eyes held me for a moment in a lambent glow, then averted. I don't remember their color, only the glow.

Bill had passed out, exhausted from several days of driving non-stop, and the company, including Freddie and Nackie, were gone, when Kitty and I slipped out into the darkness behind my new home. The sky was developing a predawn gray as we lay down in the bone-dry grass. In inland America, it crossed my mind, there's often no dew on clear summer nights.

Kitty, half drunk, talked to me like a book, congratulating me on my "soft-circling hair," in other words, the fact I haven't been near a barber since Oaxaca; also, my "tanned, athletic arms," and, best of all, my "pale, beautiful" face. Trembling, we started touching each other and were both very wet.

Just then, several lights went on one after another, inside. We could hear Bill stumping from room to room. Where is she! Where is she! Moments later, as he rushed out into the yard, Johnny undid the front door and let us in. By the time Bill reentered, I was already under a blanket in my room, playing dead. Bill and Kitty subsided on the mattress in the front room, and once again Bill passed out. Later I woke up and went to the toilet. Passing the open door of Johnny's room on the way, I glimpsed Kitty ensconced on a pile of gilt-trimmed coverlets and red drapes, with the drapes pulled up round her shoulders and Johnny on his knees in front of her, his face buried between her thighs.

At sunup I awoke. Bill was storming up and down. Again: Where is she! Where is she!

Toward noon, Johnny brought her back. Bill said nothing much but drove away with Kitty to find a hotel where they could sleep before continuing on their way to Philadelphia.

That afternoon we went back to West Labadie and persuaded Freddie and Nackie to go home with us; then left them both asleep and took off for the Zoo.

There, on benzedrine and some hash Kitty had given me in the back yard, we caught a giraffe sex act in progress. Johnny said their backs looked like hard-boiled dinosaur eggs struck by a gigantic spoon, making freckled fracturations with the lovely white oozing at the cracks under a tropic sun.

Next thing I knew, we were lying on a football field watching a black team scrimmage in their sweatsoaked shirts like cuirasses in which 18th-century artists represent the heroes of antiquity.

Dave, Johnny exclaimed, you dig that uppity little meat-ass cheerleader? Look at that tan teaser. I told him he was going to get busted for impairing the morals of a minor.

Johnny called, Say, girl!

To my surprise, she turned and answered, What's happening, suey?

After Polish heroes from the Jews on King's Highway, we stayed in. At midnight, while Nackie and I were taking a shower, I said, Nackie, what does suey mean?

She paused, then answered: "It's a new slang word they got out. My cousin Brisco made it up and it means: you sweaty honky mother."

Moments later, snatching the bigger of the two bath towels for herself, she continued:

"Dave, something you ought to know . . . Johnny's just an old-fashioned cracker who learned to copy the way black people talk. You talk like a professor because that's what you *are*."

"I'm a poet," I protested

"'A poet.'" That's what Van said. "He's a professor, too. You boys know what you're doing, or are you just playing?"

September 13. What very few people understand about the telling of these story-like streams of action that make up life, be it a soap opera or latter-day picaresque, is that the blow-by-blow rarely if ever converges with the unfolding of the true plot or thread of reality running through an otherwise inane sequence of events. This is not to say yet again that others are merely play-acting in a farce performed to beguile one's solipsistic self. Rather, everyone is focusing on a split screen, a mind's eye constructed like the Bayeux tapestry, with its grand invasion and battle running down the center, in between margins upon which tiny people are fucking and otherwise disporting themselves; and if we try and tell our story in writing nowadays, we have more than a little in common with the ladies who wove these scenes, being distanced from the heroics and deprived of the fooling around, or at least of anything like satisfaction of the real needs behind sex and war.

At an equal remove from both Venus and Mars, those ladies were no more marginal to their world than I to mine, at whose center runs this swirl of alarums and excursions around the attempted hijacking, smuggling, harvest, sale, and use of a forbidden plant, along with an ever-restless yen for esthetic and sexual excitement, while the margins are an animated cartoon of the remodeling of the White House by Jackie, fallout shelters, the killing of Patrice Lumumba, the Berlin Wall. I have all these things in front of my eyes, and they may even someday be the death of me and everybody else, yet I might as well be on another planet. None of it is real. I can describe and narrate my way into the middle of next year, and nothing of what I write in this notebook will tell the story.

Today we unhinged the fence behind Freddie's house and rolled the Pontiac into the roadway out back. I spent an hour driving slowly up and down the alley with Nackie at the wheel. She didn't enjoy our adventure in driver education one bit. I am too uptight, it seems. I told her to get Johnny.

"Fuck you," she answered, and walked to the corner store. We had been talking about driving the Pontiac to New York together maybe next month. Neither of us believed a word of what we were saying.

This morning I noticed two things that are not necessarily connected. First, a special half-ounce of the Mexican grass that I was fool enough to hitchhike all the way from San Francisco with, hidden in the false bottom of my knapsack, is missing. That's something neither Johnny nor Freddie would ever do. The second thing I noticed was Nackie's new handbag. I heard her tell Freddie she had bought it off one of their girlfriends who boosted it last week.

I am not going to say anything.

The papers and television are full of war talk.

"Prophets of hydrogen doom are way off," Van declared in a cheerful letter that got here yesterday. "Destruction imminent, now? No! We're in it already. The fire thought to be coming is actually here—always."

A hurricane is moving up from the Gulf of Mexico. They have named it Carla. I asked Freddie if she had a message for me to put in my answer to Van.

"Yes," she said. "Get fucked." She was laughing. She loves Van. If the kid is a boy they are going to name him Alden—Van's given name.

September 14. Every once in a while Johnny's car drives him places on its own. He'll be talking up a storm, oblivious to the passing scene, when unexpectedly we land smack in the midst of an interesting destination. The Magic Short is Johnny's pet name for this rebuilt, two-tone chocolate-and-beige 1958 Ford that has a knack of thinking on its own.

Last night around seven-thirty under a threatening sky, as the car radio boomed on about Hurricane Carla and a tornado in Texas, the Magic Short whisked us to a snoots 'n' barbecue drive-in with black gold-uniformed teenage waitresses and very loud soul music; then, moments later, to a bar called the Harlequin on a borderline between all-black and mixed neighborhoods that is frequented by a coterie of musicians, dealers, hookers, and a pair of permanently hung-over white drag queens in bathrobes.

Johnny had been flirting with the barmaid, a light-skinned, 30-year-old woman named Brenda, and, since the Magic Short had conveniently fetched up in front of the Harlequin, he decided to ask her for a date. We could wash down our snoots (deep-fried strips of pork snout) with a pitcher of beer and hopefully meet another favorite of Johnny's, a blind man named Bobby, a regular at the Harlequin and a living encyclopedia of jazz. Johnny had introduced me to him at the Judge's Chambers, a club owned by Vernon Davis, brother of Miles, in East Saint Louis on the eve of our first harvest.

"We can sit in a booth," Johnny said at the door. "But, Dave," he whispered, "What's her name?"

"Brenda," I answered, standing back from the door as a patron with a waxed goatee like a Pharaoh sauntered past.

Inside, Brenda, an Afro-American Jackie Kennedy look-alike, glanced our way and leaned across the bar to tell Bobby we were there.

"I knew that," Bobby said. "He got his professor friend with him, too—Dave—white boy from New York."

"What, you smoking Newports, Bobby!" Johnny shouted. "Give me five. You always gone for Kools. Now you switched to a sissy cigarette. What you do that for?"

Bobby put his face up close to Johnny's with a dreamy smile and blew the smoke in his eyes, drawling,

"So's I can blow the smoke in a sissy's face."

"Dave! Would you believe it, this sucker is my main man. Come over in this booth, Bobby, we got a bag of snoots here."

We were no sooner settled in with our beers than the owner, a big black guy with a pale gold helmet of straightened blond hair and brown horn-rimmed sunglasses, called over that there was no eating in the booth. Then turning his back as if to say, "Discussion closed," he ambled to the other end of the room.

Johnny jumped up and ran over to the section of the bar where Brenda had just paused as her boss spoke to us. They exchanged whispers, and in a few seconds he was back, exclaiming,

"I just don't know what to make of that chick's sassy high-yellow CORE-shit accent."

He reached into the bag, now half transparent with grease stains, then pushed it toward Bobby:

"Have some snoots."

"I pass," said Bobby "You better cool it, Jack."

"Jack you off," Johnny laughed. "Dave, I love this dude."

I had just noticed that the owner was back, now standing at Johnny's elbow.

"Like I was telling you, man," Johnny continued, ignoring the owner's presence while loudly crunching a chunk from our greasy treat, "the onliest thing I hate about hitting them sissies in the ass is when I have to jack them off at the same time, and then, them being stiff in the neck, generally . . . "

The owner walked away, shaking his head, smirking.

"Stop, Johnny, you killing me!" Bobby cried, whacking the tabletop with a fat palm.

But Johnny was not about to stop:

"I have to hop off to get a kiss, you know, like humping a cow, you have to run around front and jump back on the stool without missing too many strokes. It's worser than trying to hit the jackpot on a pinball machine."

At that instant the side of a moving automobile appeared right next to the window where we sat. The driver's head was slumped forward over the wheel. The car was moving very slowly. We heard it scrape the side of the building, then stop. Johnny rushed out the door. I followed, bag of snoots in hand. The car had wedged itself between the building and a box-shaped newspaper stand on the curb. The driver was a fifty-year-old white man in a teeshirt with a bald head, bloodshot eyes, and lots of grey whiskers. The teeshirt was clean; the man reeked of booze.

"Where you headed, Hoosier?" Johnny asked.

"I fucked up," the man drooled.

"You going to be more fucked up if you stay here," Johnny replied.

"I didn't want to mess up your box," the man apologized, taking Johnny for the occupant of the newspaper stand.

"My box is airtight, daddy, but if you don't want the man to mess up your box, we got to get you in the right groove fast. Now get back in there and put her in neutral."

We pushed the car backwards out to the street. Just then the bar owner appeared, a policeman's billyclub in hand:

"You damaged the building and you ran out without paying."

Johnny walked over to him.

"You gangster motherfucker, you mess over me, I do you up good. Rile me, pops, I'll restyle your chops. Swing that thing, I'll stick it up your ass."

The owner backed away toward the door, where Brenda stood frowning.

"Don't go away, please stay!" he sang out in a contemptuous falsetto. "I going to get the po-lice on you, white boy!"

"Come along now," Johnny sang back. "Your dignity unsurpassed by your fat ass. You gangstered me, I treat you like a gentleman. God damn it, Dave, what is that chick's name?"

"Brenda."

"Brenda. Yo! Brenda! I'll pick you up at closing time, okay, honey?"

But Brenda was already being shooed inside by her boss, and we were busy with the drunk's car. Johnny made him move over from the driver's seat, where he had been observing the owner's retreat with a look of unsteady stupefaction, so that I could take the wheel.

It wouldn't start. Johnny gave us a push with the Magic Short, and we bumped off down the street.

The drunk happened to live only around the corner. We got both cars parked in the alleyway behind his house just as a police car was arriving at the Harlequin. We helped Billy—that was his name—up the stairs. His wife, a skinny white-haired mulatto woman with hundreds of shiny freckles and a sagging face with alert but friendly eyes, told us that Billy had been drinking for the past three days.

There seemed to be a plastic dust cover on every horizontal surface in the apartment except the floor, which was all linoleum with carpets here and there. There was a smell of Murphy's Soap. I hadn't smelled that in a private house since a visit to a fifth-grade classmate's home next door to his dad's steam laundry whose whistle sounded at noon daily, and also signaled fires and the signing of unconditional surrender on VE and VJ Days.

After helping Billy to a plastic-covered couch, where he lay on his back fast asleep immediately after kicking off his shoes, we were invited by his wife to sit down at the formica-top table in the kitchen. Her name was Leanna. She brought us each a can of Pabst and offered glasses, which we declined. Leanna also offered to heat up the snoots, and when we declined that, too, she emptied the bag into a serving dish and set it on the table next to an item that had caught my eye from the moment we had entered, a booklet titled *Fall-Out Shelters* that Leanna told us she had ordered from *LIFE* magazine. It explained how a family can survive quite nicely for weeks, even months, underground after nuclear blasts have obliterated everything upstairs. Eventually, ground crews will have cleared away the radioactive waste, and people can come back up to rebuild, safe at last from communism. The Reds will be dead, and our side will have liberated all of their captives and slaves that have survived our withering counterattack.

Billy was laid off his Job at Union Electric in July, Leanna remarked.

"I heard they were hiring, ma'am," Johnny said. "My fiancee's dad told me that. He's been there ten years."

"But I'm sure the gentleman you're speaking about is not a drunk," Leanna said.

My thoughts flashed back to a letter received last week from Van. He and John Ceely were sunbathing at the Oakland docks. A Swedish freighter was taking a cargo of canned fruit on board. Blond deckhands were goofing on the quarterdeck, pretending to paint. An old black truckloader walked up to Van and Ceely and said,

"Don't work when you're young. Don't work at all if you can help it. Fuck 'em."

"Right," said Van.

"Right," said Ceely, slurping his Fudgesicle at the sun.

In the same letter, Van reported that his father had written saying he should either get a job in California or, if too sick to work, fly home to Rutland. My mother, when she took off for six weeks in England with her friend Muggie, ignoring the latest crisis over Berlin, on the eve of sailing wrote me something in a similar vein, one of those lengthy, gentle remonstrances that make me feel I am going to choke.

Why should I work? I don't want to. I read somewhere that the builders of Stonehenge worked no more than a couple of hours a day. The author of that may have been talking through his hat, but I'm ready to believe him. I have always felt it my duty to believe everything.

Johnny and Leanna got up and went to the phone. He had talked her into calling the Harlequin on the pretext of asking if her husband was there. (Actually, Billy had never been there in his life.) The call was answered by the owner. Hearing a woman's voice, he gave Brenda the phone. Johnny got on the line. In lowered tones, Brenda said yes, it was the man, but blind Bobby was the only person who knew Johnny's full name, yet he denied knowing Johnny at all. Brenda herself when asked had described him as "a handsome man that's going with a girl I knew in high school but I forgot her name." The boss had threatened to fire her. His vision was so poor, though, he couldn't even describe the Magic Short, much less give her license number. He even got the colors wrong. Johnny interrupted,

"You tell Bobby next time I see him I am taking him in the nearest men's room and offer him my hard wrapped in a silk ribbon. Pardon my French, ma'am," he added, with a glance at Leanna, who was already exclaiming to me,

"Goodness, how that man talks!"

"You still fruit to go out with me, baby?" Johnny continued, then putting his hand over the mouthpiece, asked me yet again to repeat the name.

"Brenda! I'm in a hurry, make up your mind. Beautiful! Corner of Page and Hamilton at three o'clock!"

He slammed the receiver down and kissed a startled Leanna on the cheek:

"Come on, Dave, we've got some planning to do."

The car radio brought updates on Hurricane Carla. As of mid-afternoon, there was flooding in the riverbottom around Kansas City. Six were dead. The Weather Bureau called the situation "grave." I wondered how we were ever going to find that stand again under five feet of water.

"Dave, we go in in boats," Johnny asserted. "If necessary, a diving bell."

When we got in, Freddie and Nackie had come and gone. Freddie had also left a letter for me, care of her folks, from Van.

Van wrote that the doctors were experimenting on him again. He is getting a sort of subsistence retainer, like a welfare check, from the med school. The arrangement sounds wrong, as though they were more interested in the science than in keeping him well.

"They're just getting their future bag together," Johnny commented. "If it means a Nobel Prize over Van's dead body, that's cool."

Johnny has begged Van several times to come back to Saint Louis, because Gaither (the intern who diagnosed Van's disease a year ago) said the best treatment was just transfusions when necessary and otherwise nothing, and he was pretty sure he could keep him going indefinitely in that fashion. Of course Van himself leaps at the possibility that there might be a miracle out there and those people have a line on it. I wonder if he really believes that. Johnny holds me partly responsible. He thinks Mexico was my idea, and I may have taken years off of Van's life just for a few weeks of mosquitoes, malnutrition, and the shits. Freddie repeated this to me in private. Johnny said nothing. I don't want to ask.

At U Cal Hospital, Van is on a so-called chrome study until the end of this month or beginning of October. The letter adds:

"Write more & keep me alive for the next 2 ½ weeks."

My immediate impulse upon reading that sentence was not to write a word. But the desperation behind it became unbearably tangible and present at the table where I sat rereading it, alone over a quart of Ballantine Ale, Johnny already off with Brenda, in the dusk before daybreak.

September 17. For three days I have been camping on this hillside facing Kansas City, the riverbottom with cornfields at my feet and hills with granite outcroppings in a middle distance on either side.

None of the immediate vicinity was flooded from last week's storm. Johnny and I brought in a bumper crop.

The sun is about to set. Cars on the bridge yonder have their headlights on, a stream of violet-pink sparks.

There are thousands of crickets within earshot. Their song rises in a crescendo like a buzz saw, then drops. Others, the soloists, have individual soprano voices like dentists' drills. Am I hearing things? Soon each of these creatures will, in Blake's words, "fold her slender bones without a murmur."

At noon today a red snake trembled on the stones in the sun where the marijuana is drying. I am invisible.

A few minutes ago the air seemed to be quivering like apple jelly. A smoky smell drifts up from the river. In his nature journals kept at Selborne, in Hampshire, around the time of the American Revolution, Gilbert White records days when a dry haze brought an odor that the local people were in the habit of saying was the smell of London smoke.

Night falls. I have a tin of corn beef and a Pepsi. I gaze at factory chimneys spitting flame in the dusk over the Missouri. There are three of them, and now also a purple cloud with an orange hairdo. A Gershwin tune runs through my head.

September 18. Earlier today I saw two speckled deer drinking where the grass in the streambed is darkest and coolest. I have a dozen half-quarts of Pepsi buried. I drink a quart a day. It's mid-afternoon now. The river looks as though it were running vertically into the sky.

Weeks ago, after our first sortie, I facetiously described harvesting in a letter to Van as "a spiritual experience." He sent a postcard: "Hirschman says 'spiritual harvest' goes back to Heraclitus."

I fired off a reply.

"The harvest is the end of the world, and the reapers are angels" (Matthew 13:39).

Van's response arrived in Saint Louis just as Johnny and I were heading out:

> *Who turned on Heaven with Kansas City weed?*
> *Not Johnny & Dave but*
> *I, mad Satan—I*
> *Sucked it back through hollow*
> *Stems & threw it into hellfire so the sweet*
> *Smoke ascended to God's lost kingdom &*
> *God fell off his throne punning*
> *With Baudelaire & W.C. Fields on*
> *The brand-names of sanitary napkins . . .*

Whenever Van sounds a sophomoric note, as in this take-off on the parable of the weeds of the field, my first reaction is annoyance. His illness worsens, yet he keeps cracking jokes as though there were nothing wrong.

Johnny and I envy Van's good looks. The other day Johnny tried on the green suit Van left behind, glanced in the mirror, and groaned: "That rascal looks like a candy boy in these threads. Why don't I?"

With the "jolly" roasting in September sun, I have little to do but think. This afternoon I had a fantasy of myself as an Algerian rebel. Like the *bled*, these hills and fields are full of people. Could I live in the midst of my fellow Americans like a fish in water, an F.L.N. fighter amid friendly felaheen? Ho, ho! Every one of these rednecks would be more than happy to turn me in.

This isn't my country, or theirs. Alongside the Indians, we are like Afrikaaners in Africa. But the idea of native ground holds no water, either. If the human race began in Africa, we should all go back there and leave the rest of the planet to the birds and the bees.

One day last winter I showed Van a new magazine from Harvard, *The Psychedelic Review*. He wasn't impressed: "Don't tell me about 'drug culture,' man. Drugs *are* culture."

Yes, but I have my doubts about being a part of this culture, or any. How about getting *outside* of the whole thing?

The first agriculturalist was Noah. He cultivated a drug—wine. Homer's *moly* given to Odysseus' comrades to turn them into pigs is a parable. Sufi and Tantric mysteries revolve around hemp. That's why I'm here. Do I want to be here?

"Outside" might mean entirely separated. Manna, water. I found a formulation of this in the 1824 diary of August von Platen:

> *To taste of nothing but the flesh*
> *Of light, forever whole and sweet,*
> *To drink of waters that refresh*
> *But never drive the blood to heat.*

September 18. Monday. At noon a fluffy cumulus sailed across an otherwise empty sky.

September 19. There was no dew last night, so I left the leaves out. The light of the full moon shone on them.

These woods are a far cry from the roach-infested hotel room in Puebla where Van and I pulled the leaves off the *mota*, or stalk marijuana, purchased after our fiasco in Nochistlán. We had paid $15 (U.S.) for a kilo. Cleaning it cut the weight to less than two pounds.

Soon after sunrise I bagged up the weed and concealed it along with my knapsack and other gear, then hiked out carrying nothing but my notebook. Next time I must bring more reading matter. At a service station a short ways down the road I phoned a taxi and hired him to take me over the bridge to North Kansas City. From there I rode a municipal bus into the center of town to a Western Union office, where I sent Johnny a telegram to come get me.

Now I am sitting in the quiet, well-lit reading room of the Kansas City Public Library. The sky is bright in the tall windows, a golden day. I pore over the Max Mueller edition of the *Rig Veda*. The two volumes of *King's American Dispensatory* (1889) just arrived. Turning to the article on *Cannabis indica*, I read:

"The drug is a useful hypnotic for the *insane*. By its influence over the mental function, it controls lascivious thoughts, dreams and desires. It also has some reputation as a remedy for *chronic alcoholism*, and for the cure of the *opium habit*."

I have had nothing to eat today.

6 p.m., Milt's. Milt's is a jazz bar where Johnny will pick me up any minute now. The entranceway boasts a row of blue neon niches with white plastic statuettes of J.S. Bach, Mozart, Beethoven, and Wagner. I arrived an hour ago with a pound of raw hamburg, which I ate secretly in the utter darkness of this booth, over a bottle of Pabst. No sooner had I finished my savage repast than Milt himself came over and offered me a candle. "I never see you without a book," he explained. Here comes Johnny, glad-handing Milt and Billy the bartender.

September 21. We recovered the stash without incident night before last, but on the way back Johnny picked up a hitchhiker who we found out from today's paper was wanted for murder. The minute he got in the car, I had the feeling he was going to pull a gun on us. Johnny's reaction was to blow hard and mean to me, completely ignoring him. Evidently our new acquaintance got the idea of what kind of people had picked him up, and thought better of his original intention. In a shy voice, he told us the police were after him for abandoning his wife and kids. Actually (it turned out today) he had murdered them and several others on his way east from Oklahoma. When we reached Saint Louis, Johnny gave him carfare to the railroad station and said, "Stay very cool, baby, you have got to." The man looked at him uncertainly, then muttered, "Thanks," and hurried away in the dusk.

Johnny and I stayed up all night talking about the mounds in East Saint Louis, left over from an Aztec-type civilization that flourished here in Dante's lifetime. There were several other mound centers. The last was going strong at Natchez when the French arrived in the late sixteen hundreds.

"Why'd you dudes have to go to Mexico? These mounds are as big as any Aztec pyramid. Same people built them."

September 22. Last night was the right night for us to be thinking about the Cahokia Mounds. The Indians had a regular wood-henge over there, for calculating, amongst other things, the exact instant of the autumnal equinox. This was the savages' cue to perform a rapid series of human sacrifices in the numinous moment's full glow, atop a pyramid now called Monk's Mound because French missionaries planted gardens on its terraces two hundred years ago.

We drove over this afternoon. Monk's Mound is a park with a grassy meadow on its flat top. It's only a little more than a hundred feet high, but that stands out in this riverbottom. We were all alone up there in a warm breeze, as rainclouds scudded past. To the east were cornfields as far as the eye could see.

Here I saw links connecting Saint Louis and Mexico. The triad of maize, beans, and rice. Pythagoras taught that beans are a food of the dead. Mississippian pyramids exactly resembled those in Teotihuacan. In both places life and death were joined in ways unimaginable to us, given the timorous distinctions that we draw between the two.

September 23. I cracked up the Magic Short on King's Highway today. It was raining hard, and the car in front of me stopped without signaling. I rear-ended him. It was a black man. The cops arrived and told me I was responsible. On inspection it turned out no damage was done to my disgruntled victim, so he drove away after advising me to look out where I was going in the future. The Magic Short was a horse of another color. The left-hand front fender was stove in, with the paint cracked all the way back to the door on the driver's side. I drove it to a nearby auto shop, the Jihad Body Service. The owner was very courteous but none too friendly. He did allow me to use his telephone for a long-distance call, reversing charges, to Everett T. Rattray at the *Star* office in East Hampton.

E.T.R. was not a bit pleased to learn about the scrape his kid brother was in. All things considered, though, he was a model of big-brotherly politesse and promised to immediately wire the money—ninety dollars—required by the Jihad Body Service.

I said, "You're a brick."

"Sweet creeping Jesus," he groaned. We laughed uneasily.

"Don't you think you ought to be coming east one of these days?" he ventured to ask. "The mother image is due back from Merry England in just three weeks. You could warm the welcome."

I thanked him and promised to think on it.

September 24. Johnny and I went to the Jihad Body Service in Nackie's Pontiac this afternoon to pick up the Magic Short. I noticed Johnny didn't talk black. The atmosphere was calm and formal. Afterwards he found fault with the work the Muslims had done. It was all right, but there were little ways in which the Magic Short was never going to be the same. All because I'm such a fuck-up, and, he added spitefully, I was so hung-over yesterday it was a miracle the cops didn't run me in for drunken driving.

A letter from Everett just arrived, written the day before the accident, enclosing my $100 check. He had agreed to handle the monthly stipends in Mom's absence. I'd written to say that I was planning to stay on in Saint Louis through Thanksgiving. I had also analyzed the present world crisis, asserting that Kennedy and Khrushchev only *seemed* to be the protagonists. Actually, I explained, there were invisible forces at work. As Heraclitus said, the most powerful connections are the invisible ones. Politely overlooking Heraclitus, Everett disagreed. He pointed out that editing a newspaper gave him a close-up view of the political process:

> *As far as I can see, Churchill is right with his theory of history determined by personality. From here, you can see upwards, dimly, as from the bottom of a cesspool, to the higher levels of politics, and the collision of personalities, as of turds in the cesspool, is all-important.*

There's an inconsistency. At twenty-nine, Everett is a nihilist, yet conforms. At twenty-five, I believe in my choices, yet find that I am hard put to defend them.

September 25. Today I came within a hair's breadth of getting killed. Here is how it happened:

Taking advantage of the clear, perfect weather we have been having, Johnny parked the Magic Short on the edge of Freddie's yard on West Labadie, and we got busy tinkering with the finish on the imperfectly repaired fender. I was still eating crow and obeying each of Johnny's many commands without protest. But he kept riding me. Finally I remarked the insults were coming out of his mouth like some kind of nasty-smelling diarrhea. In a split-second he was on his feet, coming for me with a Philips screwdriver aimed at my throat. There was a galvanic pallor about his face. I raised my arm to block the screwdriver and hauled off to whack him with the mallet that was in my right hand. At that instant, Willie and his partner Bo stepped between us, and it was over. I apologized for what I had said. We were both almost in tears.

"Dave, don't do these things. I'd have killed you and I sure enough don't want to do that."

He put his arm around me and said he knew I was sorry and he wasn't going to rub it in.

The incident brought me respect. Never mind the fact I didn't stand a chance against Johnny, at least I called him on his shit.

September 26. Last night we decided on one final harvest, so early this morning found us near the scene of our fishing expedition of a month ago. It was a mistake. We met the same sheriff's deputy, and the first thing he said was,

"What you after, boys?"

We fed him a line about picnicking.

He scratched his head and said, "Some other boys was here a

few weeks ago, putting sacks in their car. Told me 'twas orchid mulch, but I ain't no Hoosier. I knowed that was mary-huany they was picking, to dry it out and sell in town. I didn't see 'em good; sun was in my eyes . . . "

As we stood there, I wondered if Johnny was about to, in his own words, unravel like an old sock. Instead, he fell in with the deputy's way of talking and cracked a joke, incomprehensible to me, about fishing. The deputy laughed till he almost choked. Johnny was a good old boy. We drove away, wondering if he got our license number.

An hour later, bemoaning the twenty dollars we had wasted on the round trip, we drifted into a Famous & Barr in Kansas City and were on the point of boosting the best suede coats in the place when Johnny got nervous and we walked out empty-handed. "My fault," he admitted. "If we had moved just a few seconds earlier, we'd have them coats now. That lally-gagging was what blew our cool. They got hip to us."

I persuaded him to go back with me to the levee and pick some weed after all. We filled four big sacks. Considering there is a State Police barracks only a short ways up the road, I can't believe what we've been doing.

Here I am, back at my old campsite, starting a letter:

"Dear Van, I write against advancing dusk, advancing chill, and possibly advancing fuzz."

Just as I wrote the word "fuzz," there was a screech of brakes and a loud thud a hundred yards from here. Another car just stopped. In the intervening silence a dog barks, far away. The chirping of crickets continues. A cracking in the branches nearby startles me—a squirrel, no doubt. Through the trees I see red blinkers, the arriving highway patrol.

September 27. All that has kept me together for the past few hours is this anthology of Chinese poetry. Not only Li Po and Tu Fu, but Li Ho and Po Chu-I. My extreme loneliness and fear may make them seem better than they are. At this moment for me they sculpt the breath of the forest floor, the anxiety of the watch, the dread of being seen, the dialogue with passing airplanes and other vehicles, the fascination of the insects, all that invades me, breath by breath, as the reverberations of human voices and eyes subside, and the sun turns overhead. Chinese poets speak of the forest as an empty place. They mean, empty of human beings. So it must be for me.

September 29. I shivered all day and dared not go out in the sun. Now I'm warm in my army blanket. Some cows were browsing through the woods. They saw me and stampeded. I expected the farmer up here with a shotgun. Nothing happened.

I have three cigarettes, sixteen matches. The sky darkened at midday. Johnny comes in the morning.

My position is continuously exposed. I can't see cars and trucks coming up the road until they are in full view to me, as I would be to them, were I to move about.

This is a wood of saplings and looping vines, headlight beams by night. A flat, dry, leafy floor. I lie on my stomach, glancing over my left shoulder at the red dusk disappearing as these lines vanish.

September 30. At sunrise, when I awoke, a storm was coming up. I bagged the reefer, made coffee, changed shirts, even combed my hair.

Rain came down like a waterfall. Gusts of wind stripped trees. Thunder cracked, lightning flashed. I squatted low, with both the blanket and the oilcloth over me. All I needed was a Japanese flute.

Johnny arrived. The Magic Short was repainted, red and gray. I hardly recognized it. He had even got new plates. But no more magic. On the way back it suddenly skidded out of control. In a second, we spun all the way around three times without turning over, almost colliding with an oncoming 1962 Cadillac. We fetched up heading the same way we had been going. Shouting delightedly, "Wow-ee! Same old magic!" Johnny stepped on the gas.

An astonishing letter from Van awaited my return. He wrote it while tripping on morning-glory seeds, a major event from the sound of it:

> I am ready to come back to you.
> I have lived my life a million times over in a few hours, seen everything, know too much, and now burnt out, want only love and peaceful madness of America seen and shared with your eyes. Last night I saw my whole life illumined over and over . . . Don't take this unless you want to know everything, perfect knowledge, its terror, & wild hallucinations . . . hallucinations that won't stop, but devour time and leave you hung-up for eternity . . .

Continuing the letter after coming down, he said that he wanted to leave California and join Johnny and me in three weeks, after the current experiment they're doing on him at the hospital ends:

> I now know life's short, love's all. I could write okay if I was living under your mattress. Fuck our hung-up genius temperaments anyway. They won't get in the way again.

Van added that I had better tell Johnny to suck the man's dick to get his parole transferred to New York so we can all move in together. Meanwhile, he reported, all was well. He and Ceely were busy metamorphosing into sun-tanned bums, sitting in the park reciting Ovid.

All this I read out loud to Johnny. He hugged me:

"What this means, Dave, is you go there and nail down a crib. We shoot this here reefer on ahead to your bro, he'll never be the wiser. You stash her nice and safe in East Hampton, then find a pad for all of us in Manhattan. Makes sense."

Freddie looked skeptical. In the ten days since I saw her last, she has grown more noticeably pregnant.

Nackie to the contrary embraced the idea with the first show of anything like enthusiasm I have ever seen in her and immediately started talking about "our New York venture."

The thought of living with Nackie in New York had never occurred to me. I said it would be hard to find anything decent without first having made a substantial transaction. Nackie rubbed up against me and asked, "What kind of action, honey?" It was impossible to tell if she was serious or kidding. We haven't touched each other in weeks.

Johnny and I just packed my share of the harvest to be mailed off in the morning first thing.

By midday I'll be out on the interstate, hoisting my thumb.

West from Napeague

Passing through the woods at Bendigo, I note elderberries, pussy willows, and shotgun shells (empties, green and black, 12 gauge) by the road; also pines, wind-stunted, putting me in mind of bonsai trees at the Botanic Garden in Brooklyn. Today I'm wearing bright blue socks outside the bottoms of my corduroys, against ticks. A red shell casing. Nearby is that bottle dump, with the 100-year-old bottles my sister and I visited after our brother died. 25 minutes from my sister's house, on foot. At the top of the hill the trees really flatten out, and you can see both the Bay (behind) and the Ocean (ahead). Very bright. There is so much sky. A dirt road doubles back down the hill. I've never followed it. It's the old Montauk Highway from before the Rail Road. It drops off toward the tracks. Deer tracks. A dead mouse. I'm scared of ticks. A blue shotgun shell. Ant hills already open, sun-baked as if this were summer. It takes me back a mile out of my way. I don't know where it goes. Still another shell, canary yellow, this one.

2:45 p.m. Breeze freshening. I don't know where I am. A rusty paint can made into a sieve by a shotgun blast. Another canary-colored shell. Winchester Super X. 20 gauge. I turn back, facing a pale sun in a milky cloud.

3:20. Napeague Beach at last. The ocean. I found a path down the hill, across the railroad and Route 27, onto "Napeague Lane" straight to the ocean. I put Napeague Lane in quotes because it wasn't there when I was young. *Napeague* means waterland in

Algonkian. The beach is level with the ocean, flat and still. No wind, no waves to speak of. Just a quiet, steady sound of 10-inch wavelets in endlessly repeating lines. Sunlight forming spokes in the clouds west. Dead spider crabs, gulls moving up the beach ahead of me. The sun like a full moon behind moving clouds; and then tire tracks, the endless trace of a wheeled vehicle along the high tide line. It looked the same 200 years ago. I pick up a transparent egg-shape stone with pink and blue in it. A jelly fish the size of a nickel. Two horseshoe crabs. There's certain clamshells with this combination of blue and gray in shifting patches, moving over to a dirty cream color. I came to love these colors only lately. Younger, I never saw them. Nature was drab, compared with, say, a painting by Mondrian, or the color chart in Goethe's *Farbenlehre*.

3:45. Approaching Asparagus Beach, Amagansett. The sky is now the same color as those shells. Gray. Blue. Rust-pink. Except there is the vibrancy of sunlight behind it all. I keep mentioning Light in my writing, even my conversation; above all, my thoughts. It's almost like a prayer. I wonder, is this mystique of light a received idea, something latched onto at an impressionable age? It can't be. Look at the life forms, coelacanths and others, that inhabit the ocean floor entirely cut off from light, which not only make do without retinal vision but stand on their heads on the bottom for long periods, like yogis, and often swim upside down or backwards. Then there are others that are both photophobic and scototropic, that is, growing toward darkness, and I wonder about the part of myself I can feel inside doing the same; it's not toward death but toward another kind of life, without light or seeing, but in pure darkness which is what I used to call my prayer for blindness. That wasn't a plea to have my eyes put out, I get dizzy even thinking about that, or dimmed by cataracts, like Bach, but it is a side, a dark side, of the mind that reaches out into something like Novalis's all-mothering Night and wants to inhabit it as blindly as its blindest denizens in a protozoic but intensely aware darkness that would be like vision without illumination, a blackness dazzling as the intensest light.

A line of surf washes over a slight rise on the curve of the water's edge, just a sheet of water with a ruffle or frill of foam, so quiet.

4:25 p.m. The sound of the surf is very still, muffled as it were. There's hardly any breeze. The tide pool I am looking at is almost perfectly smooth. There is an ancient Chinese book titled The Classic of Pure Calm.

4:30. Indian Wells. The sand is crinkled up like an aerial view from very high over the Sahara. Water action, however, not wind, did this. The dunes here are marked with yellow tick-warning signs. Pinks and browns are coming out in the clouds round the sun, now much lower in the sky. It's ten to five.

Two Mile Hollow, five o'clock. Three sets of footprints. Shoes. Boots. Bare feet.

I pass the windmill belonging to William Simon, Secretary of the Treasury under Nixon. He had the windmill fixed up with federal funds for historic landmarks. It's in his duneside backyard, not open to the public. I once was invited in there and climbed up inside. From the top I imagined I could see all the way to Montauk.

5:20 p.m. Maidstone Club. I turn in from the beach, onto the tar-top, hiking fast over the golf links toward Main Street.

Family Business

On January 10, 1980, Bob Metzger, the doctor who had been treating my brother Joshua for several years, called me on the phone and announced, "It's the end of the road for Joshua." Metzger had just seen the chemotherapy specialist, and the two were agreed there was nothing more to be done. Joshua was in a daze, unable to put two sentences together. There was too little oxygen and too much carbon dioxide in his blood. The mechanism in the lungs that regulates the balance of the two had been impaired by the spread of the disease. I mentioned that the last time I'd seen Joshua he seemed stoned. Metzger replied, "He *is* stoned. On excess CO_2." He went on to say that he and Joshua's wife, Ruth, had taken it upon themselves to bring him to the hospital, adding, "He's no longer competent."

I had just finished reading the *Aphorisms* of Hippocrates, in which the following appears: "Those diseases that medicines do not cure are cured by the knife. Those that the knife does not cure are cured by fire. Those that fire does not cure must be considered incurable."

After Metzger hung up, I took the Lexington Avenue subway uptown to the hospital. Joshua was sitting up in bed. Ruth sat next to him, holding his hand, an untouched suppertray on the ledge nearby. He greeted me in friendly fashion, then looked away. His expression was like that of a man by himself on a train, or in a waiting room. On his lower lip there was a faint line of what appeared to be dried blood. He moved a bit and cocked his head at an angle suggesting scorn, or disdain. As if he were looking down his nose at death. His nose, our nose. The two of us have the same nose, I once heard it called "patrician." We inherited that nose from our Dad, but on Dad it had looked anything but patrician. In later years Dad's nose had always reminded me of Jimmy Durante's.

Joshua pushed his chin forward, cleared his throat, and started: "Ruth, I . . . " She tried to get him to finish the sentence. What did you say? He waved the question aside, then said: "Nothing." This happened several times. Ruth left the room. I leaned forward and asked, "You want to leave the hospital?" His eyes meeting mine narrowed with concentration, he replied, "Dan, I'm at the end of my rope. I've reached it." Then he stared at the wall. I didn't answer. Then I told of plans to visit my friend Ruthven in Georgia and mentioned Bartram's classic *Travels in Georgia and the Carolinas*. Its report of subterranean rivers in Florida was the source of Coleridge's *Alph*, the sacred river in "Kubla Khan." Joshua replied that he had heard of the book but never read it, would however very much like to. The conversation proceeded, in bursts of lucid remembrance followed by spells of apparently tranquil silence. I was put in mind of De Quincey's phrase, "blank mementoes of powers extinct."

Twice he got up and sat in the chair, then got back on the bed. There was a bustle at the door. The specialist walked in, with two junior colleagues, to say goodbye, as it turned out. A man in his mid-fifties—a very large balding head with small, pinched features, glasses, long fat-fingered hands, a white smock and a soft, fluent voice. Shaking hands with me, he turned to Joshua and launched into a paragraph-long sentence, an obscurely euphemistic preamble. I wondered if he realized Joshua wouldn't be capable of making sense of it. I imagined Pavlov pronouncing a farewell address to an animal in the lab. At last the doctor gave his blessing to our plan to return to Maidstone immediately. He phrased it in such a way to exonerate himself of all responsibility if it turned out badly.

At that point an astonishing thing happened. Joshua pulled himself to his feet and made a speech that must have lasted nearly a minute, thanking the doctor and his staff for their efforts and kind offer to let him stay on at the hospital. Having weighed it in his mind he had decided to go home and fix himself a martini, instead.

Making the most of this, the doctor suggested that the "conquering hero" could rely on such teammates as Ruth and myself to make him an excellent martini. Oh no, he said, he liked to mix his own. Then he sat back down. The doctor told us to have oxygen in Maidstone. That could be done through the local ambulance service. Joshua interrupted, "Daniel will call and arrange for all that." Once again, he stood up, indicating that the visit was over, and shook the doctor's hands, with appropriate pleasantries to each. When they had left, he lay back down, exhausted.

With the bedside phone I called Carol to tell her I was going out to Maidstone. Ruth and I then left, to take a cab downtown to pick up her car where she had parked it on Ninth Street. As we passed, on our way out, through the ward where Joshua lay, there was a commotion around one of the beds, where a black man with all sorts of tubes in his arms and down his throat seemed to be going into death throes, and a stout woman in her Sunday best, who could have been his wife or sister, groaned and sobbed loudly, her face buried in a pillow that had been left on the bedside ledge. The thought crossed my mind that something similar was about to happen in our house, quite soon, the sooner the better, no doubt.

Downtown on Hudson Street, Ruth parked in front of the Parisienne Deli, and while she got sandwiches for us I went upstairs where Carol had packed a bag for me. As I left, Carol pressed a twenty in my hand. On our way back uptown, Ruth told of an unsuccessful attempt to persuade Bob Metzger to write a Miltown prescription. I urge her to stay off drugs, they would only make what was happening seem even worse than it was. She said she knew that was probably so, but there were times when the pain of it was so unbearable she craved anything that would give even a few minutes relief. She recalled an ex-neighbor who had, as she put it, "grinned from ear to ear" and laughed at her husband's funeral, smashed on tranquilizers. She didn't want *that* to happen.

On our arrival at the hospital, I sat in the driver's seat, the motor running, because we had to park in the NO STANDING space directly in front of the door. The guards there, West Indians, tried to prevent Ruth from entering. She made a fuss. I could see her gesticulating on the other side of the glass wall, fifty feet away. At last, one of them picked up a phone, and after a further delay of several minutes she was admitted.

Next, Joshua was downstairs, being pushed in a wheelchair through the lobby to the door. At the street he stood up from the chair and after pausing to thank the nurse's aid, a good-looking woman, walked to the car, waving aside offers of assistance.

Stopping at a red light in Harlem, en route to the bridge, we watched a group of men crowding round an ashcan with a fire inside. Ruth wondered whether they were cooking something, or just staying warm. Don't ask, came Joshua's voice from the back seat, where we had imagined him already asleep.

Going over the bridge and the long causeway that rolls down from it parallel to the river, Joshua sat up straight and gazed at New

York and its lights. The volume on the radio went up, and Bach's *Chaconne* filled the car like a movie soundtrack, the kind of music that has often brought tears to my eyes, but under the present circumstances I was simply annoyed and hated it.

Soon we were passing Kennedy. Joshua was asleep. Arriving in Maidstone two hours later, we were greeted in the clear icy darkness by my sister Florrie and the two teenagers, Daniel and Peter, Joshua's sons. I glanced up at the sky. The first stars I'd seen in months and they were all out.

Joshua walked the short little sidewalk to the house. That walk was installed when they still had the 1938 Chevy, just before the war, over a previous mudtrack. Daniel and Peter brought in the luggage. While they helped Joshua get settled, I went back to the kitchen and stepped out onto the screened porch where we'd had many a summertime breakfast and supper, the screening doubled waist-high with child-proof "elephant wire," as Dad called it. We never used that porch in winter except to store Christmas turkeys and hams after the fact, making it a spot for midnight raids by the teenagers we were. I stood there, leaving the kitchen door ajar. It opened softly and Florrie was there next to me. I spent the next ten minutes hugging her as she sobbed, repeating over and over something Joshua had just said to her. I couldn't understand what Florrie was saying. It occurred to me that she was drunk.

Back inside, Joshua was sitting up in bed. He was in the same state as at the hospital, except that he had developed a wheeze and his breathing had become somewhat labored. I concentrated on petting the cat that had jumped up on the bed, making him purr. I asked Joshua, "Is he the kind to purr and then scratch?" Yes indeed, he replied. Ruth and Florrie frequently paused from what they were doing, to come past the bed and kiss him or squeeze his hand. He liked that, and smiled every time. I wondered if there would be a blowup between the two women. Things were strained between them at the best of times.

I suggested to Ruth it would be a good idea for me to go home to Bendigo Road with Florrie. She agreed enthusiastically. She sent us off with admonitions to drive safely. "She must have thought I was smashed," said Florrie fifteen minutes later, under a night sky ablaze with planets and constellations, adding, "She was right, I *am* smashed."

We talked for a couple of hours in the kitchen. Although on the wagon, I drank a can of beer. The words with Joshua that Florrie had sobbed out to me earlier had been a whispered, conspiratorial exchange, as she remembered it. She had asked him, Josh are you tired, *really* tired? and he had replied, Yes I am. *Yes*, "Clear as a bell," she said again and again.

She had jumped to the conclusion that he wanted us to give him an overdose of something. When I was a kid, the newspaper term for this was "mercy killing." Maybe it still is. I didn't think Florrie was right. That is, I didn't think Joshua was sufficiently alert to nuances to have caught the drift of that question, "Are you *really* tired?" On the other hand, the bond between my brother and sister was so close, it was conceivable that the faculty to communicate on unspoken levels had remained intact, despite his present state. Florrie's ideas about this were based mainly on past events, however. In the first nights at the hospital long ago, after Grandma fell down her basement stairs with a stroke and cracked her skull, Florrie had had the opportunity to "pull the plug" and refused to do so. Grandma had lingered on another year, wretched and half-crazed. As Florrie said, "What little brains she had left went sour on her."

Then there was the story of Aunt Flo. Florrie and Grandma spent a lot of time together a few years before Grandma's accident, and despite a gap of fifty years the two women became close friends. Grandma was Uncle Dan's first nurse at age 20 when he opened his medical practice in 1901. When Aunt Flo, her sister, was dying, sometime in the mid-1950s, Uncle Dan eased Flo out on morphine, according to Grandma. She watched him giving Flo progressively bigger injections. Nobody ever said anything about it at the time. Grandma told Florrie the story by way of a request for herself, should the need ever arise, so Florrie felt that she had let her grandmother down.

At this point, I told Florrie that Bob Metzger had given Ruth a bottle of morphine. Florrie said she thought that was a cop-out on his own responsibility toward Joshua, not only as his physician but as his friend. She asked if "it" could be put in Joshua's food. I said it was well nigh impossible to administer a lethal dose of morphine orally, especially to a person who wasn't eating or drinking much of anything. Besides, it tastes nasty. It works only if injected, preferably in a vein. "Nonsense," Florrie interrupted. "Can you picture Ruth there, filling up the syringe?" I suggested we forget about the morphine. Nature would take its course.

The next morning I took the train back to New York, to work, and after work a judo class. I couldn't keep my mind on it. My reflexes were slow. At supper with Carol, I felt uncomfortably distant. Ever since this began, I was spending much more time away from Carol than I had been expecting or wanting to. Also, impending death has a way of making her even more circumspect and reserved than ordinarily.

The next day was a Saturday. I learned from a telephone conversation with Florrie that Joshua's state was unchanged. I decided to take the 7:58 a.m. train Sunday, to spend the day with him in Maidstone.

During the train ride, I tried to summon up my earliest memories of him. 1939. I was three, he was seven. He got to go to the World's Fair. I stayed home. They told me the Fair was west, like the setting sun. I started, crosslots, through the fields, heading west, meaning to go the whole way on foot. I remember the vermilion disk, the sun in the trees.

In 1942, first year of the war and of victory gardens, our mother served as den mother to a group of Cub Scouts including Joshua. I wanted to be a cub, too. They told me I was under age. I crashed the meetings anyhow, only to be led away in tears. I tried to join them outdoors, after the meetings, but there too I was excluded. From this time on, I was an embarrassment. One day I made a scene in front of the other Cubs and hit Joshua with a hatchet. He shouted furiously. I was told the Cain and Abel story. I imagined I had indeed attempted to murder my brother, being only one year short of the age of criminal responsibility as set forth by canon law.

Meanwhile, Grandpa Hedges showed his preference for Joshua, maybe because he exhibited a knack for boat and water lore. By the time he was ten or eleven, Grandpa was taking him out on seine-hauling and gunning expeditions. Joshua was already an apt pupil, a useful companion.

Another episode paralleled my attempt to walk from Maidstone to the World's Fair. This happened when I was seven or eight. I was awakened in the middle of the night by a commotion in the next room, Joshua's room, as he got up to leave for Grandpa's house on Daniels Lane. It must have been three in the morning. They were to join a gunning party at Napeague. Lying there in the dark, I couldn't bear it. I got up, put on my warmest clothes, and walked through the rainy night to Daniels Lane. They were already out in the barn, loading the trunk of Grandpa's 1936 Dodge coupe with shotguns, decoys, and other gear. There were several other people, men and boys, present. My entrance created a sensation, and much laughter. Joshua flushed with anger. I don't recall Grandpa's reaction, but he couldn't have been too pleased. I was taken home, where my parents gave me a lecture about how I couldn't go because I wasn't old enough. I was made to promise never to do it again. I never did. By the time I reached the age Joshua was on the morning of that scene, our grandfather was already dying.

The train raced past a parking lot in Babylon in which stood a hundred orange school buses. My thoughts drifted back to a conversation with Carol in New York City. She had remarked that there was anger in my voice when I spoke about Florrie's going to pieces at Joshua's homecoming three days before. According to her, I had sounded a heavily disapproving note. She said it was as if I were more than a bit frightened to see my big sister acting like a child. I ought to look at the situation from Florrie's standpoint. Joshua was Florrie's little brother, and it might well frighten *her* to be watching him die. I ought to bear in mind that unlike myself Florrie had been in the firing line for a long time with Joshua's illness. I should go easy on her and consider that this whole thing was likely to stir up a lot of unexpected feelings in all of the nearest and dearest, including me. So, she concluded, you had better keep an eye on yourself. When she said that, I remembered something that had happened at the time of Joshua's first operation, seven years earlier, when they removed the kidney that was the original site of the cancer. I wrote to the surgeon and offered myself as a transplant donor but was turned down for some reason relating to immune reactions. Carol was horrified when I told her about that letter. "There is only one person in the world," she said, "just one I'd do that for, and that is you."

At the Maidstone house I found a crowd of people, including Dorothy, a college friend of Ruth's, who had come up from Washington D.C., to stay and assist. The boys were in and out of the house. In the middle of the day, Daniel climbed to the top of the forty-foot pine tree behind the house and looked at the ocean with binoculars. Descending, he told me he had been able to see a mile of beach between Main Beach and the bluff at the end of Egypt Lane. I went inside and told Joshua about Daniel's exploit. "Knew it could be done," he whispered in reply.

Sitting with him became unbearable. He was rarely altogether conscious and that only for seconds at a time. Mostly he stared blankly, at the same time groaning, muttering to himself, and wheezing. It seemed to be getting harder for him to breathe. I considered the abyss between the actual reality on the one hand and our everyday talk on the other. Confronted with the reality, there is little we can say. Art and literature may prepare us for many of the great experiences—love, for example. But there is nothing in art or literature to prepare us for death.

Florrie entered the room and asked me to go pick out some music for the stereo, preferably Mozart. *He* would like that. I chose a Mozart piano concerto. At one point during the first movement, Ruth leaned forward close to Joshua's face. He smiled and puckered his lips for a kiss.

Things are said and done at a deathbed that would seem bizarre, or inappropriate, under any other circumstances. An instance of this was enacted by Florrie who after disappearing for a couple of hours returned with a piece of fresh seaweed from Cartwright Bay. With this she wet Joshua's lips. He thanked her and said it tasted good.

The night before, Ruth and Florrie had discussed the impending funeral. Ruth opposed cremation, although Joshua had once mentioned wanting it. At one point in the conversation, she suggested a memorial service for family and friends at Bendigo Beach, to be concluded with a fireworks display. Florrie talked her out of that.

In the middle of the night, Joshua said to Ruth, "I am lacking." This cryptic statement she took to be a self-reproach for not being "strong" to the end.

Later in the day he woke up briefly. I told him I had read his latest column for the *Maidstone Sun*. Written barely two weeks earlier and now in galley proofs, it told of a crazy man who had recently walked into the Southampton police station brandishing a shotgun. Surprisingly, the cops had managed to subdue him without injury to anyone. I congratulated Joshua on the column, assuring him that it was a marvelous piece of writing. In reply he chuckled self-deprecatingly, "Yeah, that was really something . . . " I couldn't tell how much of this was automatic, reflex-action affability and how much of it represented real presence of mind. He was making sense only in response to things said to him, but seemed to have lost the power to initiate, to say something on his own. Early that afternoon, he had said to Ruth, "Leave me alone." In the context, he might just as well have intended to say, "*Don't* leave me alone." Whichever was meant, Ruth broke down and cried, at which he seemed momentarily to focus on her distress and said, "Hush, hush!"

At suppertime, Florrie brought in a chowder she had made from some Cartwright Bay mussels. Joshua declined to touch it. A bit later, Ruth gave him a few spoonfuls of ice cream. Shortly after that, she had a telephone conversation with Bob Metzger in New York. He told her not to feed Joshua anymore, and not to give him much to drink, either, because it would only lead to pain later on. At the same time, he warned Ruth that there was a possibility of seizures. Seizures were always a possibility in uremic poisoning, which was bound to set in, or, to be more precise, had already set in. Sitting alone with Joshua after the conversation with Metzger, I noticed a solitary tear streaming down his cheek. He was flushed, breathing with difficulty, staring at me, and groaning. I put my hand on his shoulder and squeezed. Whether he knew what was going on, I couldn't say.

The end didn't come until the next day, sometime between six and seven in the evening, and I wasn't there, having gone back to New York. A few minutes after five, on my way out to a judo class, I spoke with Florrie on the phone and she told me Ruth had just noticed a change. Joshua's pulse had sunk very low, and he was getting cold. She still expected him to last through the night. However, when I came home from judo, Florrie called to say Joshua was dead. During the hour following our previous conversation, he had sunk steadily lower until very cold and breathing hardly at all. Finally, they could feel no pulse. All at once, the color drained out of his cheeks, which had been flushed with the effort of breathing. There were two or three more breaths. "But," Florrie added, "those were mere reflex actions. He was already dead, I am convinced of that . . . " His eyes remained open, as they had been for hours. Ruth couldn't bear it. Suddenly she said, "Joshua, close your eyes!" Then she turned to Florrie and said, "Close his eyes. I can't stand to see his eyes like that." Florrie put her hand across his eyes, with the thumb and forefinger pressing his brows, merely covering them without making any attempt to push down the lids. She kept her hand there a minute, at the same time trying to soothe Ruth. At length, Ruth turned away and Florrie lifted her hand to glance at Joshua's eyes, wondering how she was going to go about closing them. To her amazement they were closed. Had he heard Ruth at the last instant and closed them himself? This seemed unlikely. Florrie speculated that the closing of

Joshua's eyes represented yet another "reflex." Or, possibly, the warmth of her hand had somehow caused them to close.

It occurred to me that even while dying, Joshua's waking and sleeping hours, as well as his rising and falling phases of vitality, coincided with the day-night cycle. He always slept at night and stayed awake by day. Even that last day, his final glimmerings were in the morning and at midday. All that day a passage from the Bible rang in my mind: "And Joshua said, 'Sun, stand thou still at Gibeon, and thou Moon in the valley of Aijalon.' And the sun stood still, and the moon stayed. And there was no day like that before or since."

The terminal plunge into deep sleep coincided with the coming of night. This is what Hippocrates says about the actual instant of death:

> The boundary of death is passed when the heat of the soul has risen above the navel to the part above the diaphragm, and all moisture has been burned up. When lungs and heart have cast out the moisture of the heat that collects in the places attacked by disease, there passes away all at once the breath of the heat, wherefrom the individual was originally constituted, out into the universe again, partly through the flesh and partly through the breathing organs in the head, whence we call it the 'breath of life.' And the soul, leaving the tabernacle of the body, gives up the cold, mortal image to bile, blood, phlegm, and flesh.

In the above there is more than a hint of transcendence, I feel. As the Commentary points out, it is an obscure passage, but the gist seems to be that the warm life of the individual gets reabsorbed at death into the warmth of the cosmos. Over that last week I had observed the entire process closely, and there was nothing about any of it that could be described as "transcendent," with one possible exception, a little incident that was later described to me. A fellow Naval officer stopped in to say hello, or rather goodbye, to Joshua a day or so before the end. This man had taught him how to fly, in a Navy training plane, in the sky over the Pacific and the San Diego base. His presence in the sickroom triggered luminous memories, and for some minutes Joshua talked nonstop in what everyone except the man who had taught him to fly took for delirium. He imagined the two of them were flying in a perfectly cloudless sky and began ticking off the main features and landmarks of the vista several thousand feet below, the islands on the horizon to the west, the brown coastline of Baja California, and so forth. For a few seconds there was something like exuberance in his voice. It had the ring of the twenty-two-year-old he had been at the time of the actual experience.

The day before the funeral found me still in New York. At a gallery on Fifty-seventh Street there was an opening that I wanted to attend, a show titled "ADS" by Les Levine. My friend Giancarlo agreed to meet me there at six. A few moments after his arrival, I ran into Michael Codrescu, the author of an article on my brother-in-law's paintings that appears in the Akademie der Künste catalogue I had just finished translating. We decided to go over to the Parsons. As we moved out of the crowd of art world people, down an elevator, and into the noisy street, to thread our way single-file through a sort of catwalk on the edge of a construction site, Michael said he had just heard that my brother had died. He went on to talk about a book titled *The Meaning of Illness*, by the psychiatrist Georg Groddeck, who viewed cancer as a psychosomatic syndrome, a view of the matter that he, Codrescu, also considered to be correct. I wondered whether he was saying all that to make me feel bad, or because unusually insensitive, or perhaps out of honest conviction.

I decided to leave New York immediately for Napeague. I spent the night in the room where I always stay, on the second story of Florrie's house, overlooking Cartwright Bay. The room is bitter cold in winter. I love it anyway. I wrapped up to the ears in blue bedsheets and three blankets.

Over breakfast, my brother-in-law Harold went over my translation of the German introduction to his new catalogue. There were minor points to be cleared up. Florrie was annoyed to see us, her husband and her brother, occupied with a catalogue on the day of our brother's funeral. Not very annoyed. Just a bit. Harold said, "Do you remember what we were doing the week Ann Hedges McCormick died, and the day of her funeral?" "Yes," I replied, "The day Mom died we were working on my American translation of your Lehmbruck Museum catalogue." "Right," Harold said, "I wondered if you had noticed the coincidence." I had in fact imagined I was the only one to notice it.

When we got to Maidstone, I was told that they wanted me to read a poem by John Hall Wheelock at graveside. I went to the *Sun* building, got out the Wheelock books, and took them into Joshua's private office there. I found a ten-line poem titled "Silence."

Back at the house, the pinewood coffin had a wreath, made by Florrie the day before, of seven white roses, three daisies, some baby's breath, and pine boughs laid on top of it. I was one of the pallbearers. We actually carried the coffin, a plain box made by a carpenter friend of Joshua's only three days earlier, four times. From the house to the hearse. From the street to the church door. Then after the service, from the church steps back to the hearse. And finally the cemetery, from the hearse to the grave. The pallbearers at either end of the coffin lifted it on carrying sticks. Those in the middle steadied it with their hands. Going down the aisle and coming out, we marched with it mounted on a stainless steel frame with wheels, our hands on the coffin lid. Ruth and the boys, together with Florrie, marched immediately behind us. At the church door I noticed the sixteen-year-old Daniel Hedges McCormick behind me, almost at my elbow, weeping bitterly.

In the street, once the coffin was inside the hearse, various people came up to kiss and shake hands. It was a fairly warm day for January. A light rain was falling. I noticed a tremor in my face and hands. I wondered if this was the spectacle people had come for. A middle-aged woman, heavily made up, with blue eyeshadow and lavender lipstick, introduced herself as Joshua's highschool classmate who, in the Senior Variety Night Revue, had sung, or rather, lip-synched to a record, as I vividly remembered, "I can't give you anything but love, ba-by . . . " That would have been in 1948. She had no way of knowing it, but her rendition of "I can't give you anything but love" had haunted me for twenty years. I wouldn't know why, it was just one of those things.

Bob Metzger and his friend Pat interrupted this colloquy to ask if they could "hitch a ride" with me to the cemetery. I led them over to Harold's car, where the three of us sat in the back seat, awkwardly jammed together. I had thought there would be two in front, but in the end it was only Harold, driving as if he were our chauffeur. Bob Metzger and Pat held hands all the way to the cemetery. My thoughts flashed back to a summer day six months earlier, on a picnic with Joshua at (or as older people including Grandpa used to say, "on") Montauk, when Metzger and Pat and I went skinny-dipping in the bay, much to the amusement of the others.

As the car swung into the cemetery, I glanced at the names on the stones nearest the road. It seemed that every one was a family name well known to me. Arriving at the grave, we placed the coffin on a contraption with straps to lower it into the hole, which was in the center of a square of Astroturf. Several baskets of funeral wreaths surrounded the coffin. The crowd looked expectantly at me. Before I had a chance to start reading the poem, Peter caught my attention and asked me to remove the flowers from in front of the coffin. "They look horrible," he said. They did look horrible. I moved them. Then I turned and faced the crowd. After a long silence I shouted, "I'm going to read a poem by John Hall Wheelock . . . 'Silence' . . . " I wondered if anybody in the crowd thought I was calling for silence. Mortified at the thought of the pointlessness of what I was doing, I read off the poem in a voice big enough to be heard by all of the several hundred persons present.

As soon as I finished, Mr. Richards, the funeral director, pressed a button on the contraption, and the coffin was automatically lowered into the ground. This happened with excruciating slowness. We stood there until the coffin disappeared. Then everyone dispersed, and we returned to the house, where a large crowd was given food and drink.

Among the guests was a very old black man who had come uninvited. He had worked at the Napeague fish factory, he explained, at a time when our grandfather Captain Joshua Hedges used to bring little Josh to the dock and buy him a Peter Paul Mound from the company store. Also, the man had had a lot of trouble paying his water bills. So, knowing Captain Hedges was President of the Water Company, he had approached him to ask for more time to pay the bill. Captain Hedges had said that he would speak to Miss Garrupie and get it taken care of. And, would you believe it, the man never got another bill from the Water Company. All thanks to Captain Josh, Captain Hedges that is. So today he had thought he would come by and pay his respects. As I listened, Florrie kept the man's glass filled with bourbon and ginger.

Still on the wagon, I didn't take a drop of alcohol. Just about everyone else did. At one point an old woman walked up and informed me that I was "a dramatically romantic-looking man." The carpenter who made Joshua's coffin came over and asked me, in front of Ruth and several others, if I was a black sheep. Ruth said, "Oh no, he is 'The Count,' the romantic aristocrat, the poet." After a couple of hours, I rode back to New York with Jane Poe, a grand-daughter of Uncle Dan Hedges.

That night I had two dreams about Joshua. In one of them I was an old man living alone at the Hotel Chelsea. It turned out that Joshua was not dead at all, but had remained the same age he was when we first thought him dead, forty-seven. I visited him in a loft in Soho, which he was sharing with a young woman I had never met. Joshua was a forever youthful-looking forty-seven, whereas I had gone on aging and was now much older than him. He and his Soho girlfriend invited me to stay for a drink. I complained of the rigors of living at the Chelsea. In the other dream I opened a new rock and roll album and discovered that the lyrics were by John Hall Wheelock. One of the songs was titled "Silence."

A month or so after the events I have just described, one sunny weekend in February, I spent a couple of days at Napeague with Florrie. On Sunday afternoon, we went on a hike over the meadows, into the woods and through a swamp, out to a beach near Islay. From there we walked back to her house along the edge of a Cartwright Bay half-frozen like the Arctic Ocean in summer, brightly roiling under a high wind. In the woods, however, there had been no wind, but great patches of sunlight in amongst the scrub oak and pines. We were looking for a bottle dump. We found plenty of bottles but not a single good old one. As we searched among the half-buried bottles, Florrie told me about the last week before they had realized Joshua was dying. She mentioned that he had found a pretty little medicine bottle out in the Northwest Woods, while looking for a tree just before Christmas. He had been so out of breath he could barely walk. At one point he had sat down to rest on a bank of frozen moss. It was there that his hand had happened to alight on the little medicine bottle. It now stands on the mantelpiece in the Maidstone house.

I asked Florrie exactly when it was that she had become aware of Joshua's final decline. She said no special time, he'd simply started sleeping more and more, really an inordinate number of hours every night, with long naps during the day. Ice cream sodas or milkshakes were his only nourishment for weeks. Apart from that, he had no appetite. During the last week before he died he probably ate nothing at all, save for an occasional spoonful of ice cream. On our way out of the woods, we bushwhacked through a frozen swamp. Neither of us had any idea of where we really were, but that didn't seem to make any difference. As we pushed forward, Florrie told me how Harold had once panicked, or nearly panicked, when they got lost in the woods near the Maidstone airport. It had started to rain, night was coming on, and Harold was scared. Florrie and I are similar in one respect and different from most other people. Neither of us has ever been afraid of getting lost in the woods.

The Darkened Chamber

"Vile daguerreotypy, perverter of the artistic instinct!" Thus Gérard de Nerval on Photography, 1854. Yet one of Gerard's best friends was the great Nadar, whose portrait of Nerval stares (squints, glares) from the cover of his *Complete Works*. A redhead, Nadar sat Gérard through a few bad nights when suicide loomed.

Is Photography a perverter of instinct? To answer the question, let's get down to brass tacks and the mystery of the *camera obscura*. In my grandfather's barn, in East Hampton, New York, there was a small upstairs room, sandwiched between the hayloft and a ground-floor workshop, connected with the latter via a stairway closed off by a trapdoor. At the turn of the century and for some years after, the room had lodged a hired man. In my childhood it was completely bare, its single window boarded up. One winter, a knot hole developed in one of the pine boards covering the window. On Easter Sunday, 1947, upon entering the darkness of the room from a brilliant cloudless day, I was startled to see that the entire wall facing the window was alive with the greens, yellows, and blues of the privet and forsythia and April sky outdoors, all of them floating upside down, like Edward Lear's wonderful tree, the *Many-peoplia upside-downia*.

It has been forty years since I stepped into that darkened chamber as into a glory robe, and I have not given up trying to elucidate the moment. It dawned on me as it was happening that I had just stepped inside a giant Kodak, sort of. The analogy didn't stop there.

The room could also be equated to a skull, the knot hole to an eye, and the hole to the mystery of visual perception. This in turn led to a reflection on the mind's eye, the nature of thinking itself. A few years later, I was to encounter the comparison, in Plato's *Republic*, of our perception of the visible world vis-a-vis the higher realm of the Ideas with that of a man who spends his life seeing images of the daylit world projected onto the wall of a darkened cave, and in the absence of wider referents imagines what he sees to be reality. Other readers of Plato link this simile to the experience of watching a magic lantern show, a slide show, a movie, or TV. My starting point for the whole train of thought is that room in my grandfather's barn.

Getting back to the natural lens formed by the knot hole in the board covering the window of the room, my first experience in practical photography, soon after that day, was prompted by a passage in Steichen's memoirs, telling of boyhood experiments with a pinhole camera. An 1890s boy's book of things to make and do supplied the concrete instructions. My first camera was an outsized shoebox lined with black paper. At the business end I cut out an inch-square hole and covered it with an oblong of the same opaque black paper. The center of this I punctured with a neat hole, using a needle. The size of the aperture and focal length were given in the book. The film was on a coated glass plate. A jam closet in the cellar of my home became the darkroom. The shoebox pinhole camera worked only a couple times. One used it on a sunny day. The exposure was half an hour. Both Steichen and *The Boy's Own Book* gave reproductions of outdoor scenes, exhibiting high contrast and sharpness, produced by pinhole cameras. My results were disappointing.

The next camera was a 1914 folding affair that had belonged to my mother as a girl. Using it, I did time exposures by candlelight. With equipment like this, I never came close to action photography.

The 1914 camera's maximum speed was a hundredth of a second. I did get some excellent shots of runners coming through the finish line at an East Hampton High School track meet in 1949.

In 1932 my Dad had bought a Leica while visiting friends in Germany, and this camera became a household god, a recording angel. My father was a newspaperman; his pictures were mainly the kind that tell a story. In the 1930s and 40s, contacts came in a long strip, rolled up in a tight roll like the film itself and stored in a cylindrical can.

Looking at these postage stamp–sized shots through a magnifier, I step back into a place where the expression "pre-war" (pre-WWII) stood for a magical era like that of the Golden Age. However, the world of these snapshots was no Eden but a 20th-century family circle where the mind and face of sibling rivalry, in silver nitrate writ, stares at a beholder who is as much a stranger as anyone could be to the world his own eyes were gazing at when photographed a half-century before. The smaller of the two boys at table, the one wearing a bib, mooning over an untouched meal, is me. The purposefully masticating redhead is my brother. Two of the living room shots surprise him and me, squeezed together in a leather armchair in friendly converse. A third shows all three of us, my sister, brother, and me, in a pose prefiguring our lifetime relationship—my brother standing apart, obstinately staring past the photographer, at some-thing in back of the felt perceptual center; while my sister and I cuddle in the same chair, giggling over some private joke. Behind us is a white wall bare save for a Chinese silk hanging and a couple of red-framed photographs, by Arnold Genthe. Genthe was to photography what Thomas Moran was to painting, my parents said. They possessed several of his 1904 Chinatown, San Francisco photos and a number of portraits including a 1936 one of my grandfather in oilers amid his nets, like a heroic bronze statue. Genthe had published that picture with a gallery of ten photographers invited by *Vogue* to submit a portrait of the most handsome man they had ever photographed. This story led to a childhood ambition to make friends with a photographer of Genthe's rank so as to guarantee future status as one of the world's ten handsomest men.

Together with his first group of regular playmates, at around age seven or eight, my brother built a little shanty with a tarpaper roof, over against the side of my grandfather's barn. The doings of this little clique were recorded in great detail by the Leica. Looking at the contacts dated 1940 and '41, I recognize each boy by name. They used to sleep overnight in the shanty—it was a clubhouse with bunks, a table and chairs, pictures torn from old magazines nailed to the walls, plus a large store of Batman, Green Lantern, and Torch comics, Wild West magazines, flicker books (by flicking the pages you got a movie image in the upper right-hand corner of the book for a second or two), and back issues of *Reader's Digest*. My brother's friends made up the first in-group to which I was denied access.

The shanty actually descended to me for a brief spell when the older boys had outgrown it, but it was falling apart; and so, in the summer of 1942, around the time the German saboteurs landed in Amagansett, one of my grandfather's hands spent a day demolishing it, removing every trace.

In 1949, at age 13, a fascination with the war that had set brother against brother, father against son, led me to idolize Matthew Brady. I had met several very old people who had clear memories dating back to the 1861–5 period, but in Brady I had a fixed, unwavering gaze and what to me seemed an almost superhuman objectivity. I went to the Library of Congress that spring and spent a day in a basement room filled with Brady plates and a light table. The librarian showed me how to handle the plates without smudging them. I managed to weave into the conversation the fact I'd been dealing with photographic plates for the past couple of years. I have never gotten over that day. The Gettysburg casualties haunt me still in the faces of men nowadays euphemistically termed "the homeless." Those desolate eyes—now I am speaking of living men and boys on both sides, Union and Confederate—I have met many times on skid row up and down America; and in my teens, reading Cotton Mather and Edward Dahlberg and Leslie Fiedler how my native land is a howling wilderness, always was and will be, I panicked and wanted out. My sister had preceded me to Paris, so that is where the iron filings within tended for several years until a reversal of magnetic fields drew me home, where I remain, dividing my life between New York, northern New England, and an East Hampton that, with the invasion of the city already minutely detailed by my parents and my brother in their writings, has become a country of the mind only, having ceased to be a social or even a physical reality.

So is Photography a perverter of the artistic instinct? Consider the question in Nerval's terms. When he said artistic instincts ("le goût des artistes") he wasn't talking exclusively about that not-necessarily important minority, the makers of art, nor did he have in mind that even less important although numerically superior group, artistic people, in the sense of Nero's last words, *Qualis artifex pereo.* ("What an artist dies in me!") When Nerval said artist he always really meant those who were seeking the philosopher's stone, the alchemists, those who believe reality can be transmuted into a shape of light outweighing matter. And by *goût* (taste, I would say here instincts) the French language ever since Rémond de Saint-Marc and Couperin's time has meant that mysterious faculty that helps you make the right move instinctively, without having to figure it out in advance. Does Photography pervert taste in this sense? I say, No. Nerval was wrong. What he couldn't have known, since the documents were not generally known in his day, was that Photography was in fact invented by artists in Nerval's own sense of the word—alchemists, initiates. Photographs reflect Nature, as everyone knows; but Photography the process imitates her, in that the *camera obscura*, the box, the aperture, the inverted image captured in a light-sensitive emulsion and subsequently fixed—all this is a crude mechanical analogue of visual cognition and thinking. The light-sensitive medium was discovered during the 1600s, when the quest for light-containing minerals reached a fever pitch among natural philosophers. Match the discovery of silver nitrate's properties with the *camera obscura* idea and the myth of the magic mirror that could hold an image, and you have the concept. But does the acceptance and use of photographic technique, a technique that mimics our mental structures (the viewing screen, nowadays the cathode-ray tube of the mind's eye, and the very process of visual thinking) somehow pervert or subvert higher faculties? The answer is that its drawbacks are no worse than those of any other mechanical adjuvant. Literacy increased literature while decreasing memorization. With guns, archery declines. The faculty of visualization as cultivated by yogis and lamas lies beyond the mental reach of anyone who has grown up with print books, photography, and TV. By way of compensation, the modern person's ability to process photo-image information has looped back so far into the deep structures of everyone living within electronic reach that memory itself refers less and less to the past than to the faculty of selectively retrieving bodies of contemporary information from a logarithmically expanding base, in a universe where each night in one or another library one more great book goes out like a dying star.

French Film Friends: A Memoir of the 1960s

One day after arriving in Paris in the fall of 1965, I went to the studio where Chris Marker was editing *Far from Vietnam*. (Before getting on with my story, I had better tell a bit about Chris Marker and Mario Marret in two of whose works I played a tiny role, as a translator—Marker, born in 1921, assisted Alain Resnais in *Night and Fog* (1955) and has done many films since then. Founder of SLON filmmakers' cooperative, Marker has helped and in general ways influenced a whole generation in France—Mario Marret is about the same age as Marker and has directed a dozen documentaries, most on nonpolitical subjects; however, in the work of this veteran of the Resistance there is always an at least implicit political content, even when the subject-matter is as far afield as sled-dogs of the Far North, as it actually is in one of his films . . . The dominating figure was of course Jean-Luc Godard, whom I never did meet, though many of my film friends were deeply involved with him and his projects. 1965 was the year of *Pierrot le Fou* and *Alphaville*.)

Far from Vietnam is a composite film in which several French directors explain their position, or lack of a position, on the war. (This film was to be issued under Marker's name, as supervising editor, in 1967.) It was my first visit to a film studio. I'd come to Paris to write about Artaud. My translations of works by him had just appeared in Jack Hirschman's *Artaud Anthology* (City Lights, 1965) and a number of the poet's close friends, including his editor Paule Thévenin, were about to kick up a storm over it because of the book's numerous and inexcusable errors, a typical Parisian flurry in which I was to contribute my two cents in the form of a protest against the sloppiness with which the *Artaud Anthology* was put together, published in *Le Monde*, which identified me as "American poet writing his Harvard dissertation on Artaud." It was during the calm before this storm that I had got in touch with Chris Marker, because someone had told me Marker had known Artaud in the last phase of his life, in the late 1940s. The phone call to Marker was one of the most mysterious I have ever had. I never found out whether my interlocutor was really Chris Marker, or not; nor have I to this day learned anything about his relationship (or nonrelationship) with Artaud. The conversation simply skipped a groove, and the voice at the other end informed me that they needed an American at the studio, for a couple of seconds on the soundtrack of a film on Vietnam.

As I entered the cutting room, Defense Secretary McNamara's face filled the movieola screen, then receded a bit, to reveal a classroom map of Indochina next to the Pentagon chief's snarling visage. McNamara turned to the map and glared at Haiphong, jabbing at it with a pointer, gesturing and making faces at the camera, his lips forming words that we couldn't hear because there was no soundtrack.

I was asked to create an imaginary newscaster's script, to last maybe 10 seconds, and provided with an issue of the Paris *Tribune* featuring a McNamara press conference, to stimulate my imagination. I read my 10 seconds several times to a tape recorder.

(Two years later, when I saw the film at Lincoln Center, the McNamara scene had been edited to a point where, like the Cheshire cat's grin, it almost wasn't there; as for my voice, I thought I recognized *something* for one split-second, but couldn't be sure; such was my cinematic debut.)

The sound technician, Isidro Romero, was a husky fellow with wavy brown hair, pale freckled face, Midi accent, and the air of a Spanish grandee. He seemed distracted, annoyed, when we were introduced, and increasingly upset as I ran through my McNamara number. "Why?" I wondered out loud an hour later, at the bar next door where I had elbowed my way in to a spot alongside Isidro. Because you are an American, that's why, Isidro rejoined, switching to an insultingly familiar tone. If a clairvoyant had materialized at that moment to inform me I was preparing to square off with a future best friend, I would have told him he must be working the wrong Ouija board. However, the scene was all too tediously familiar from the annals of adventure, from G. A. Henty to John Wayne, and besides, Sylvaner in a long-stemmed green bulb glass (regulation for Rhinewine in a French proletarian bar) has a magically soothing effect. In *The Red and the Black*, Julien Sorel's nerves are soothed at a similar juncture by the timely administration of "*un verre vert de vin du Rhin*."

So Isidro Romero (militant filmmaker) and I (American poet writing his Harvard etc.) made friends. We pushed off into a cold wet evening—it was only about 7 p.m. but the nights were already closing in fast. We had just heard news of a giant black-out in the States, the whole Northeast, according to the French press, which hinted sabotage. "Is it true the Blacks are preparing to rise over there?" Isidro asked. "Yes," I replied, "Definitely." "The entire U.S. system is like those power lines, with or without sabotage—overloaded, ready to give out any day," he pursued, as we headed for supper.

In the course of that evening it transpired that Isidro's favorite poet was Rimbaud. He could recite the booklength *Season in Hell* from start to finish. Listening to him do that was an amazing experience. When called up for the draft, he had so intimidated the psychiatrist (he threatened to kill him) that the Conseil de Révision (their draft board) had released him as a nut case. He had gotten into the film world by a similarly direct approach. He was working in a bedspring factory somewhere in the south of France when Truffaut appeared, to shoot a scene in a factory. Isidro volunteered as an extra, recited highlights from *Season in Hell*, and was hired, then retained as an apprentice technician.

That first evening was to be the last for several months, because Isidro was on the point of leaving the country to shoot a documentary on a liberation struggle, a hot war, in fact, that was being conducted in a postage-stamp size country in West Africa, Guinea-Bissau, a territory grabbed by Portugal during the late 19th-century imperialist rush on Africa, presumably because Portuguese explorers once stopped off there in 1446. In 1965, the country's official name was Portuguese Guinea, or, as supporters of the Guinean nationalists were wont to say, "So-Called 'Portuguese' Guinea." So Isidro was off to Africa, to be smuggled into the liberated half of So-Called "Portuguese" Guinea as a guest of the PAIGC, or African Party for the Independence of Guinea and Cape Verde, and their armed forces, led by the charismatic Amilcar Cabral.

At length Isidro returned and invited me to a screening of rushes from Guinea-Bissau. The film's director Mario Marret was a short, stocky guy in his 40s with bushy, brown hair and a long record of documentaries from far-out places such as Antarctica, Lapland, the Sudan, and the Algerian desert. He had gotten into film while serving as "Sparks" on the French Antarctic Expedition of 1950–51, led by the famous Paul-Émile Victor. The filmmaker assigned to document the expedition died en route. Mario, with no previous film experience, filled the slot and taught himself as he went along.

Among the results was an award-winning documentary, on the lives of penguins.

The African footage opened with an air raid. A village of grass huts in flames. A Portuguese plane shot down, PROPERTY OF U.S. AIR FORCE stenciled on a portion of the wrecked fuselage glimpsed amid jungle greenery. Next, a 12-year-old boy, his face half blown away, huddled in fetal position on the ground. A medic cleans out the wound, the camera zooms in for a close-up of the inside of the hole as you would see it if you were the medic. The boy's village had been massacred hours earlier by Portuguese soldiers; he was the sole survivor. Marret noted that the boy was alive and well in a hospital in neighboring ex-French Guinea a few months later, a fact to be included in the narration. Next there were scenes of PAIGC troops playing soccer after returning to base from a patrol. Some of the most exciting footage showed a company of PAIGC men (or to be more precise, teenage boys) attacking a Portuguese column. The countdown. Faces of guerrillas waiting in ambush, sound of approaching trucks, explosion of sounds and images as the shit hits the fan. There wasn't much usable footage from that point on, but Isidro handling the sound had managed to get a great tape by the simple expedient of concealing the equipment in the ground so that it could be abandoned and recovered later. In the course of the firefight the guerrillas gave ground and let the Portuguese chase them back into the woods a certain distance. On the tape you hear enemy soldiers directly overhead, yelling in Portuguese.

Other scenes included a jungle schoolroom, where teenage militants taught children to read and speak Portuguese. (As in many similar countries, the colonial language was to remain the official language after liberation because there was no other way—Guinea-Bissau's million inhabitants are divided among 17 separate groupings, with corresponding linguistic and cultural differences.) Likewise, many scenes of open-air political meetings. These, surprisingly, were very interesting. Unlike May Day in Union Square, such meetings involved entire populations of a given area living under fire, in a state of day-to-day emergency, and the matters debated and publicly resolved were matters of life and death. What impressed me was that the PAIGC militants seemed to be playing a role more like that of discussion moderators than of "Commissars" as one educated in the United States during the Cold War might have expected. There was a seriousness and cogency in everything said that put one in mind of a town meeting in some rural part of New England. Marret's main objective in the film was to show a revolutionary society, in its day-to-day workings, and the meetings in the liberated zones of Guinea were a major part of the picture. Far from being dreary, the footage made one feel like rolling up one's sleeves and joining in. The film aimed to promote the liberation cause on several fronts— it was submitted to the Committee of 24 (the UN anticolonial committee) as part of PAIGC's charges that the Portuguese were committing atrocities in Guinea; it was shown in many French-speaking countries with Mario Marret's voice on the soundtrack; finally, it was shown in the States with Julius Lester narrating. This is where I came in, as translator.

A couple of scenes from the film remain with me to this day. An endless column of Black people, men and women, with gun components and other hardware—brought in from the USSR, China, and Cuba, via ex-French Guinea—they are carrying these things on their heads along a jungle trail—there are hundreds, perhaps thousands of people in the scene—as far as the eye can see. In another scene, a couple of buxom women, in dresses made from giant burlap bags, guard the entrance to one of the base camps, guns in hand.

"Those are Guranov submachineguns," says the narration. Alongside this scene, similar material we'd been reading in the States, such as Robert Williams' *Negroes with Guns*, had a shrill, slightly false ring—here, in the film, were Negroes with guns in a real life situation, not a race riot or a fantasy of revenge, but a genuine revolution in which they were winners, not losers. The shooting and editing of the film aimed at a sort of epic realism. I remember Mario and Isidro saying they wanted the film to convey a sense of what was really happening, with maximum fidelity to the felt vibes of the situation, without trying to suck the viewer in and turn the viewing experience into an emotional jag. The purpose was informational, after all—information presented from a straightforward engagé viewpoint, to be sure, but solid and accurate, nonetheless. For this reason, a lot of gorgeous footage was eliminated in the editing process—specifically, many fine close-ups and a few acci-dental sequences where the action is blurred but the visual effect could have been great, in the hands of another editor. These things were cut. That's not to say that *Nossa Terra (Our Land)* as the film was titled when released the following year, 1967, is "dry." To the contrary, both visually and contentwise, it is rich, lush, lyric—it would be hard to be any other way, dealing with the people of Guinea-Bissau and their country.

Nossa Terra is about 45 minutes long and premiered in 1968 with the Julius Lester narration in my American version at the New Yorker Theatre. The film was ignored by critics and public. 1968 was an apocalyptic year, worldwide. Looking back, it's no wonder that *Nossa Terra* bombed, the May revolution bombed, Mao's call for a Third World uprising bombed, many good things bombed. At the same time as I was translating the *Nossa Terra* narration, I met the writer whose work was responsible for my filmmaker friends' getting invited to Africa in the first place—Gérard Chaliand. His *Armed Struggle in Africa*, based on a visit to Guinea-Bissau in 1964–65, had just been published in French in the Maspéro *Cahiers Libres* series, and the Guineans were pleased with it. Following my return to the States, I spent the summer of 1967 translating that book with Robert Leonhardt, and it was published the next year as a *Monthly Review* paperback, in New York City. The shot of the two women with machineguns, taken by Isidro Romero, adorns the cover.

Artaud's Cane

Anyone opening volume one of Antonin Artaud's Complete Works for the first time is bound to be struck by the final words of the Preamble inserted by the poet shortly before his death in 1948, where Artaud declares that the *cane* he wrote of a decade earlier and subsequently lost is about to be replaced, and that armed with the new cane he will wage war on "monkeys," in other words Art, Ideation, Sex:

> The cane of *New Revelations of Being* fell into the black pocket, and the little sword fell in, too. There yet another cane is being prepared, which will accompany my complete works in a hand-to-hand combat, not with ideas but with the monkeys that keep mounting them from the top to the bottom of my consciousness, in my monkey-riddled organism . . . My cane will be this weird book summoned by ancient now-extinct races that have been branded into my fibers like daughters flayed alive.

Artaud's cane dates back to 1934 when he was doing research at the Bibliothèque Nationale in Paris and chanced upon the story of Saint Patrick and his wonder-working cane, the *baculum Jesu*, or "Jesus-stick." The image of a cane came to represent for the poet a badge of initiation, a master magician's wand, and, eventually, the power he was seeking when in January 1936 he left Paris in despair for

Mexico after his adaptation of Shelley's tragedy *The Cenci* had bombed. A year and a half later, the actual stick acquired in Paris a few months after his return from Mexico came to stand for the power he thought he had at last truly acquired, when in late summer 1937 he sailed for Ireland, only to be returned in irons two months later and confined to mental institutions for the next nine years as a schizophrenic exhibiting symptoms of religious mania. Following the lead of Artaud's poet-psychiatrist Gaston Ferdière, a number of writers have claimed that Artaud was a mystic. I don't believe he was. Consider his words:

> *Take the body from the human*
> *Take it out by nature's light*
> *Plunge it raw in nature's glimmering:*
> *The sun will wed it that same night.*

This is not mysticism, but acquisition and exercise of power. From time immemorial, magical identification of spirit and matter has meant power. That is its secret. Why is this power inaccessible to the uninitiated? Because initiatic identification, or mental union (*unio mentalis*), acts solely on that which although not immaterial is so subtly hidden as to be undetectable in the fabric of the universe.

Such identification acts in imitation of nature, but more quickly. The artist becomes in Artaud's words "an actively sentient force of nature whose thought-process is patterned by its activity." And the civilization in which the artist is a participant becomes "an image of the cosmos, the revelation of a system of interacting forces."

A century earlier, the same insight had filled Artaud's Romantic precursor Gérard de Nerval with a sensation of invincible power: "How could I have existed for so long outside Nature and not identified with her." Such a cosmos-imaging civilization and such initiatic powers were precisely what Artaud was looking for in Mexico in 1936.

A port of call on the voyage to Mexico was Havana. There Artaud met up with a voodoo priest who gave him a miniature sword, which he was to carry on his person up until his arrest in Dublin in late September 1937. The swords of the 19th-century master Eliphas Lévi and of Lévi's spiritual ancestor Paracelsus spring to mind.

Arriving in Mexico City without money, Artaud happened to meet the Mexican Rimbaud translator José Ferrer (not to be confused with the Puerto Rican actor, writer, and director José Ferrer who died in 1992). Ferrer soon arranged for publication of two of Artaud's lectures on the theatre, and got him a job writing a weekly column for the literary *Nacional Revolucionário*. Eventually Artaud obtained a small grant enabling him to make a trip to an inaccessible region in the Chihuahua Mountains of northern Mexico, homeland of the Tarahumara Indians.

In Mexico as elsewhere, Artaud was out of step with the world around him. He had nothing in common with his intellectual contemporaries in Mexico City or with the left-wing atmosphere of the Cárdenas revolution. In 1936 he was vehemently anti-Marxist as a result of his earlier break with Surrealists who had embraced communism. At the same time he quite accurately observed that the Cárdenas regime when stripped of its fiery rhetoric tended rather to philanthropy and reform than to revolution.

Artaud was in fact a much more radical revolutionary than any of his friends or enemies, proclaiming total revolution, not only of production modes and political and class structures, but of the family and of sexual mores. He went even beyond that, to prophesy an unimaginably radical *physiological* revolution: If the flesh is weak, said the logic of Artaud, we must revolutionize the flesh—and our first step will be to *burn* it.

An occult conception of burning runs throughout Artaud's works, from his famous precept in *The Theatre and Its Double* that the actor should reach his audience as if he were being burned at the stake and signaling through the flames, the vision of "a soon-to-be-generalized combustion" at the end of *Journey to the Land of the Tarahumaras*, and the "FIRE" that dominates *New Revelations of Being*, to the "eternal cremation" with which the late (materialist) Artaud threatens all "parasites" of the occult and maintainers of present-day "digestive humanity."

Nevertheless, it was not inspired certainty but wishful thinking that carried Artaud through months of social and drug withdrawal in a Mexico that didn't want or need him. He tried to persuade himself that he had at last found a country where "the overflow of dream in real life" seemed a concrete possibility and not a mad dream. In Mexico, he told his Gallimard editor Jean Paulhan in a letter written from there, "like anywhere else, there's the straight world (*le monde officiel*) and the *other* world. Only here the other is so strong that the straight is turned upside down, in spite of itself." In the same letter Artaud writes that a cataclysmic revolution is imminent: "Madness, utopia, fantasy, the absurd are about to become reality." All this, however, was only a dream. To the Mexican intellectuals he met at the time, Artaud seemed a crank, with his talk of total metaphysics and of a return to the authentic redness of the Maya and Aztec past.

Artaud was to come back disappointed from his stay among the Tarahumara as well. The journey and the peyote ritual were valid only as ordeals along the way to initiation, but initiation itself was denied. In the peyote priests Artaud encountered the same resistance that Nerval had met with from Druse initiates. The Tarahumara priests obstinately refused Artaud access to the central mystery of the peyote cult, without which the peyote itself could have none of its true magical efficacy.

The central mystery of the Tarahumara peyote rite is embodied in an object: a *grater*. This grater is at once each priest's badge of power and the actual source of that power. The sorcerer receives his grater from the invisible lord of the peyote with his nine assessors after a three-year waiting period that starts with the first Easter after the candidate has received the vocation of the grater. This corresponds in Artaud's life to the period from late 1934, when he first read of the Jesus-stick, without realizing the tremendous meaning it was to have for him, until April 1937, when upon emerging from a lengthy stay in a detox clinic (like the third Easter retreat of the Tarahumara candidate sorcerer) he received from his friend René Thomas a strange cane covered with thirteen knots and various magical signs. The number thirteen not only corresponds to the Tarot trump Death, but to the Hebrew letter *mem*, which in turn corresponds to the number 40; and 40—apart from its universal cyclical signification as well as Jacob Boehme's attribution to it of the meaning "eternal Hell"—was Artaud's age when he received this cane. Forty was also the age of Muhammad and of the Buddha at the beginning of their ministries, and it was also the age at which, in A.D. 429, Patrick received the Jesus-stick and set forth on his mission to chastise the Pelagian heretics of Britain and convert the Irish.

The cane Artaud received in 1937 was none other (he proclaimed) than that same Jesus-stick, the staff of Saint Patrick. The thirteen knots on Artaud's cane were for him a Kabbalistic representation of his age [1 + 3 = 4 (0)]. He had already written in the account of his frustrated quest for initiation among the Tarahumara, that the graters "had as many notches as the sorcerer had years when he acquired the right to grate and also became free to perform the exorcisms by which the Elements are drawn and quartered." He could feel the impending cosmological upheaval already vibrating in the cane, just as he had written that the whole mystery of the peyote was "inside the grater."

The graters bore signs at either end, "with one dot for the Male principle and two dots for the deified Female of Nature." When Artaud received his cane in 1937 he was astonished to find that it bore a similar symbol at its head—that of the Female ("a prenatal symbolism," he called it ten years later in one of the *Letters from Rodez*). To complement this feminine symbolism, he made his only addition to the cane. He had it tipped with iron, so that sparks flashed when he struck the sidewalk. This he explained by saying that "the ninth knot bore the magic sign of thunder," a phrase repeated more than once in the obsessive refrains of *New Revelations of Being*. The idea of tipping the cane with iron also relates to Artaud's observation in Mexico that the peyote graters were "gray like iron ore."

On the subject of the cane, Artaud's student the actor Roger Blin said many years later, in an interview published in *Lettres françaises* (21 June 1965), "the famous cane was a simple stick with knots and pointed ends. Artaud had had it steel-tipped and dipped in holy water so as to obtain, as he put it, its consecration by the elements. But when all was said and done it was nothing more than a big stick someone had given him as a present. Artaud was no magician. Nevertheless, this was the wand that attracted him to Ireland because he associated it with the cane of Saint Patrick, patron saint of the Irish. Now I ask you, was this Magic or was it Humor?"

Artaud's cane was anything but humorous, even if there was sometimes a bit of black humor in the way he brandished it. What is essential to a cane such as Artaud's is not humor, but humors. The humors innate to wood. No matter how funny it might have been when Artaud twirled it or struck sparks from its tip, the cane was still a piece of wood, once a tree-branch, hence a bearer of sap, of life energy, of the cold fire that rises from the abyss to drive forward the leaf trembling in broad daylight via innumerable tiny ducts in a grand vertical upflow of desire, the erotic ascent of pure crystal darkness transmuting into light.

It is no accident that Artaud, who in the period before his failure in the theatre could be said to have been one of the last Romantic dandies in the tradition of the Bouzingos (mods of 1830s Paris) and of the young Baudelaire, should have become interested at the very moment when his own personal crisis was intensifying, in that more recent dandy whose obsessions caused Society to crush him—Oscar Wilde. With the same literal-mindedness that he had brought to bear on the Marx Brothers, Artaud studied the calculatedly outrageous, paradox-studded text of Wilde's *Intentions*.

Wilde's famous statement that his talent lay in his art, his genius in his life, applies to the Artaud of the mid-1930s, the man whose perpetual temptation, as he put it, was "to pass from this imitation of life to life itself." It was not until his last months on earth, however, that Artaud was to fully succeed in this, and achieve that identity of work and life that he called "human reality," alongside which "the rest is not us but the nothingness we are clothed in."

Artaud's cane is also like the pet lobster Gérard de Nerval took out on a leash to parody what in the 1830s was a brand-new fad of the Parisian bourgeoisie, the fad for pets on leashes. Artaud's cane similarly affronts the world of swagger sticks and canes. As long as he lived, Artaud was never to forget the grandiose and outrageous appearances he made all over Paris with this cane that was at once wildly funny and deadly serious, the emblem of his resolve to destroy the world by fire.

To Artaud's description of the cane's 13 knots compare the passage in his postwar text, "I Never Studied Anything," where he parodies the idiocy of all systems of numerology: "Because 9 and 4 give 13" (the speaker is a giant flea), "and we really must transcend 13, which by addition within and upon itself . . . "

Jung's caveats against the exclusively sexual Freudian interpretation of hermetic symbols apply to the cane. At the same time, the dominant theme of *New Revelations of Being* is that of the domination of the female by a male in a conflagration in which the female is to be separated from the male once and for all. In other words, sexual domination simultaneous with flight from sex.

In 1937 Antonin Artaud's father had been dead for ten years. His mother, ever anxious and watchful, had moved to Paris in order to be close to her son. The relationship—always ambiguous—became more and more antagonistic.

The winter of 1936–37 witnessed a major event in Artaud's life, his engagement to a wealthy Brussels artist named Cécile Schramme. Something held him back, however, from consummating this prospect of emotional and financial stability. He postponed the commitment first by dosing himself daily with laudanum and heroin, and then by a protracted stay in a detox clinic. When he at last came out of the clinic, it was not to Cécile, but to the cane.

The cane became his passion. It represented an immediate prospect of magical initiation. There was no question of reconciling this with marriage, although Artaud seems at first to have hoped that there might be, and even made a long-delayed trip to Brussels, to be presented to his fiancée's family. From there he wrote in mid-May to a friend in Paris: "I'm putting twenty years of my life behind me now. I sense that Another Man is about to come out of me. I don't know exactly what he is. I don't know where he will lead me. Although I was instructed by a number of uncommon, even extraordinary, signs that I must change my life. A Man can't be erased overnight. I shall have to wait a few weeks, even months, before I see my true light."

A few weeks later, Artaud began work on *New Revelations of Being*. Immediately after writing the letter, however, he gave a deliberately offensive lecture titled "The Decomposition of Paris" in front of an audience of Brussels culture-vultures, armed with the magic cane and brandishing it. His listeners, including the Schramme family, were scandalized. Artaud left the same night for Paris. His engagement with Cécile was broken.

Soon afterward Artaud finished correcting *Journey to the Land of the Tarahumara* for publication in the *Nouvelle Revue Française*, and he made a strange request in connection with it. The text must be published anonymously. "My name must disappear."

Ten days later, he was already deeply absorbed in the Tarot readings from which *New Revelations of Being* emerged:

"Shuffling the cards and cutting the deck with the dexterity of a master magician, he flung the cards out in threes and fours, which he doubled, then split, in a firmly articulated whole, where the beginning touched the end, returning to its point of departure like the tail-devouring world-serpent. In this little north-facing room, Artaud sat as if in a trance, his gaze fixed on the Pole Star, attracting the astral flux polarized in his eyes . . . " (Manuel Cano de Castro, in *Revue "K,"* No. 4, 1948).

The first of the "triangle" of readings underlying *New Revelations of Being* took place on the night of June 3, 1937, a date both of "spiritual energy" and of "division," because the Kabbalistic reduction of 3-6-1937 gives 11 = 2. On that night, according to Artaud, "the Macrocosm was illuminated" and "the construction of the Abstract Man" achieved. Yet that night's reading is omitted from *New Revelations of Being*, whose text is entirely based on the two readings made later that month.

Manuel de Castro published the latter readings along with Artaud's marginal notes on them in "*K*," in the article just cited. By omitting the readings, Artaud was making a book of commentary and interpretation *minus* the main text.

This hole-in-the-donut effect is integral but not unique to Artaud. In his study of Raymond Roussel, Foucault remarks:

> The work and the illness revolve on the incompatibility that links them, a basic incompatibility whose hollow core nothing can ever fill. Artaud, too, tried to get close to this void in his work, yet he kept being separated from it—separated by it from the work, but also from it by the work. And at this medullary ruin he kept hurling his language, hollowing out a work that is the absence of a work.

The outline of *New Revelations of Being* is that of the classic three-part *explication de texte*: 1) Introduction; 2) Analysis/Synthesis; 3) Conclusion.

This burlesque of "French clarity" Artaud was to repeat a decade later in the radio broadcast *To Pass Final Judgment on God*, with its mock-Cartesian demonstrations.

Whereas Artaud's imaginary world in *The Theatre and Its Double* and *Journey to the Land of the Tarahumaras* had been abstract and utopian, it became esoteric and occult in *New Revelations of Being*. What were the "new revelations" made by this Being? What was this Being?

The Being of *New Revelations of Being* is a "double" of Artaud who reveals to him his initiatic self through the Tarots, "as the Astrologers no longer know how to read."

From Mexico the year before, in 1936, Artaud had written to Jean-Louis Barrault: "So far the horoscopes and my personal faith haven't let me down. They prove that Mexico will yield what it must." But he had returned to France soon afterward, feeling that the stars had cheated him.

The Being reveals to the poet that if he is now simultaneously a sage, a madman, an "extravagant lout," and a desperate, tortured man (and, in the language of the Tarots, both Juggler and Fool, i.e. the first and last, the two great arcana of magic and madness), he will soon be transmuted from the Tortured Man into the REVEALED ONE. The Abstract Man is actually the cane, and the cane is fire. In Tarot symbolism Staves, or Sticks, stand for fire. Not ordinary fire but the ethereal fire of Heraclitus, the fire of Boehme's Light World, as against that of his Fire World; or Paracelsus' "Iliastric Fire," which is the fire of pure substance, as against the grossly material "Cagastric Fire."

The Being is also the Macrocosm that has been illuminated and "turned *earthside*." Like Nerval, Artaud italicizes words and phrases that he intends in an occult rather than a literal sense. Since the Being is Macrocosm, *earth* plainly refers to the "corpse" of Artaud who is dead to the world. The cane which is the Abstract Man works as a link joining the two; the expected result will be a universal conflagration. The cane is *abstract* in the sense that it has been *abstracted* from the corpse, the earth, the old Artaud, in the same fashion as the graters in *Journey to the Land of the Tarahumara*: "They sleep there in the high Mexican sierra waiting for the Predestined Man to discover them and make them *go forth by day*." Once more, the sense is underlined: Artaud will be that same regenerated man of whom the Egyptian Book of the Dead promises that he will "go forth by day." The cane represents, as did the graters, that which the initiates "have torn from the forest and the *forest yields to them so slowly*." In the terminology of the occult, *forest* means "body." Artaud is abstracting a new body from the old. The new body is itself fire (in Paracelsian terms, Iliastric Fire) and the old body will be utterly consumed with fire (the Cagastric Fire of Paracelsus, fit for *le caca*, Artaud's expression for both flesh *and* spirit). There will be fire everywhere, total destruction.

Shortly before breaking off his engagement to Cécile Schramme, Artaud wrote to Breton: "A woman is going to give me the willpower to separate all that must be separated . . . She will give me the Star that will enable me to see my destiny with clarity." By the time *New Revelations of Being* came to be written, three or four months elapsed, and the star of the letter to Breton became "a Star that shall occupy the total surface of the Air in which the Spirit of Man has bathed." By the light of this terrible star, the sexes will be separated, all will be humiliated, enslaved, and finally burned. Elsewhere Artaud has designated the Tarot trump 17 as "Star of the Magi = regeneration." That is precisely what it means here. The tortured Juggler/Fool stands at the center of this star, awaiting the first fruits of the burning. The star itself marks the focus of the process.

The star of the Magi has returned in order to make the Tortured Man manifest. Manifest as a God-Man "to be recognized by the whole world, as THE REVEALED ONE." How will the fire do this? What does Artaud mean when he says that "we must consent to burning, burning in advance and immediately"? The burning, like the star, means regeneration corresponding to the *incineratio* of the hermetic Phoenix. Of the Tortured Man, Artaud says: "HE FIRST PLAYED WITH HIS OWN FLAME. AT FIRST HE PRETENDED TO BE AN EXTRAVAGANT LOUT." The very lout for whom the star of the Magi shines.

He played with his own flame. Here we have the alchemical operation known as *combustio in igne proprio* ("burning up in one's own fire").

The Magical burning of *New Revelations of Being* has an exact parallel in *Thus Spake Zarathustra*. Nietzsche's chapter titled "Path of the Creative Man" opens with these words: "Solitary one, you follow the path to yourself! And your path leads you beyond yourself to your seven devils. You must have the willingness to burn yourself up in your own flame. How did you expect to be made new if you did not first turn to ashes?"

Artaud's idea of a fifth element potentiating the revolution of the four elements corresponds to the Manichean image of the First Man armed with destructive light. The idea keeps resurfacing. A 17th-century Italian alchemist had a dream in which he discovered a quintessential "spirit" that could destroy all of nature and reduce it to nothingness.

On November 3, 1937, Artaud wrote, the world would be coming to an end. "On whatever side one turns, Destruction will be given free play everywhere." There would be a "fundamental, absolute, terrible" overthrow of all received values, because "the Man within us has liberated himself from humanity." In the *Conclusion*, Artaud says, "I also preach total Destruction, but *Conscious* and *Rebellious* Destruction," and adds that by "burning" he means a magical operation—not the burning of things but rather that of "*everything that represents things for us* in order not to expose ourselves to being burned up whole."

The two Tarot readings that form the basis of the text are read out in oracular style with extended commentaries. They are diametrically opposed to each other. The first (chronologically the last) is titled "On the Initiate." The figure is surmounted by the Juggler, upright—signifying to Artaud "well-directed will"—and based on the King of Cups (= "domination") and completed by cards signifying self-mastery, spiritual energy, regeneration, harmony, and willpower at the service of the senses (in Artaud's personal interpretation).

A synthesis of the cards themselves, the date on which they were drawn and the number representing Artaud's age leads to the prediction of "DESTRUCTION BY FIRE."

The cane returns as five serpents appear in the sky. For Artaud the serpent represents vibration, energy. The serpents' "STRENGTH OF DECISION IS REPRESENTED BY A CANE!"

What does this mean?

It means that I who am speaking have a Cane.

A cane with 13 knots, and this cane bears on the ninth knot the magic sign of the thunderbolt; and 9 is the number of destruction by fire and

I FORESEE A DESTRUCTION

B   Y   F   I   R   E

I see this Cane in the midst of the Fire, provoking destruction by Fire.

The second reading—a reading of death and despair—was titled "On the Tortured Man." It is surmounted by the Devil trump, based on the Fool, and completed by cards signifying division, destruction, badly directed willpower (an upside-down Juggler occupies the mid-position between Devil and Fool), ruin, and transformation (the Death trump, LA MORT).

Remarkably, the protagonists of *New Revelations of Being*—the Being (or Macrocosm), the Juggler, the Fool, and the Hermit (sage)—correspond exactly to the only four major trumps in the Tarot to be endowed with "canes": the androgynous Anima Mundi and the Juggler dominate the occult forces of the universe with their wands, and the Hermit and the Fool go their ways with simple sticks. In the course of the operation prophesied by Artaud, they are all melted together into a single identity, that of the cane: "For these double Rods of Fire, where the Fire turns on itself, like the Flame around the Focus, show that the Fire will flame from the Focus,

> Like the Lightning of Fiery Ether
> Of which Heraclitus has already spoken . . . "

Wands and sticks are the "double Rods of Fire." The "Fire" itself is the cane.

What does this mean? The question is repeated over and over again throughout the text of *New Revelations of Being*, an ironical refrain. What is this "insolent prediction, the language of which no one but visionaries and madmen will understand"?

Is it really—as the hallucinatory intensity of the writing suggests— a prophecy of the end of the world? Or is it an occult apocalypse, a manifesto of initiatic intent? It is both at once. Neither constitutes a tenable position. Artaud was aware of this: "*If I can start to say it now, it is because I have left reality behind.*"

At this point it seems clear that Artaud knew he was getting close to death, a death of some kind or other ("OUR DESTINY IS A

DESTINY OF DEATH"), but hoped to achieve through it an occult victory of regeneration. He did indeed obtain something of the sort, but not before he had passed through the darkness of utter insanity could he say, like the great Renaissance magician Cornelius Agrippa von Nettesheim, that he was *Ipse philosophus, daemon, heros, deus, et omnia* (Philosopher, Demon, Hero, God, and Everything). Only then could he "unlearn his spells entirely" as did the old Faust, and stand up in the solitude of absolute freedom.

In 1945 or '46, shortly before Artaud's release from the Rodez asylum, Jean Latrémolière—one of the doctors there—asked him why he was correcting some of the language in *New Revelations of Being* but none of the dates. With magisterial sarcasm, Artaud replied that the end of the world had come exactly on schedule but that Latrémolière had been prevented by black magic from noticing it. In an article titled "I Spoke of God With Antonin Artaud" published in 1959, Latrémolière cited this incident as proof of Artaud's incurable schizophrenia. The poet's latter-day renunciation of the occult struck Latrémolière as "a failure of mystical faith."

In August 1937 Artaud was hurrying toward the greatest disaster of his life. Armed with the cane, he sailed for Ireland. In less than two months he would be lying in a straitjacket, strapped to a bed in the "violent" section of a narcotics ward in an asylum near Rouen.

In August, however, he imagined he was setting foot in that part of the world where his cane would work most effectively when (as he had written at the end of *New Revelations of Being*) "on the 7th [of September, 1937] the Portal of the Infinite is opened for humanity. The Tortured Man is at last prepared. He can enter. He stands on his own feet before his work. He can begin."

Why did Artaud go to Ireland? The foremost expert on Artaud's life and works, Paule Thévenin, has speculated that he sensed death or some terrible madness approaching, and that he did not want any witnesses. He was certainly *not* thinking of a "return to God," as the Catholic critic Jean Hort has suggested (in a very bad book titled *Antonin Artaud: The Man Suicided by Society*, Geneva, 1960). The specific choice of Ireland was dictated by the cane. In *New Revelations of Being* he claimed to have obtained it from God; also, "it was already mine in other centuries." In *Letters from Rodez* Artaud states that the cane had belonged to Lucifer, Jesus Christ, and Saint Patrick.

Lucifer: A Luciferian self-identification runs through several of Artaud's works, notably *Life and Death of Satan-Fire*. For Artaud as for Walt Whitman and many others before him, the Devil was none other than the Fourth Person of the "Square Deific"(as Whitman called it). However, in the end Artaud was to uncompromisingly reject all manifestations of divinity, even Satanic ones.

Christ: From Ireland he was to write to André Breton that Christ was a magician who struggled in the wilderness against demons, armed only with a cane. The idea of Christ as a magician (nowadays fashionable thanks to the work of scholars like Morton Smith) must have delighted Breton by its seemingly blasphemous originality in 1937. However, to Artaud himself, immersed as he was in the literature of late antiquity and the Church fathers, it would have been a self-evident item of common knowledge. The "cane" of Jesus Christ is none other than the wand with which he is often depicted in early Christian and medieval art.

Patrick: Artaud's discovery of the Jesus-stick motif in his readings at the Bibliothèque Nationale in 1934 was the seed from which the whole cane obsession sprang in the first place. In *Letters from Rodez* Artaud writes that he first found mention of the cane in a "Prophecy of Saint Patrick" published in a dictionary of Christian saints at the

Library. The "prophecy" in question was an oracle delivered to the pagan king of Ireland by his wizards, according to which "Adze Head" (Patrick) would come over the sea *armed with a cane* to overthrow the king and chiefs and destroy the power of the druids, and his reign would last forever.

Reading further, Artaud must have discovered that Patrick's pastoral staff (Latin *baculum*, naturalized in Irish as *bachall*) was the most characteristic emblem and chief instrument of his power. Following Patrick's lead, all the Irish saints carried magic canes. When people saw a saint in a dream the saint carried a cane. Saints exchanged canes as tokens of love or esteem. Canes were used to curse and to administer oaths. A saint's cane cured the sick, raised the dead, stopped floods, divided the sea, opened cracks in the ground, led streams uphill, split rocks so that sweet waters could gush forth, brought mountains down on the heads of enemies, deflected attackers like a "druid's hedge," tamed wild animals and monsters, flew through the air to kindle or extinguish fires, returned to its owner when lost, enabled its owner to become invisible, caught fish, divined the presence of gold, overthrew pagan idols, and expelled demons. The medieval library of the Priory of Saint Martin at Dover listed in its catalogue a book with the double title "On the Cane of the Beatified Patrick; Patrick on the Jesus-Stick."

There can be no doubt that Artaud saw Patrick's life as an anticipation of his own. Before acquiring his cane, Patrick had had to undergo ritual journeys and labors, just as Artaud did. Patrick successfully rebelled against both God and Jesus Christ, fasting against them, to compel them to grant him certain special privileges. One of these was that he should have the right of judging the Irish on Judgment Day. (In *New Revelations of Being*, Artaud proclaims: "The Man in us . . . has ascended to judge us for being human.") Moreover, Patrick will sit on the right hand of the Almighty on that day, which stops barely short of saying that he will replace Jesus Christ. In hundreds of statements, Artaud was to replace Christ all the way from His miracle-working ministry through the Passion and on to the Last Days. Patrick's very acquisition of the cane exhibits a close parallel to Artaud's. It is preceded by a sojourn in a cave with three mysterious initiates, "The Three Patricks." The future saint's relationship to these magi is the same as that of the Tortured Man with a parallel group of three—the Being, the Other Man, and the Revealed One, in *New Revelations of Being*. (In the Old Irish Hymn of Fiacc, when Patrick dies he takes his cane with him to join The Three Patricks, and they go to Heaven together.)

Later, Patrick lands on an island where he meets a young married couple who tell him they have been waiting for centuries to give him a magic staff that Jesus Christ has left there for him to help in the adventures that lie ahead. Jesus has left them young until Judgment Day. The old people on the island are their descendents. Patrick refuses to take the staff unless he can receive it from the hands of Jesus Christ in person, which he does in the end, but only after much debate. This corresponds to the two versions Artaud gives of receiving the cane. According to *New Revelations of Being*, he has the cane from God. According to *Letters from Rodez*, he has it from a Savoyard sorcerer ("mentioned in the Prophecy of Saint Patrick") and his daughter who must likewise, he writes, be fabulously old. (The sorcerer and his daughter correspond to the young couple in the Patrick legend, although the latter do not figure in the "prophecy," as Artaud has it, but in the *Tertia Vita Patricii*, or *Third Life of Patrick*.)

An "authentic" cane of Saint Patrick existed in medieval times. According to Saint Bernard's *Life of Saint Malachy*, it was ". . . a stick covered with gold leaf and studded with precious stones, believed to have been fashioned by the divine Carpenter Himself for Patrick. Anyone bearing it was recognized by the mere fact of its possession as the spiritual leader everywhere in Ireland." This cane was preserved in the Cathedral in Dublin until 1538, when it was burned as an object of superstition. The Dublin Cathedral is precisely where Artaud was arrested with his cane in 1937. The cane vanished at that moment, no doubt confiscated by cops who took Artaud in custody, and has never resurfaced.

Having acquired the Jesus-stick Patrick stormed a city of monsters and forced open its gates.

To Artaud the magic cane was a key with which "the gate of the Infinite is opened for humanity." He was to repudiate the same idea a decade later in a contemptuous attack on Goethe's archetypal image of "The Mothers," titled "Mothers to the Stable": "Oh if all rooms were only as bright as they were in the days when, from the mountainside, opening the gateway of the immensity before me, I saw infinity without locks and without a key!"

Artaud had already found the cane "imperfect" because of the prenatal signs connecting it with the female reproductive function. These signs interfered with the cane's magical principle and fulminating power, preventing it from having all the action it should, he explained. In fact, this maternal symbolism "made a criminal attempt to channel this fire toward the idea of the predestination of beings which, regardless of what sins they may have committed, must infallibly be saved eventually." This last statement will appear less cryptic in the light of Patrick's first mission while en route to Ireland. His instructions were to overthrow the Pelagian heretics in Britain. The Pelagian heresy was threefold. It denied the Fall; it asserted free will as against predestination, and it denied the inevitable damnation of the unbaptized. In these three points it harmonized with the position Artaud himself arrived at in the last years of his life. He repudiated the Roman Catholic concept of the Fall, he rejected baptism, and he exalted the idea of pure will above all else.

Patrick disembarked near the sacred city of Tara on the night of the fire festival of Beltaine. Defying pagan prohibition against any fire not duly taken from the magically kindled *bel-tine*, "bright fire," sacred to Bil, god of the dead, Patrick kindled his own fire on a nearby hilltop, using the staff and tracing with it a magic circle round the spot. Soon the fire of pagan torches came crowding around, and Patrick's fire was like that "fifth element" of *New Revelations*, "the fire [that] will flame from the focus," a new fire round which other fires turn. The moment that Artaud calls "an infernal confrontation" had come. The wizards told their king that if he could not extinguish this fire it would burn forever.

Important as background for Artaud were two recent books by the esoteric historian René Guénon. Guénon's recent *Spiritual Authority & Temporal Power* (1929) had sections on "sacred islands" and on the scepter as link to the "world axis" that could not have failed to interest Artaud. Even more importantly, from Guénon's *King of the World* (1927) Artaud learned the occult geography of Ireland: That it was anciently divided in five kingdoms, one of which was called Mide (present-day Meath), meaning "Middle." That Mide was formed from portions taken from the four others and was the seat of the high kings of Ireland, to whom the other four were subordinate. That in Ushragh, at the exact center of the country, was a megalith called the Earth Navel, also known as the Portion Stone because it marked the point where the four primitive kingdoms' original borders converged. That Ireland was known as Island of the Four Masters. That the name of Saint Patrick was originally *Cothraige*, "Servant of the Four." That the Four Masters correspond to the four cardinal points and also to the elements. That the supreme Master, the fifth, who is seated at the center, represents Ether (Akasha), the Quintessence of the Hermeticists, the primordial element from which the others sprang, the Pole.

Irish myth presents a perpetual succession of combats between young and old gods. The burning of the old god and the emergence of the youthful champion from the flames is the theme of all the Irish fire festivals, a drama of death and resurrection that has continued to be reenacted in them down to the present day. Patrick's arrival in Ireland was simply one more in the series of divine combats. When Artaud went to Ireland in the summer of 1937 he was deliberately seeking to replay the ancient hero-role.

Patrick's victory, like that of previous divine champions, had represented a liberation from the demons and snakes (= mental sexuality?) of the old ways. All of Patrick's occult powers issuing from the Jesus-stick came into play in these contests. His fingers became luminous and gave off light like a chandelier full of burning candles (*Fourth Life of Patrick*, chapter 55). Artaud possessed similar powers in later life. Visitors to the gatehouse of the Ivry asylum where he spent his last years experienced the feeling that some sort of tremendously powerful occult waves were passing through their bodies when he looked at them or touched them. In the *Letter to Pierre Loeb*, likewise, Artaud describes the "human tree" of pure will that he was in a previous existence:

> *He was all electric nerve,*
> *flames of an everlasting phosphorescence . . .*

One is put in mind of Gérard de Nerval's idea of having a very large body "entirely flooded with electrical forces."

The self-image projected in many late Artaud texts is that of a free-floating, self-propelled consciousness in the shape of a huge tree or stick or bone that repels or burns off on contact all the "lice" and "bacteria" of alien intelligences that are trying to invade, subdue, and devour it.

The Irish fire festivals are also festivals of hellfire, because Irish gods are gods of death. Men and gods have a common descent from Bil, chief god of death. There are dead men among the living. Ancient Ireland teemed with zombie-like creatures, one of whom says, in a medieval legend text: "Even though we are alive, we are actually dead." (The week Artaud died, the newspaper *Combat* published an interview with him in which he stated, "Toward the year 1000 there were whole villages of the living dead such as exist nowadays only in a handful of remote corners of Asia.") All, whether dead, alive, or living dead, whether gods or humans, are subject to what Artaud calls in a letter from Ireland to André Breton "the unconscious and criminal law of Nature . . . [and] we-the-gods are its victims jointly." Magic is the only way to transcend and master the upheavals of the four elements, to become, as in *New Revelations*, the master of a fifth element. This, Artaud says, is the "pagan truth" manifested by such magicians as Jesus Christ and Saint Patrick. And a drop of Christ's blood (= fire) has remained on the cane: "It goes away when you scrub it with water, but it returns."

Among Patrick's principal attributes in medieval art are snakes turning round his magic cane, and *the flames of Purgatory* coming out of a hole dug at his feet by drawing a circle with the cane.

One of Patrick's feats was to point the cane at a hilltop idol, and the gold and silver covering it immediately melted and ran onto the ground, and the wood underneath crumbled to dust.

The "opening of the body" (an alchemical operation) is performed using a "fire rod." The fire rod must be used by a *chaste* operator. Celibacy is often a precondition for pacts with supernatural powers. All the medieval sources insist that Patrick was chaste. Artaud's well-known abhorrence of sex, long in the making, became crystallized in its final form at precisely this time, 1937, year of the cane.

The crook in the pastoral staff or cane did not appear in Ireland until the ninth century, 400 years after Patrick's lifetime. The earliest type (e.g. Saint Fillan's staff at Edinburgh) was shaped *exactly like a modern walking stick, or cane.*

The medieval *Three-Part Life of Patrick* states that when Patrick set sail for Ireland *nine* was his number, and it was then that he came to the volcanic island [Tenerife?] where he received the stick from Jesus Christ on the mountaintop, and upon arriving in Ireland he had nine companions, raised nine dead persons, called down nine ranks of angels, and saw nine druids struck by lightning. Nine— Artaud wrote—is the number of destruction by fire.

Artaud cannot have overlooked the connection between a cane and illness or handicap. The object of alchemy is the redemption of sick matter, its transmutation to the goldenness of health.

An *imbecile* is one who lacks a *baculum* or stick.

Bacteria = rodlike microorganisms.

In the *Seventh Life of Patrick*, the saint plants a staff in the earth and it grows to a tree (folk motif of blooming staff as chastity index).

Six Latin hexameters in a margin of the medieval Irish Calendar of Oengus explain the meaning of the Jesus-stick:

> *Its curved end represents its crown*
> *And shows good morals by its upright hardness.*

Its lower end prefers to stab Earth's guts.
Fair priest, see how the stick shapes you, that you,
A dancer, learn its laws and win your stick:
Its curve attracts the meek; rebels its point impales.

In early Christian times itinerant prophets called themselves "sticks" of the Holy Ghost.

"Stick" (*baculus*) was an epithet of Jesus Christ. A medieval poem states that this epithet is given because the stick helps the fallen to get up and the sick to stay on their feet.

With his cane, Patrick turned an ice floe into a sheet of fire and splashing waves into dancing flames.

Artaud's philosophy of a sadistic Nature had led him in the years before his initiation to attempt to embody the old Cenci and Heliogabalus, monsters of evil both, and both destroyed by women. It now happened that Artaud needed a woman's help and advice. And so in August and September 1937 he searched the Western Isles for a certain old woman, last authentic descendent of the Druids, who "knows that humanity is descended from the god of death, Dispater, and that humanity must soon disappear by water and fire."

This sentence echoes his reading at the Bibliothèque Nationale of a passage from the Durkheimian sociologist S. Czarnowsky's *Hero Worship & Its Social Background: Saint Patrick, National Hero of Ireland* (1919): "The Irish are all descendents of the same god of death who was also the progenitor of the invading peoples' tutelary genius. Bil, father of Mile, is identical to the god Bel. This genealogy is confirmed by the existence of an analogous belief among the Gauls who according to Julius Caesar claimed descent from Dispater" (p. 160).

Reference to Patrick's sending a flood to engulf Ireland seven days before the final destruction by fire appears on the preceding page in the same work. It seems likely that Czarnowsky's book was the "hagiographic dictionary" that Artaud claimed as the source of his information on Patrick.

Toward the end of September 1937 Artaud returned to Dublin with the cane. What actually happened there to cause his forced repatriation is still largely a matter of conjecture. He spoke, much later, of street riots centering around the cane. These riots were surely imaginary, since his late writings tirelessly evoke riots and other disturbances concerning himself "all the way from Greenland to Sumatra," as he put it. The cane itself was lost, either in the Cathedral or the adjacent Jesuit establishment or the police station.

With the lost cane went the power to strike fire, the virile fire burning in the depths of the universal ocean. The deep is female. The agony of the flame embraced by the dark is the agony of the panic the male feels at the danger he will not be able to keep it up and will suffer the mortification of a desire ungratified. When sharp flame drives back darkness, it is a victory of desire, not only of desire to possess but desire to be. It is life exploding walls that shelter and nourish but devour. When Artaud had walked into the Cathedral brandishing his cane, he imagined he would set a fire that would destroy the world and put him in the place of Patrick and Jesus and every other savior, to make the light world from which he was a sojourner in this universe suddenly manifest itself in the here and now. If this world was in the dark, it was also in the darkness within the body. Artaud heard from inside himself a clamor as of a voice, or a million voices, crying out, proclaiming that all, everything that is, is gathering, girding, opening a path, to rise and go forth by day.

But something else was happening even before Artaud entered the Cathedral: "The cane was useless as a means of defense, and I myself was becoming very evil, in other words, inept, idiotic, and spiritually insipid, as a result of using it. This cane seems to have been the same one that legend says was the cane of Lucifer who thought he was God but was only God's vampire." Did Artaud fear that he was becoming a vampire of God?

One reason for the cane's loss of power may have been the ambivalence attached to it from the start, the ambivalence that Artaud had endeavored to resolve by tipping the cane with iron. He may have inadvertently betrayed deep dread when, on one of those extravagant rambles with the cane through the Paris streets, he jokingly addressed the cane: "You are the daughter of Cenci." He had himself played the role of the old Cenci who raped his daughter and was later murdered by her. In Shelley's tragedy Beatrice Cenci metamorphoses from abused innocence to the grand impersonality of an avenging angel. "I am as universal as the light," she declares.

"And the Revolution that we did not know how to make will be made by the Universe against us. For Revolution, too, remembers that she is a woman." These words, from *New Revelations of Being*, did not fit anything else said in that book. They were an incongruity in its vision of a male-directed cataclysm. But they came true when Artaud's cane changed from a phallic rod into a female wand "as universal as the light" and (for its thunderstruck possessor) as blinding as the most intense vision of supreme terror.

Difficult Life: René Crevel

In 1977 the art historian Gert Schiff lent me his copy of *La mort difficile* by René Crevel on the same day a big Brassaï show was opening at the Marlborough. Crevel I had heard of, thanks to an essay by Ezra Pound, "René Crevel," published in the English magazine *Criterion* in 1938. According to E.P., Crevel was the best of the post–World War One generation in France, although mainly unrecognized by his compatriots, and too bad for them: "A nation which does not feed its best writers is a mere barbarian dung heap . . ." I had never gotten around to reading him, though, nor had anyone else I knew, apart from Gert Schiff. But of course everyone is conversant with flapper-era Paris By Night as captured by Brassaï. It's a classic. Lovers in a cafe at dawn. Sleepy petulant sailors with bee-stung lips. Transvestites at the drag ball. Tweedy opium-smoking dowagers. On my way home from the show, I opened *La mort difficile*. Out popped a cast of characters very like those in Brassaï's photos. Within a short time, I found myself like Charlie Chaplin on the conveyor belt in *Modern Times*, being translated from hilarity to consternation, in other words, to the grind of transposing that experience into my own language under a new title: *Difficult Death*.

I had never met with the likes of René Crevel anywhere. Consider his description of the moment of falling in love:

Hands pressed against hands, palms wedded palms. Pierre shuddered and then was nothing but a droplet of blood transfused

*into another life's bloodstream. Little by little, he altogether ceased
to exist.*

Or, on a more mundane level, the experience of finding oneself
trapped at an avant-garde event in a gallery or performing space or
loft in a great city of the 20th century. Let's say you are boxed in
with a galaxy of break dancers and graffiti writers in the New York
City of 1985. Here is Crevel's 1926 equivalent:

> *Having invited a handful of snobs to watch a couple of juvenile
> delinquents bump and grind to the sound of a pianola, they
> imagined themselves to be prophets.*

Similarly, take Crevel's observations on various individual sorts of
people and their psychologies. For example, his characterization of
someone who had "a special way of walking that could never quite
help turning very rapidly into a dance" as a person who "fit inside his
ego as naturally as an orange in its rind; never uncomplicated but
always harmonious." Or his remark about Diane, heroine of *Difficult
Death* who has made up her mind to remain a virgin forever—She
doesn't know that ignorance of the joys of love makes them easier to
give up. Quite possibly Saint Augustine beat Crevel to the punch on
this one. It's so true, though, that it can't be repeated too often.

For years I wondered what the French see in us Americans. Not
until I read Crevel's characterization of the American Arthur
Bruggle in *Difficult Death* did I ever find the whole thing summed
up in just a few words:

> *The power that is Bruggle's has nothing to do with intelligence
> in the European sense of the word. Come up out of the depths of*

his being, Arthur's is a potency transcending all means of conscious self-expression, and it would be both unjust and inexact to speak of cunning with regard to him, but a mysterious energy bursts out of him like electricity from a cat's fur. A feline floating in a baggy jacket, a feline with big shoes ("The French," he says, "love shoes, not feet, clothes but not bodies, and that's why they live in such narrow, velvet-and-leather-lined rooms!"). Arthur, lost in his raglan overcoat, with each of his gestures puts one in mind not so much of all the hard work and study implicit in the elasticity of his movements as of the very instincts that predetermined the nature and direction of that study.

There was another Bruggle in Crevel's first novel, *Detours*. In *Detours*, Bruggle is an American member of France's gilded youth who is capitalizing on his magnetism and good looks to eat, drink, and fuck his way through a world very similar to that portrayed in Raymond Radiguet's exactly contemporary *Count d'Orgel*. Like the Bruggle of *Difficult Death* (and the actual person he was based on, the American painter Eugene MacCown who was the love of Crevel's life), this Bruggle is bisexual. In Crevel's parlance, this term denotes a male homosexual who occasionally sleeps with a woman, one who

if he was still capable of being aroused by a woman's warmth, it was more in response to the warmth than to the woman.

Predisposed to misogyny by a murderous relationship with his mother, Crevel was to succeed more than once in breaking out of the confining fear of the opposite sex, only to fall back into it soon after. His manifesto on bisexuality in *Putting My Foot in It*, where he boasts of having "fornicated with both sexes of the species and even several dogs," uncovers a deep streak of morbid fear and hostility. In vain he disguises it as just one more item on the agenda for social and intellectual liberation:

> *Do you view erotic activities as subversive? Do you support the rebellion of the reproductive instincts against their preordained functions?*

The undercurrent remains one of anger against women for representing a stifling conformity to preordained function, leading to home, family, and responsibilities.

Crevel suffered from a very deep ambivalence about homosexuality itself. This ambivalence informs every page of his books where the subject comes up, and there are many. *Difficult Death* contains several paeans to cruising as a mystic communion and release, including Crevel's "anonymous continent" image, which occurs in virtually all of his books. But other passages in *Difficult Death* picture cruising as a descent into hellish degradation. In one instance, the anonymous encounters of men in dark doorways are fervently described: " . . . the body leaps, flies, weighs no more than a song under the midnight sun," and in another the protagonist castigates himself as one who "calls himself a man and is in fact nothing but a child in the grip of a nightmare." Of his lover MacCown, Crevel wrote in a letter to Marcel Jouhandeau: "He was sent to punish me by the people I have hurt."

Although at the time of writing *Difficult Death* Crevel was not yet "official," he had been involved with Eugene MacCown for a couple of years, while actively cruising on the side. He never made any effort to hide it from friends. This took courage. Most of Crevel's fellow Surrealists, including especially André Breton, were if anything rather more homophobic than your average middle-of-the-road Frenchman of that era. From 1921, when they first became acquainted, up until the final hours of René's life, in mid-June 1935, Breton was to loom large for Crevel. From start to finish, Crevel's behavior toward Breton exhibited a remarkable mix of timidity and intransigence. I have seen the inscription to Breton, in Crevel's hand, on a copy of his pamphlet *Mind Against Reason*, which is arguably a more powerful exposition of Surrealism as a philosophy than anything Breton himself ever wrote. This inscription meekly assures Breton that he and Crevel are "for and against the same things," although Crevel never once backed down on the issue of homosexuality. That same year, 1928, Breton published the following statement in his magazine *Surrealist Revolution*: "I accuse the homosexuals of affronting human tolerance with a mental and moral defect that tends to advocate itself as a way of life and to paralyze every enterprise I respect. I make exceptions, one of which I grant to the incomparable Marquis de Sade." One must assume that a similar exception was graciously extended to René Crevel. *Difficult Death* was a risky book to put forward in 1926 because it was a public statement of the author's ambivalent sexuality. Now, in 1985, *Difficult Death* is a risky book because of the author's disregard of received ideas on the subject, of ordinary prejudices attached to it, combined with a bone-deep honesty in his disclosure of his own feelings and experiences. Honesty of that order threatens Order. It's a security risk; and as Crevel observed in *Mind Against Reason*, there is nothing in this world that intellectuals dislike so much as risk.

The risk-taking that leads up to the suicide in *Difficult Death* has one thing in common with the audacities and failures that led to Crevel's own suicide, and that is that neither has anything to do with sexual problems. In 1925, the year Crevel was writing *Difficult Death*, *Surrealist Revolution* canvassed its contributors on the question, "Is Suicide a Solution?" Crevel responded:

A solution? Yes.

People say one commits suicide out of love, fear, or venereal disease. Not so. Everyone is in love, or thinks they are. Everyone is frightened. Everyone is more or less syphilitic. Suicide is a means of conscious choice. Those who commit it are persons unwilling to throw in the towel like almost everyone else and repress a certain psychic feeling of such intensity that everything tells you you had better believe it is a truthful and immediate sense of reality. This sense is the one thing that allows a person to embrace a solution that is obviously the fairest and most definitive of them all, the solution of suicide.

There is no love or hate about which one can say that it is clearly justified and definitive. But the respect (which in spite of myself and notwithstanding a tyrannical moral and religious upbringing) I have to have for anyone who did not timorously withhold or restrain that impulse, that mortal impulse, leads me to envy a bit more each day those persons who were hurting so intensely that a continuing acceptance of life's little games became something they could no longer stomach. Human accomplishment is not worth its weight in horse mucus. When personal happiness leads to even a modicum of contentment, this is more often than not a negative thing, like a sedative taking effect. The life I accept is the most fearful argument against me. The death that tempted me several times was lovelier by far than this downright prosaic fear of death that I might also quite properly call a habit, the habit of timidity. I wanted to open a certain door, and I got cold feet. I feel I was wrong not to open it. I not only feel, I believe, I want to feel, I want to believe it was a mistake not to, for as I have found no solution in life, notwithstanding a long and diligent search, I am not about to attempt to pull myself together to give life another try unsolaced by the thought of this definitive and ultimate act in which I feel that I have caught a glimpse at least of the solution.

"The life I accept is the most fearful argument against me." In the 1920s French publishers used to tuck a loose insert in a book, containing the blurb and author's biography, stuff one sees on the back cover nowadays. For the blurb that came with *My Body and Me*, Crevel wrote his own bio, and it characterizes him in words he was to repeat almost verbatim in his portrait of that minor figure named Lucas in *Difficult Death* who is remarkable in that (apart from young Diane, who is Pierre's alter ego, good angel, and twin sister) he is the only decent person in the book. Of Lucas, Crevel says:

He had never yet had the grace to change fads with every changing season, nor to share, according to the taste of the day, his contemporaries' enthusiasm for opium dens, Oxford trousers with outsized cuffs, and dance clubs of so-called ill fame.

Of himself, in the blurb, Crevel writes:

Hates fads, be it the mystique of Oxford University and trousers with outsized cuffs, or that of movie palaces and related funhouses, Negroes and jazz, music halls, and player pianos.

Yet Crevel spent half his life smack in the middle of all that. The blurb continues:

> *In search of characters for future novels, men and women naked and alive as knives and forks, to figure in tales as unprintable as the ones he used to make up when he was a little kid.*

This shows Crevel was already mulling *Babylon* over in his mind, with its famous opening chapter, "Mr. Knife, Miss Fork," a good two years before he actually wrote it. More importantly, the image of "men and women naked and alive as knives and forks" conjures up a vision of a new humanity, of people as clean and sparkling and smooth and hard and shapely and bright and tuneful and functional as so much good silver. Further: it suggests simplicity and candor. Qualities that contradict what he referred to as "the life I accept," in his statement on suicide. Crevel disliked trendiness of all sorts, regardless of social or sexual markings, but the Surrealist camp of which he was a leading ideologue represented an apotheosis of camp, camp for camp's sake, and the Surrealist association with the world Communist movement was preposterous—as only Dalí seems to have had the wit or the sense of humor to grasp at the time. Bear in mind that the René Crevel who was caught up in all this was the same guy who "intended to give all his attention to an immediate sense of reality" (Breton's words in discussing the motives of his suicide). A striving to capture and share that "immediate sense of reality" against all odds is present in all of Crevel's writings. By the summer of 1935, Breton says, Crevel was in despair "at not being physically able to maintain himself at that level." What is meant by the phrase "not being physically able?" Incurable pulmonary disease, hereditary syphilis, plus liquor and drugs. But there was something more at the end, a failure of language that Crevel himself equated with a moral breakdown. He had once observed to René Char that words are shovels. With language we dig our graves. Char referred to the remark in a poem inspired by Crevel's suicide:

What if words are shovels?

Death will have only put your echo under
Winter sows our coats with frost.
Your curly way of talking keeps blending
*   with the steam out of our mouths.*
Mind means not to petrify.
Its adversary clay tempts it to try.
But sleep, sleep shovels a spoonful at a time.
You want to get out, go. Vanish in the night
*   where pain can hurt no more.*

Shortly before Crevel did just that, he made an appearance in front of a working-class audience with a talk on Art and Love and Revolution, subjects about which he supposed himself to be on common ground with his listeners. Art, Love, Revolution. Steam shovels, not spoons. This was by no means his debut as a lecturer. Already a decade earlier, when *La mort difficile* was first published, in 1926, Crevel had given such a talk in London. The event was described by the critic Logan Pearsall Smith:

All the young lions, or rather the young tom-cats of Bloomsbury were there, a few older celebrities trembling for their thrones and reputations among those hoping to replace them, and a few ladies of fashion anxious to be in the intellectual swim. This audience was addressed by a pert, self confident French boy with a big mouth and a brazen voice [Crevel] who dinned our ears with a galimatias of what I thought pretentious and incomprehensible nonsense, a new gospel of *surréalisme* composed of Freud, Rimbaud, Valéry, Keyserling and Mussolini—an anti-intellectual gospel and attack on reason, chanted and bellowed at us in a kind of figurative and bombastic prose which, though we pretended to follow it, I am sure not one of us really understood. The whole thing—the brazen pretentious boy and the anxious pretentious audience— was extremely funny. (Letter to Cyril Connolly, dated Autumn 1926.)

Unlike the bright young things of 1926, the workers of 1935 were unimpressed. The talk was a flop. Here, considering the lifelong thirst for reality that was Crevel's, I see a thread leading straight to the final chapter. To understand what happened in the question-and-answer period that followed the talk, it is necessary to have some idea of how Crevel viewed himself up to that moment. Over the past decade he had grown accustomed to thinking of himself as a poet, a witness of the truth, an "unacknowledged legislator." The world, at least a sophisticated segment of the reading public, had recognized him in that role. His view of himself as a poet rather than a novelist, even though his published writings consisted almost entirely of fiction and essays, reflected an allegiance to Surrealist literary theory, which had it as a basic tenet that the old genres were finished, and all that remained for a writer in today's world was the pamphlet and poetry, on the writing front, at least.

Pamphlets. In other words, philosophy and criticism in the service of a worldwide Communist revolution. To actual Communist

Party members, the Surrealists' efforts along those lines, including Crevel's, were a laugh. Crevel's essays certainly do cut a bizarre figure if viewed as contributions to Marxist-Leninist theory. *Diderot's Harpsichord* and *Mind Against Reason* present the most powerfully argued defense of the irrational since Nietzsche, and the essays on Klee, Sintenis, and Dalí reveal a critical eye of penetration and originality linked with an extraordinary breadth of historical perspective. Anna Balakian has written that Crevel would have been the philosopher of Surrealism had he survived. These five pamphlets, actually booklength essays, represent the unfulfilled juvenilia of that philosopher.

Poetry. Crevel believed in the programmatic restriction to pamphlets and poetry and conformed to it in his own way, as a poet, in that his novels are not novels so much as they are richly poetic discourses with elements of narration and a storyline. The novella *Detours*, his first book, was an exception (which Breton returned to Crevel without comment, while other members of the Surrealist group marveled at his temerity in asking Breton to read it in the first place). The other five—*My Body and Me* (1925), *Difficult Death* (1926), *Babylon* (1927), *Are You Crazy?* (1929), and *Putting My Foot in It* (1933)—have much more in common with Richard Pryor than with Marcel Proust. According to Klaus Mann's memoirs, Crevel was in the habit of electrifying friends with raps very similar in style to his novel-writing. The manner varies from rapid narration to slapstick and beyond, to lyric flights with a shapeliness of the language itself that adds up more to a storyteller-poet than a poetic storyteller. Present tense and indicative mood predominate from start to finish, creating a myopic closeness to the details of what is being stated or told similar to that which characterized the cinema verite of the 1950s and again the structuralist film of the Sixties and Seventies.

The whole point of all this was to communicate an immediate sense of the reality and life that is right at hand for every one of us the moment we exercise our freedom to reach out for it and live it in our own minds and bodies: "Poetry is the highroad of freedom." Crevel used a couple of analogies to illustrate this slogan: "A contemporary of Diderot's imagines a color harpsichord; Rimbaud in the *Sonnet of the Vowels* revealed the prism of sounds; Poetry bridges the gap between our senses, between image and idea, idea and precise fact." A color harpsichord, a prism, a spark. What they have in common is that all three are mediums. Sometime in 1921 Crevel had obtained initiation as a medium. He in turn initiated Breton in the experiments with hypnosis and automatic writing that were to open up the dark continent of the unconscious to the Surrealists. The barriers separating the unconscious from the conscious mind, dream from reality, had long been perceived to be chief among the walls that hem life in, and it is thanks to Crevel that Surrealism developed the techniques that it did for breaking down those walls with a view to realizing, if only in some small measure, Rimbaud's brave program to "change life."

To avenge herself on a faithless husband in the year 1903, Madame Crevel had had little René circumcised at the age of three, an event that was to burn henceforth at the center of his mind in images of sperm and blood, an obsession the Pythagorean teachings associate with a soul wavering on the brink of a fresh descent into material existence. The ancients pictured such unborn souls as brides of Neptune, sea nymphs hovering in a white mist over the flood of materiality: "They are in love with blood and semen, just as the souls of plants are nourished by water" (Porphyry, *On the Cave of the Nymphs*). As is well known, a chief power of poetry is to foreshadow the future. In *Diderot's Harpsichord* Crevel had written,

"All Poetry worthy of the name is a menace." A poet in the act of making poetry is a soul forever at the edge, on the brink. In the encounters between poets and the unborn whom they address, there is an overlap of two worlds, of the here-and-now with the elsewhere, the hereafter. "Their death we live, and they ours," Heraclitus wrote of these moist souls that are always just about to be, but are never quite yet, reborn in the mind, invincibly wet behind the ears, of every fully conscious being.

In 1926, the year of *Difficult Death*, Madame Crevel died. According to Klaus Mann (who says he was appalled), up to the very end the mere mention of her in front of René was apt to touch off fireworks. Jouhandeau, however, quotes a letter in which René says he is yearning for a day of mutual forgiveness but fears it will never come. Be that as it may, Madame Crevel served as the model of the hateful Madame Dumont-Dufour in *Difficult Death*, just as her son, the book's hero Pierre, was René himself. The same year, 1926, marked an encounter with psychoanalysis. Crevel soon abandoned therapy in disgust. He refused to believe in the Oedipus complex: "I was one of those who would have preferred to kill their Clytemnestra of a mother, rather than their Laius-like father." Before the Twenties were out, the youthful Jean-Paul Sartre was to dismiss Surrealism: "These turbulent young bourgeois want to wreck culture because it represents their Papa." With an appropriate transposition of parental gender, these words apply (although somewhat unfairly) to Crevel, who appears to have been the only Surrealist who actually felt the sting of this kind of criticism.

It may have been the last sensation he ever had. When those working-class guys from the factories showed up for his talk on Poetry and Art and Love and Revolution in June 1935, and after hearing him out, asked him questions he couldn't answer, something happened and René was blushing, then stammering, then reduced to speechlessness and left deeply humiliated. He had now to figure out for himself (like Pierre at the end of *Difficult Death*, stripped of everything and everyone, with no more hate, no more friendship, no more love) that to the insulted and the injured of this world who were getting it together at last to write their own script, he was just a rich kid with problems, slumming, or at this point a burned-out once-fashionable junkie in a world all his own, out of touch, spinning his wheels, completely and irretrievably full of shit, and it was the realization that this was the truth of the matter that burned to the very core of an at last absolutely honest man, true poet that he was, and killed him. Fifty years after the fact, it is clear that René Crevel wasn't the burn-out he thought himself in those last hours. What triumphs today is the inheritor of Rimbaud and Lautréaumont and Orpheus making language sing with a freedom, an openness, a candor so total you want to drop everything and, just as he did, take it from there.

Roger Gilbert-Lecomte

The bowl of an O pipe is convex not concave. It is shaped exactly like a doorknob. O is not a hip abbreviation for Opium. I am using it for convenience.

The code word for O that was in fashion in the Paris where Roger Gilbert-Lecomte smoked it long ago was Ondine. Ondine means "water nymph." *C'est une véritable ondine*, they say of a graceful swimmer. Undines appear, Paracelsus writes, when tender subtle things change color in the wind.

In a video performance made in New York City in the early 1970s titled "The Suitcase," Larry Miller displayed the contents of a suitcase containing the possessions of an alcoholic who had died in a flophouse on the Bowery. In these possessions a whole life and mental universe unfolded on the screen.

When Roger Gilbert-Lecomte died in a Paris hospital after a week-long agony, in and out of convulsions, from tetanus caused by a dirty needle, on December 31, 1943, his possessions were all in one small briefcase in the backroom of a working-class bar whose owner Mme Firmat had taken him in three years before for kindness. She had found him, a stranger, unconscious in the street. To his friend and famulus the future playwright Arthur Adamov she gave the briefcase. It was filled with letters, prose writings, and poems, a hundred or so, not much else. Three and a half years earlier, in May 1940, Adamov had pleaded with Lecomte to leave Paris. My dealers are here, Lecomte replied.

The bowl of an O pipe is like an empty eggshell, one that has been sucked. The smoker sucks the smoke from within, via the pipe. To a smoker, that bowl is like the walls of the firmament as pictured in ancient cosmologies, and we're inside. *Flammantia moenia mundi*, flaming shell of the world, is the expression in Lucretius.

Lecomte had been jabbing the needle into a thigh muscle through a pair of trousers he hadn't changed in months. He had been a medical student and had once attended a dying tetanus victim.

Baudelaire writes of Poe: "He drank as if he were performing an act of homicide, as if he had to kill something inside of him, a worm that would not die."

Lecomte was 36 at the time. At 16 he had written a poem about the disappearance of ancient Alexandria, titled "Mystic Tetanus." Much was made of this coincidence after his death. In the 1960s an association was organized at the initiative of the writer Pierre Minet, a lifelong intimate, under the name "Friends of Roger Gilbert-Lecomte's Works." Apart from Mme Firmat, however, who played Mrs. Clemm to Lecomte's Poe, and Adamov, who was his assistant and at times collaborator, the only people Lecomte had any contact with during the final months of his life were the patrons of Mme Firmat's cafe whose back room he occupied. They seem to have liked him for his educated speech, his simplicity of manner, and occasional flights of fancy. With tears of retrospective tenderness, they spoke of his childlike purity and staggering naivete.

The woman he had been involved with for the past decade, Ruth Kronenberg, had been sent to Auschwitz in mid-1942. She was never seen again. She had been arrested in 1940, but somehow had got out and obtained false I.D. Then, according to Adamov, somebody denounced her to the police. Ruth was German and had left Germany in 1933. She had fallen in love with Lecomte soon after arriving in

Paris. Lecomte's father had threatened to disown him if he married this Jewess. The father was a right-wing Catholic businessman, an executive with a champagne-manufacturing company in Reims, ancient capital of Frankish Gaul where the kings of France were traditionally crowned. The Cathedral had been shelled to smithereens by Big Bertha some time after a German army dashed for Paris in the summer of 1914, when Lecomte was seven, an event of which he later retained a vivid memory, that of running hand in hand with his mother down a street in flames, but the front lines remained just outside city limits throughout the war, and it was a town leveled in part by bombardments, a feature Lecomte was to dream of all his life and record in an unpublished dream-book of masturbatory fantasies played out in the cellar holes and ruins, a town occupied by Allied Armies and their high commands up to the eve of puberty, a town of nightclubs and whores. Lecomte's father had rescued him more than once from drug busts, paid his fines and hospital bills. Lecomte couldn't make up his mind to defy the man and marry the woman.

Ruth, however, tall, with a mane of red gold and ethereal pallor, thin like a Poe heroine, wore the pants, as the saying used to go, and from the time she met Lecomte until the beginning of the Occupation she was employed as a seamstress, and supported both of them, so far as her means allowed. In the interim between her initial release and final disappearance, Lecomte and Adamov published a series of jointly written articles on 19th-century German Romantic poets. These appeared in an arts magazine, *Comoedia*, which had the blessings of the Occupation authorities. The series dropped in mid-career when Éluard, speaking for the Resistance, suggested to Adamov that it might seem inopportune to be writing panegyrics about German authors in the collaborationist press at that particular moment. Their actual motives would have been a need for money, and—especially on Lecomte's part, since the articles were mainly his—a very deep sense of identification with especially Novalis, together with a certain high-minded and cavalier contempt for the appropriate or seemly occasion that seems to have characterized both Lecomte and Adamov.

The bowl of an O pipe also resembles the head of a mushroom with the tiny vent hole through which the column of O-charged vapor passes on its way into the pipe and down the inside of its wooden stem and out through its ivory mouthpiece into the smoker's mouth and thence in a long slow pull back through the esophagus and into the lungs where the particles dissolving on the walls of the alveoli break down to their active principles, the opiate and other alkaloids, which are at this stage absorbed into the bloodstream mounting to the brain to trigger signals of blissful release. The bowl of the O pipe doubtless resembled the image of the mushroom of immortality in the mind of its inventor. The smoking of drugs through pipes began of course with the American Indians, but they never had this mushroom-headed pipe which was invented only after the Portuguese introduced tobacco to the East Asians and the latter set out to develop a pipe that could smoke O to the best effect. This took place in the 1500s and all three, mushroom, bowl, and O itself, came straight up out of black earth. *Papaver somniferum* is a white flower.

From the Front near Reims, on October 10, 1918, Wilfred Owen wrote:

> *I have found brave companionship in a poppy, behind whose stalk*
> *I took cover from five machineguns and several howitzers.*

Owen was of course talking about a poppy of the red sort worn to commemorate absent youths.

One of Lecomte's last publications in his lifetime was in the establishment avant-garde magazine, *La Nouvelle Revue Française*, shortly after Ruth Kronenberg was deported to Auschwitz. It is a twelve-line poem, written a decade earlier, yet every line reverberates with the absence of Ruth:

PALACE OF THE VOID

To a palace made
Of wind

To a palace whose towers
Are pillars of fire by day

To an opal palace
In the sky's zenith hear

The bird of pale air
Flies

In a swift white line
On black space

A brushstroke
Signifying absence

A physician in the court of Louis the Fourteenth did a treatise on O and reached the conclusion that O had formed the sap of the tree of the knowledge of good and evil in the Garden of Eden.

"Who's the traitor, Lord?" the well-beloved disciple whispered. "It's the one I'll give the morsel to that I dip." And so, having dipped the morsel, he took and gave it to Judas. And with the morsel, Satan entered inside Judas. And it was night.

The morsel, *to psomion*. This word, *psomion*, was used in the Eastern Rite to designate the Host. The wafer of the Host is white. O comes from a perfectly circular white flower. Yet O the sap is black. Is the O flower the wafer and the O sap "night"? Communion, according to Simone Weil, is equivalent to nakedness which in turn equals Death. Of this state, Vaughan (Henry) exclaims:

> *O that I were winged & free*
> *And quite undrest just now with thee*
> *Where freed souls dwell by living fountains*
> *On everlasting spicy mountains . . .*

The blackness of the O stands for the night enveloping Judas, the womb of absence, out of which light is about to break.

At the moment of birth, the infant Lecomte nearly died of suffocation, an event which entering the family saga was often recalled in the child's presence, so that in later years he was convinced that he could remember it himself.

"There are no two ways of being a seer," Lecomte wrote. "The only way to see is via asphyxia or congestion, whether by yoga, drowning, or narcosis."

He used to maintain that the first men and women on earth were human-sized lizards with three eyes that walked upright on their hind legs, and that, with the third eye linked to the pineal gland, they communicated directly with the invisible world.

This theory—it goes back to the mysteries of Greece and India, with modern elaborations by Descartes and Blavatsky—Lecomte set forth in an essay, "Pineal vision," written in 1927 at age 20. In his teens he had done experiments to prove a physical basis for the theory with a philosophy professor named René Maublanc who had written a book on the subject. That same year, pineal vision was lampooned by Georges Bataille, whose essay, "The Pineal Eye," identified the organ with the extruded anus of a monkey seen in the zoo.

Lecomte's earliest extant poem, written at age 14 in 1921, is a sonnet titled "The South Pole." In it he plays with classical diction just for the hell of it, and a kind of humor at once saucy and warm. The French admire Lecomte's poetry for its lovely sound, but the humor is what makes it sing.

At fourteen, also, he announced to friends: "I will kill myself slowly by smoking O."

Lecomte's friends at the lycée in Reims made up a group of half a dozen boys; he was the undisputed leader. They called themselves *les Phrères simples*, or *les Simplistes*, the Simplicissimi, one might translate. Almost everyone in the English-speaking world has by this time read Alain Fournier's *The Wanderer* and seen the movie *Zero for Conduct*. What we don't realize unless it is pointed out is that these works are faithful depictions of the real universe of schoolboys in France from the turn of the century up to the very recent past. As Waterloo was won on the playing fields of Eton, much of the 20th century's philosophy, art, and literature began in the lycées of France. Exactly such a group—dominated by the mysterious Jacques Vaché, a young poet in uniform André Breton knew during World War One who killed himself with an overdose in 1919—was the direct ancestor of Surrealism. Lecomte and his Simplist chums were too young to have gotten in on the Surrealist Manifesto, but they were in Paris five years later to challenge Breton and his comrades with a new movement and magazine, which they called LE GRAND JEU, "The Great Game," a phrase with idiomatic meanings. In older usage, it meant high stakes in gambling. Nowadays it means something like "the full treatment." *Jouer à quelqu'un le grand jeu* means "to give someone the works." It was a provocative title.

It's hard to summarize The Great Game. At the center of it, for Lecomte and for his classmates and best friend the poet René Daumal, was a vision of the unity of everything in the universe arising from experiments at age 16 with carbon tetrachloride. Lecomte was to define the essence of the experience with a phrase: "the impersonal instant of eternity in emptiness." In the essay "A Fundamental Experiment" (translated by Roger Shattuck, Hanuman Books, 1987), written twenty years later, Daumal attempted to disclose the discovery that came out of this impersonal instant of eternity in emptiness. It was a discovery both were to spend the rest of their lives explicating. It led to The Great Game; it *was* The Great Game.

At around that time, coincidentally or not, Lecomte and Daumal lost their virginity at the same hour and with the same hooker, having picked her up in the entranceway of a club they were barred from by reason of their age, using several bottles of good champagne for bait. The pimp, a taxi driver, drove them in his cab to the whorehouse and sat next to the bed drinking up the champagne while they fucked his sheila, a good-natured fellow, Lecomte wrote in a breathless letter to a friend who had missed the fun because away at school in Paris—just the sort of thing immortalized in Brassaï's photography, from which we are separated as if by a Grand Canyon of discontinuity in the history of mores, having discovered, as Tennessee Williams once put it, that there are plenty of good times to be had outside the good-time house.

Years later, after *The Great Game* had folded, the GRAND JEU magazine, that is, and the two friends had quarreled irrevocably, Daumal was to become a full-time disciple of Gurdjieff. He had been studying Hinduism, yoga philosophy, and Sanskrit, and was writing the poems titled *Counterheaven*, the novel *A Night of Serious Drinking* (note, by the way, that Daumal was no addict or alcoholic, early experiments notwithstanding) and a masterpiece, *Mount Analogue*, not to speak of numerous essays and versions of Vedic scriptures, and a booklength translation of writings by Suzuki on Zen. So much for René Daumal who started out as Lecomte's kid brother, far surpassed him in measurable achievements, and died a few months after him, of TB, in the spring of 1944. That impersonal glimpse of eternity in a void, Lecomte dreamed, might just pop out of a book whose leaves unfolded an arithmetic of higher unity—he could go on about it by the hour, yet in his actual writing he shunned every model or format that might lead to a finished work, and this, he declared to friends who visited him in the hotel room where he held forth daily in his bathrobe after several pipes of O, was precisely his intention.

Back in Reims in his mid-teens, Lecomte had fallen in with a coterie of O smokers, an odd assortment, as such groups always are, of age, nationality, and sexual orientation, not that the latter is of much significance to a true smoker. Still, Lecomte was a good looker, and his letters dating from that period hint that he was putting out for drugs and curious as to whether this was going to turn him into a homosexual. He soon found that an entirely different sort of attraction rated top billing in an O bed.

Finished in black lacquer, the classic O bed was big enough for three. Its side to the wall was built up in a screen, one panel of which was typically painted with a hell scene, rank upon rank of demons swirling round a central point at which karma-racked souls were being stuffed into waiting ovaries, to be projected back into the cycle of earthly life and death. The side of the bed facing the room was provided with a drawer containing the so-called trousseau, which was a tray or box with all necessary accoutrements, a bamboo pipe with silver fittings, and a detachable bowl of glazed porcelain, the pipe being shaped like a flute, with a metal fitting on its side for the bowl, which had to be a perfect fit because the assembled pipe must be airtight, for the slightest leak made it impossible to smoke, and the O would be burnt to a crisp without any of the euphoriant fumes reaching the smoker's lungs.

Lecomte was a big reader, one of those who skip to the end, spoiling the middle. He was obsessed with the old idea that the end and the beginning of things link up, that Mind is the union of the two. But our mind, he insisted, knows nothing of cosmic awareness. "Human life does not mirror the universe but shuns it in horror. Yet the only way to be free is to grasp i.e. embrace the Law on which all things revolve."

In the vent hole there is a small depression designed to hold the pea-size bead of O being smoked. This bead is pierced and squashed round the smokehole in the shape of a tiny donut. To smoke, it must be brought sufficiently near the heat focused above the lamp in order to cook, and as it cooks one draws steadily on the pipe. The ring of O dwindles, sizzling round the hole, until gone, part of it reaching the lungs but much more in the form of dross coating the insides of the bowl and pipe.

Lecomte's writings remained for the most part incomplete, as if he challenged readers to complete them. The vast majority of published books are finished in name only, he pointed out. He felt he had been born too soon, and detested the easy successes of those who to all appearances were long overdue. On the other hand, given his turn of mind that in many ways would seem stuck between archaic Greece and India, one could also say Lecomte was "too late" for his time. Too soon, too late. These reproaches, for that is what they are, have been applied to others.

In all of this there were no love poems to Ruth, only one brief mention of her in a poem addressed to Adamov, "Eternity in a wink." There she is referred to spitefully as the *provider slaked with insults at the source*, the source being Lecomte, and as *this self-styled double who is more "you" than you are*, but only in passing, as he moves on to the true subject of the poem, which is the meaning of death by drugs.

No trousseau is complete without the special gouging tool used for cleaning out dross, which must be done after each session; otherwise, the accumulation gives fresh smoke an unpleasant bitter taste and eventually clogs the pipe. A dross box forms yet another necessary part of the trousseau. When it fills up, one cooks the dross, simmering it for many hours. It is then drained off into another vessel by siphon action through a length of surgical cotton, a filtration process that removes impurities generically known as *terre*, or earth. By allowing the contents of the second vessel to evaporate, a new quantity of pure O is obtained. Dross may be twice recycled in this manner. The third time it must be put up in drops, because the product of a third filtration would crumble or burn before it would smoke.

Lecomte published only sporadically. At 21, he had the honor of editing some newly discovered correspondence of Rimbaud, and this appeared with an essay, "Rimbaud and the Death of Art." Then there were his prose contributions to GRAND JEU and other magazines, titles such as "The Horrible Revelation," "Terror on Earth," "The Enigma of the Human Face," "The Prophecy of the Magi," and "Mr Morpheus, Public Poisoner."

In his preface to an Italian-language anthology of Daumal and Lecomte's GRAND JEU writings published in Milan in 1967, Claudio Rugafiori traces Lecomte's "wind" mystique back to ancient India, citing *Rig Veda* 10.168.4. The latter, a hymn to the gale wind, is in fact to Lecomte's "I'm not scared of wind" what Mayakovsky's sun poem "An Extraordinary Event" is to Frank O'Hara's "A True Account of Talking to the Sun at Fire Island." (The Vedic poem is available in Wendy Doniger O'Flaherty's *Rig Veda* anthology published in the Penguin Classics series.) Daumal reacted coldly to this magnificent text. In his view it was loose, sloppy, and extravagantly overwritten. This view formed the object of a sharp exchange reflected in the poet's correspondence of 1933.

Nevertheless, The Great Game meant the same thing to both men. As Rugafiori suggests, both highlight "the play of opposites that makes emptiness and fullness, inside and outside, front and back identical, not only poetically but conceptually . . . The abolition of space and distance, the co-penetration of the visible with an 'astral plane' that is seen not as the other world but this one inside out, a state one enters at death, may justify Death's attractiveness insofar as it is a step toward the realization of that vaster state that Lecomte and Daumal experienced in its most extreme form during their discovery of The Great Game through 'experimental metaphysics.'"

In 1923, year of his initial experiments with carbon tetrachloride undertaken with Daumal, Lecomte wrote:

> *Wind of Infinity, when you churn past*
> *And make my hair stand on end at a breath,*
> *The seer I'd like to be shivers, aghast*
> *At the touch of a Space vaster than death . . .*

Next to the pipe itself, the most important part of a smoker's trousseau is the olive oil lamp, whose wick must be kept trimmed to yield a clear, steady flame. It is impossible to smoke off a flickering heat source. If the flame is smoky, the pipe will soon stink of olive oil, and so will the O. The taste of O and burnt olive oil is particularly nauseating.

In 1933 Lecomte published a booklength collection of poetry, LIFE LOVE DEATH VOID & WIND, which went pretty much unnoticed in the literary world, except for the enthusiastic review by Antonin Artaud in the *Nouvelle Revue Française*, which appears as the Foreword to my translation of selected poems by Lecomte that was published under the title *Black Mirror* (Station Hill, 1991). René Daumal typed the entire manuscript of this book for Lecomte, and dealt with the publisher for him. It was the last project he and Daumal ever collaborated on. Daumal's future wife Véra was doing her best to persuade Daumal that Lecomte was a drag on both their lives, that the relationship was parasitical, and they ought to be out of it. So that's what happened. An old member of the group, the poet Pierre Minet, who many years later was to edit Lecomte's works in the Gallimard edition, sometimes acted as a go-between but afterwards wrote that Daumal eventually forbade him to mention Lecomte's name: "He is dead to me." Nevertheless, Daumal's *Counterheaven*, which in 1936 was awarded the Jacques Doucet Prize, the jury consisting of Gide, Valéry, and Giraudoux, is dedicated to Lecomte. One of the Great Game friends had once taken a picture of the two, Daumal and Lecomte, when they were teenagers, reenacting a scene from a Bela Lugosi film. Daumal makes as if his hands were bound behind his back and cringes with an expression of mock horror as Lecomte puts a knife to his throat. The scene prefigures the reality of their future relationship, and Daumal was to shrink from his former friend as from a vampire.

Shaped like a bell-jar with a circular opening at the top, the lamp's chimney focuses heat at a point one inch above the lamp. Final preparation of the bead of O for smoking is the most difficult part of the operation, much simplified if the supply is stored at exactly the right consistency, which is that of a product that looks and handles like cold molasses, a state maintained by storing in an airtight container.

An addict is a person who never stops needing a refill. Whenever Lecomte was out of drugs he used liquor. At the center of everything he wrote was the idea of being absent. Here are some notes by him, titled "A Metaphysics of Absence."

Lab Experiment: Inject hamsters with a 1 cc emulsion containing ordinary garden soil in order to provoke "gas gangrene." Treat Group I with a 14 percent dilution of human blood. These recover with a simple induration.

Group 2. 9 percent dilution. These die.

Group 3. 22 percent. These die sooner.

Group 4. 30 percent. These recover.

Such homeopathic triturations represent a ratio like that of one geometric point to an entire solar system. They are so infinitesimal that there is neither a molecule nor an electron left.

A homeopathic dilution represents a specific absence.

This poses a problem of both cosmic and biologic order.

How can the absence of a substance count more for a living organism than the actual substance itself?

Why shouldn't each entity have an "absence characteristic" in which a qualitative sense of what it was would persist when it was no longer there? (In fact, this would be its phantom.)

Life, in order to exist, needs absence more than it needs reality.
Life occurs between two nonexistences: past and future.

Rhythm is movement linked to absence.

Life is the rhythm of quality and quantity. Energy is the force of matter as it disappears—sign of absence.

Life is a fragile hybrid pulsing, instant by instant, between being and nothingness.

Even if every person on earth were to vanish suddenly from time and space, the mere fact of the absence would suffice to make humanity remain identical to what it already was.

The smoker scoops sufficient O for several pipes out of the jar and places it in a small shallow cup shaped like a *sake* cup. This is done with one of a pair of wrought-iron needles specially made for handling O. An O needle is about six inches long. Its upper half is somewhat less than 1/16 inch in diameter, and flattened into a spatula at the end, for lifting the soft O from its dish or jar, for scraping hardened bits off the bowl, and at times for pressing and shaping a piece of O round the vent hole. Its lower extremity tapers to a point on which the bead of O is twirled over the flame just before smoking. "Thou hast the keys of Paradise, O Just, subtle, and mighty O!" (De Quincey.)

Pierre Minet lived as a vagrant in the streets of Paris, a shivering pagan, a hippie long before the fact, a honeybee circling the electric rose of Pigalle, only to return in later life to respectability and to the Catholic faith in which he had been raised. When Lecomte was dying, he sent Minet a desperate plea for help. Minet postponed action on the appeal until it was too late, and never forgave himself for it. This was to be the pivotal event of his memoirs, published under the title *Failure* in 1947. Writing soon after Lecomte's death, in the literary magazine *Cahiers du Sud* (June/July 1944), Minet reported: "Those who saw him just after death, before he was taken home to Reims for burial, were unanimously struck by his resemblance to Christ. This, although it might have been better left unsaid, I note with a special pang." Lecomte was not the only French writer of his generation for whose life or manner of dying the imitation of Christ was an issue. Simone Weil and Artaud were to carry it to their respective limits. It is no accident that Lecomte and Artaud were attracted to each other. What made for the attraction was not a shared craving for O so much as an even more deeply shared metaphysical craving. The real imitation of Christ in Lecomte is not in the manner of his death but in the special way he embodied the absence he intuited at the heart of things, which is precisely the subject matter of a key passage in the so-called Discourse in the Upper Room, where Jesus says, I have to be absent in order for the Helper coming after me to be here for you and fill you with memory of what you forgot and knowledge of what you don't know. My Helper is a breath of air, no more, just thin air. Shortly after saying this, he breathes on them and vanishes.

The object of rolling the O over the flame is to obtain a material that is sufficiently hard to cook round the vent hole without completely melting and getting sucked through, into the bowl and pipe, which is what does happen when a bead of soft O gets stuck round the hole. By rolling, the material is cooked through and not just hard on the outside and soft within. Smokers can be snobbish about the way they roll. "We are a happy few," said Gabriel Pomerand to me in 1965. The classic Chinese style is at once the hardest and the best. With the spatula end of one needle, the smoker lifts a bit of O across the flame, and as it starts to expand into a spherical bead, picks it up with the point of the other needle, which, if there is the slightest likelihood that the O may crumble, the smoker will have previously moistened with glycerine. The bead is now transferred from one needle to the other, point to point, rapidly twirling them to and fro over the lamp. Each time the bead changes needles, some of it is turned inside out, and a bit of the soft core is directly exposed to the heat. At the slightest jarring, the bead may drop off into the oil; at the least hesitation, it will burn. Jean Cocteau was a master of this technique.

Lecomte's way of relating to the world was so awkward! Yet behind it all was that constant wish to vanish. Take the name. In 1928, upon turning 21, he decided to change it from Roger Lecomte to Roger Gilbert-Lecomte. Friends with René Crevel, Lecomte would have heard Crevel's view of hyphenated names, which in the latter's novel *Difficult Death* (1926) are ridiculed as "a key to what the aristocracy might be in this century if anyone still cared to recognize the merits of the French middle-class which, my dear, has never ceased to provide an elite in the service of our country." What motivated Lecomte, however, was not social climbing but its opposite. He had already been born into the upper middle class, and by temperament and intellectual bent he was already an aristocrat. In adopting the hyphenated name, he was emulating a close friend and patron, Léon Pierre-Quint, who was at that time editor-in-chief at one of the best houses for new writing, Sagittarius Books (Editions Sagittaire) and not only gave Lecomte the assignment to edit Rimbaud, but put up the money for *Grand Jeu* magazine and for Lecomte's first book.

Pierre-Quint had by this time known Lecomte for a while. He recalled: "At 18, the mere prospect of going into a store to get a ham sandwich seemed so difficult and repellent that he would have preferred to die of hunger. To talk with a shopkeeper made him blush like a girl and shiver like a bum. In the face of such acute distress, his friends used to spare him these mundane worries. At that time he was loved as though he were a lovable child, a young god, and admired as though he were a being made of finer stuff than the common run."

Lecomte knew his Bible. For example, "This brilliant sky without a sun," a short poem, is an admiring vignette of a madman, a seer, actually, seen in the Paris subway. The sky was brilliant without a sun, according to the Book of Genesis, during the first day of the Creation, from the moment Light appeared until subsequently when on the second day the sun and moon were made. A similar example is the long poem "Mystic Tetanus," where reference is made to *Nicolaitanism*. This was a form of Gnosticism. Mainstream Christians accused the Nicolaitans of indulging in fornication and violent crime so as to destroy sinful flesh even more rapidly and thereby liberate the soul. Nicolaitans got their name from a group combining esoteric study with illumination, sexual license, and the eating of meat dedicated in pagan sacrifices, and were said to be disciples of one Nicholas, a follower of the sage Balaam whose oracles were connected with the visit of the Magi to the infant Jesus. They are denounced in epistles of Peter and Jude, as well as in the Book of Revelation.

Writing after Lecomte's death, Pierre-Quint remembered: "His clear transparent blue gaze had a hard purity; he had a sensual mouth; a very straight nose; an androgynous oval face; he was tall and skinny. He lived in a private world that stretched back to the state he had existed in before birth, a distant but splendid vista."

In a no longer extant manuscript—quoted by Pierre-Quint—Lecomte summarized a section of an unfinished book project titled *Totalling Out* (*Retour à Tout*) as follows:

A man is disgusted with life and world. He rejects bit by bit everything that his upbringing and education had inculcated. Systematically from memory he erases history, personal names, dates, the days of the week, numbers. He unlearns reading itself and becomes illiterate. Soon the signs making up the written word become in his eyes mere incomprehensible ink blots on a white background, like movie images blurred to the vision of a viewer who gets too close to the screen. He withdraws yet further, in order to merge with the cosmos. He can no longer use his arms and legs, or eat. He can't even leave his miserable room. His body starts to melt. The negative effort, which he had pushed with a raging self-destructive zeal, at last succeeds. A chambermaid enters and finds a blob of jelly on the floor. But this slow and total disintegration of the individual was ideally supposed to lead back to a wondrous prior existence. Mind never stands still. If it shrinks from Progress, a future paradise, it imagines a Golden Age, a lost Eden. Present-day civilization and science have nothing but holocausts and cataclysms in both nature and society to show for themselves, where love is ever linked with sadism and stupidity with malice.

The second phase of rolling is to pack and shape the bead of O into a cone round the point of one of the needles. This is accomplished by rolling it with a twirling motion against a glazed surface such as the side of the bowl. When a bowl has seen much use, however, its glaze loses some of the original smoothness, and the bead tends to adhere, in heart-rending little streaks and splotches. Although rolling against the bowl is the classical way, rendered more elegant by the economy of its means, there is greater security and ease in rolling against a palmleaf strip. Strips used for this purpose are a common and cheap religious article in India. About ten inches long and two wide, flexible but fairly stiff, with a hard, smooth surface, they are covered with mantras in Sanskrit, Pali, Tibetan, and other languages. A good trousseau will contain a stack of them, cut in half. Held in the palm of the left hand, one of these strips makes an ideal surface. One twirls the bead back and forth from the heat to the rolling strip, pressing it against the palm of the hand again and again, gradually shaping it into a little cone. Smooth and perfectly shaped, with a patina like that of polished shoe leather, the bead is at last ready to mold round the vent and smoke.

The helper or spirit spoken of in the Upper Room has a tangible or at least more readily imaginable analogue in yoga philosophy, where it is called *prana*. By the closing decades of the 20th century the latter has been so completely popularized in both Europe and America it has entered folklore if not experience. *Its sound is heard but its shape is unseen*, says the *Rig Veda* (1.164.44) of this wind.

The last step is quickly accomplished. One takes the pipe in the left hand, grasping it between the third and fourth fingers, with the stem cradled between the thumb and the heel of the hand. The bowl is held over the lamp long enough to make it quite hot. The needle is then brought in the right hand over the lamp, to twirl the O in the heat for a couple of seconds until just about to start cooking. Then, very rapidly, the needle is jammed into the hot vent hole with a counterclockwise twirling motion until the tip of the needle touches the inside of the pipe, at which point one reverses direction and twirls clockwise and out. If this is done correctly, the O detaches from the needle and adheres round the vent perfectly, with a little hole straight down through the middle.

In the summer and fall of 1932, when Lecomte and Daumal were still friends and Daumal was typing the LIFE LOVE DEATH VOID

& WIND manuscript in Paris, Lecomte was living with his parents in the family apartment at 52 rue Hicmar in Reims. Lecomte would mail the poems out piecemeal and hold his breath for Daumal's reactions. These were not always favorable. The unevenness of the writing—its mix of intensity and slackness, of high and low style, of rare originality and ordinary vulgarity—bewildered and irritated a more conventional Daumal. At the big wind poem, "I'm not scared of wind," Daumal drew the line. He found it loose, all over the place, overdone; on the whole, an exercise in bad taste.

In a letter dated August 2, 1932, Lecomte replied:

> *Properly speaking, I don't consider 'I'm not scared of wind' to be a poem at all, not in the incantatory sense I like to give that term, but rather as a dumping ground for all that an unconscious decanting process prevented me from including in the other two texts, which I did consider to be poems, in the Wind series . . . For me, it's a joy of the automatic-writing variety to let myself whizz through a grand farrago of eloquent nonsense as fast as the pen will carry me, the ends of verses or lines marking only the pen's microscopic hesitations . . . I don't see why others shouldn't enjoy declaiming it as much as I do . . . On rereading, this document strikes me as curious in the measure that its realization betrays a striving for compositional balance that is certainly not me. Take, for example, its unpremeditated blend of the corniest sort of hamming in the same breath with the most rarefied flights of fancy . . .*

No other French ear was attuned to the Mayakovskian rant in 1932. The closest thing they had was Victor Hugo. For example, the vast grotesquerie of Hugo's rant on the Trumpet that shall wake the dead on Judgment Day, in the *Legend of the Ages*. To a Frenchman of 1930 this was a poetic equivalent of Jules Verne plus Doré, a blend someone like Daumal would find neither interesting nor funny, even though in earlier days he and Lecomte had agreed that the most aggressively bad taste ought to be a basic characteristic of every move they made. Within a couple of months after this exchange, Lecomte was arrested and beaten up at the stationhouse, an experience that was to inspire the poem, "Son of Bone Talks." Soon after that, he underwent emergency treatment for an abscess caused by missing a vein while shooting morphine. His mother had a stroke at around the same time. Her speech became slurred and garbled. The doctor put her on chloral hydrate. Mother and son became invalids together. Morphine was cheaper, easier to obtain, and quicker than opium, Lecomte discovered.

The message in Lecomte is what comes through between the lines. Something was always lacking in this man, "missing." He didn't even have his own body,

> *Body being the one place I have no sense of being*
> *The only place I don't exist*

and so he had to make a body for himself by writing, a body of thought, while at the same time filling himself with drugs so as to create a vacuum, making himself into an empty vessel in order to be filled. What would fill him? His deepest intuition told him that at the prime origin of everything there stirred something like a breath of wind. This he hoped would fill him.

Toward the end of his life, in 1942 and '43, Lecomte helped Arthur Adamov write the book that was to make Adamov's reputation when published in 1946, *Confession*. According to Lecomte's biographers Alain and Odette Virmaux, Lecomte was actually the book's coauthor. Here are lines from *Confession* that surely come from Lecomte: "I want to fill the emptiness that eats out the inside of my head. I want to get away from nothingness, to put a mask over the horrible facelessness of empty space." The idea calls to mind lines by one of the poet-seers of India that Lecomte had been reading all his adult life, a prayer from the *Isha Upanishad* addressed to God in the form of the Sun by one who is about to die:

> *A gold dish covers the face of truth:*
> *O Sun remove it, that I a truthseeker may see.*

A recently discovered poem by Lecomte titled "Anti-Sun" dating from the last months of his life (in a handwritten copy made by Adamov and published by Alain and Odette Virmaux) embodies the very same idea. Only it's not a prayer but an imprecation:

> *You sunbeam-blooded heart of heaven you pump*
> *Of the energy transmuting into azure*
> *The asphyxiating black gel of deep space*
> *I hate the sight of you you golden mask*
> *You ring of fiery mist blind monster blinding*
> *The prey caught in your orb you dazzling phantom*
> *You dirty veil between my dizzy gaze*
> *Avid as filings round a magnet's pole*
> *And the vision of the colorless abyss*
> *In back of your false face the true black hole.*

To an English-speaking reader these lines echo the words that Milton makes Satan speak from the margin of Paradise:

. . . To thee I call,
But with no friendly voice, and add thy name,
O Sun, to tell thee how I hate thy beams
That bring to my remembrance from what state
I fell, how glorious once above thy sphere,
Till pride and worse ambition threw me down
Warring in Heaven against Heaven's matchless king.

Lecomte was no Satanist, however. He was if anything a Gnostic like Artaud. And this poem, "Anti-Sun," which may have been the last he ever wrote, mirrors yet another passage in *Confession* that, although an uncharacteristically exuberant confession of faith, is surely by him: "To be liberated is to pierce the future with a destructive gaze that vanquishes omens and exposes the future as nothing but an illusion. What can be yet to come in a world that is absolutely full, where everything that has ever been still is, and where everything that will ever be, is already here? Let the fire of love devour future and past and deliver me into the jaws of a perpetual present . . ."

As one of Lecomte's editors, Marc Thivolet, put it, "Lecomte's poems are like road signs which are meaningful only to someone on the road; they are not for stationary reading."

The *Isha Upanishad* also contains a prayer to be recited at the moment of death: vayur anilam amrtam. *Breath enter immortal wind.* Baudelaire wrote of Edgar Allan Poe: "Part of what gives us pleasure today is what killed him." He adds: "Part of what sustained my will to translate him was the pleasure of presenting a man who resembled me somewhat in certain ways, that is to say, a part of myself."

Honey-Winged Song

Which of these two lines of poetry is better?

1) *With your advent roses burst into flame* . . .

2) *When my sugar walks down the street, all the little birdies go tweet-tweet-tweet* . . .

This question kept popping into my mind as I read *The True Subject*, a selection of forty-five poems by Faiz Ahmed Faiz (1911–1984), translated by Naomi Lazard (1988). Which is better, the classical or the popular? There are still parts of the world where the classical *is* the popular; the Indian Subcontinent is one of them.

"The true subject of poetry," wrote the 30-year-old Faiz in 1943 while serving in the British Indian Army, "is the loss of the beloved." To Faiz as to many poets of the East before him, "the beloved" meant more than one's most dearly beloved; it also meant one's own inmost self experienced as another; it could mean one's own people; maybe it even meant an idea, such as ideal Justice; for the earlier mystical poets it meant, above all, God. With the end of World War Two, the still youthful poet was to seek the lost beloved not only through poetry but through political militancy, as a labor organizer and then, with British rule coming to an end in India and the partition of India and Pakistan, as editor of the *Pakistan Times*. By the early 1950s, Faiz was in deep trouble, a Death Row prisoner for four years for taking part in an attempt to overthrow Pakistan's right-wing regime. Even after his release in 1955, the poet's life was often in danger, as the country went through one crisis after another. By 1962, when he received the Lenin Peace Prize, Faiz had been Pakistan's unofficial poet laureate for years. The man was to accept such honors as they came; his poetry refused them all. Despite the integrity of both the man and his work, the language in which that work survives is an idiom inaccessible to anyone living in present-day Western countries, save as an antique, even though its translator has created a persuasively eloquent English-language equivalent.

Faiz's poems focus on that sense of separation, estrangement, or loss that is not only the true subject of poetry but is perhaps inseparable from each person's emergence into self-awareness as a conscious being no longer symbiotic with the womb. That primal separation is the basic "loss of the beloved" common to us all; all subsequent losses refer back to it.

Very few Americans have even heard of Faiz, yet in his native Pakistan crowds of *fifty thousand* used to gather to hear him read, and the best musicians of the land set him to music. (Recently in New York City, a Pakistani cab driver exclaimed "God bless you, sir!" when I told him that I had read and enjoyed Faiz in translation.) Everyone in India and Pakistan who has ever paid any attention to poetry or song, and in the Subcontinent that means millions of people, can tell you all about this legendary champion of the downtrodden who braved torture and the near-certainty of the gallows or the firing squad and yet, alongside all these perilous and distracting feats, managed to compose poetry as sweetly perfect as any ever written. The very appearance of the original Urdu text, with its flowing calligraphy, suggests that sweet perfection.

What is Urdu? The word itself means "language of the camp" and is related to our word *horde* as in *Golden Horde*. Along with its sister language Hindi, Urdu descends from Sanskrit. It is in fact

Hindi as spoken by the populations converted to Islam in the centuries following the Moghul conquest of India, with the addition of many Arabic, Persian, and Turkish words, and written in the Arabic alphabet, rather than the Sanskritic script used to write Hindi. The relation between the two languages is somewhat similar to that of German and Yiddish, which were identical 600 years ago but grew apart as their speech communities diverged, and yet to this day remain mutually intelligible.

To read Faiz is to be transported into another world much further removed from ours than the mere hours of air travel that separate the United States from Pakistan. It is a world in which the clatter of horses' hooves, the swaying of torches in the night, the reek of strong perfumes, the intoxication of hot and flowery rhetoric, the extremes of tenderness and savagery enter into ordinary everyday experience as they have not in our half of the world since Elizabethan times. During the reign of Elizabeth, in fact, the very first Englishmen ever to visit the Moghul realms of India came back home with enthusiastic reports of an exciting, colorful, prosperous, well-governed, hospitable, healthy part of the world, in other words, a country as different as it could possibly be from what the British Colonial system was to relinquish 350 years later. In 1987 a French artist named Michel Nedjar, who by reason of his Jewish background was a victim of the Nazi terror in France when still a child, could write: "It's in those countries of great poverty that you find what we have lost here—the true and violent sense of life; there is cotton-wool all around us here." He was wrong. True, that violent sense of life predominates in Faiz's poems:

> *Today, as usual, the mind goes hunting for a word,*
> *one filled with venom, a word*

sultry with honey, heavy with love,
smashing with fury.
The word of love must be brilliant as a glance
which greets the eye like a kiss on the lips,
bright as a summer river, its surface streaming gold,
joyous as the moment when the beloved enters
for the appointed meeting.

The word of rage must be a ferocious blade
that brings down for all time the oppressor's citadel.
This word must be dark as the night of a crematorium;
if I bring it to my lips
it will blacken them forever (. . .)

Just think how many Third World streets, including many in New York City, qualify to be described in Faiz's words describing Karachi:

If you look at the city from here
there is no one with dignity,
no one fully in control of his senses.
Every young man bears the brand of a criminal,
every young woman the emblem of a slave (. . .)

I'm not convinced that degrading poverty is what creates this kind of vividness, a vividness observable in the arts of so many Third World countries. We have a lot of the same thing right here, yet our sense of life is muted by comparison. The key difference has got to be one of continuity. The accelerated rate of social and political change in the industrial countries has broken the old continuities and brought us to a point where art in the old sense is dead, or the next thing to it. We don't make music and poetry and painting the way the oldtimers did, in a tradition passed from master down to pupil, from generation to generation. The arts of every nation and period are of course available to us through museums, libraries, and other media. We can examine and compare what others have done, are doing; and this is making us so self-conscious and paralyzed that we have very little to say for ourselves. That "violent sense of life" was there in those other cultures when they still enjoyed a condition of relative well-being, long before Imperialism or the population explosion.

Faiz exercises flawless mastery of an idiom that has been *the* language of lyrical and elegiac utterance all the way from North Africa to India for the past four thousand years—the rhetoric of the Bible and the Koran, of ancient Egyptian love poetry, of the Song of Songs; of Arabic poetry both before and after the coming of Islam; of Attar, Rumi, Omar; of Bilhana, Kabir, and Tagore. The surface of all these poets' language is flowery and sugar-sweet. Even when straightforward and unadorned, it more often than not echoes earlier tradition. Faiz:

> *I made some love, I did some work.*
> *Work kept interfering with love,*
> *love got in the way of work.*
> *At last I got sick of it all*
> *and left both unfinished.*

Seven hundred years before, the great Rumi summed up his life's trajectory in three words: "green, ripe, dried-out." The greenhorn, the great one, the husk. Three centuries later, Kabir noted that the flower blooms for the fruit but when the fruit is there the flower dies. Like Dante and Sir Walter Raleigh, these were political-minded people who made a habit of sticking their necks out and often paid the price of their audacity. Several of Faiz's best poems relate to his own experiences on Death Row. "Prison Meeting" and "The Day Death Comes" lift and soar on a note of transcendence similar to that in Bilhana's (11th-century Sanskrit) "Black Marigolds," wherein the poet sees "white eternity" pouring out of the now-lost lover's body and is henceforth ready for the executioner's knife. Which of us present-day American poets is laying it on the line the way these folks did? In a culture where "risk-taking" is a high-prestige activity, we're a low-profile crowd. I do recall a recent tongue-in-cheek letter to a literary magazine editor by Edouard Roditi, daring us to emulate Ezra Pound's courage, if not his particular convictions. It doesn't always work. What comes to mind is a "Conversation in a Solitary Cell" by another poet writing in Urdu, Shamsur Rahman Faruqi, who participated in the Festival of Indian Poetry at the Museum of Modern Art two years ago. The "conversation" (really a soliloquy) is a queasy blend, a modernist poem with all the old trappings—peacocks, tigers, perfume, blood—ending with a direct invocation of the Almighty. What a vast gush of passionate energy was here piddled away, leaving only a faint, blurred outline to mark where it had passed. One of Faiz's jail poems does the same, breaks into the language of prayer and it's successful, a great poem in fact. Yet the Marxist that he was can't have really meant it. The tradition in this case was stronger than the individual; and the tradition prescribes the language of prayer and mystical experience. Faiz overflows with it, and it would be easy, too easy, to fault him for all the perfumes, the wine, the roses, jasmine, tulips standing for "nights and nights of love," pomegranate flowers, and eyes like diamonds that populate his poems. And those ankle-bells! There are ankle-bells in at least three poems. (Why not? Open any anthology of Sanskrit poetry and you will find ankle-bells jingling on every page.) Or the oncoming darkness drinking from "the gash of sunset," while advancing "with the balm of musk in its hands, its diamond lancets." One could ask, Is it Dracula or Florence Nightingale? Often, though, these very means achieve startling effects—when, for instance, a lightning flash is called "the white hand of Moses," or the evening sky "a Brahmin priest, body smeared with ashes, forehead stained vermilion."

All this is tough for an American to accept as 20th-century poetry. To us, it has an anachronistic ring, undeniably. After all, we grew up on Fitzgerald's Omar, on Kipling, Laurence Hope, Sir Edwin Arnold. However, virtually every one of Faiz's poems has multilayered personal and political meanings that have resonated so powerfully in his own world that millions still love him for that resonance and treasure his words all the more for the sweetness of their sound and imagery, their mastery of the age-old poetics. Can a Westerner stomach them on the strength of that?

While reading Faiz, I tried to imagine the voice whose grave lyrical accents electrified crowds of fifty thousand at a time. It must have been a hoarse, velvety, very soft, caressing basso. Did Faiz recite to any sort of instrumental accompaniment? An almost inaudible drone, perhaps?

How did the crowds respond, I wondered, when a high-flown fancy linked extremes of public and private anguish, as in "Don't Ask Me Now, Beloved":

> . . . the trappings of the rich are woven
> by the brutish spell cast over all the ages;

human bodies numbed by filth, deformed by injuries,
cheap merchandise on sale in every street.
I must attend to this too: what can be done?
Your beauty still delights me, but what can I do?

Did they weep when Faiz paid tribute to "the ones who have freely given / the shining coin of their blood / in our streets"? Did they groan to the refrain, "Beirut, the world's beloved" in the heartrending elegy "Battleground"? (This poem, incidentally, offers a more vivid and doubtless more accurate insight into the state of mind of those now fighting in Beirut than a thousand Op-Ed articles on the subject in *The New York Times*.)

Why are we Euro-Americans so turned off by sweetness in art, when the grand old traditions put it up front? What makes "unutterable sweetness" so sickly-sweet to us? The instinct to equate sweetness with goodness would seem innate. In a recent experiment, medical researchers somehow transmitted a glucose signal to an unborn fetus and the infant's lips were seen to pucker up eagerly; it wanted to suck that sugar. The Sanskritic heritage of which Faiz was a latter-day incumbent is the most sugary of them all. It's no accident that sugar is an originally Sanskrit word, since the substance is a Hindu invention. There may be an association with bees as well. Honeybees are emblematic of prophecy and poetic truth. Flowers are the fountains at which they drink. We Westerners detest all that nowadays; it forces us to remember we're cut off from our old nostalgia for the lost source—that nostalgia which according to Faiz is "the true subject." For us, the evocation has got to be airier, drier, more rarefied, if it is to work at all. It must be like the wind that makes love so long-winded, as Robert Creeley light-heartedly describes "its moving colors of sound and flight" in his *A Form of Women*. But the wind bloweth where it listeth. Wherever people hear its song must be a place where the heart is longing for the river that has no name and waters no country.

Nelligan

Émile Nelligan (1879–1941) was a poet who lived in a house named Peek-à-boo Villa before vanishing forever in the summer of 1899 at age 19 into an asylum in that chunk of an Old World capital crystallized in a North American glacier, Montreal. The critic Edmund Wilson called Nelligan the Rimbaud and Nerval of French Canada. I discovered Nelligan only to find that he was no such thing, but someone entirely other and much nearer to me, while on a visit to Montreal in 1988.

I'd gone there for a poetry festival but really because the idea of the North had attracted me ever since I read the legend of the Hyperboreans, a race who dwelt somewhere above the north wind, neither east nor west, in ancient times and may be up there yet in some favored enclave where they have a climate like that of Southern California, live a thousand years on sweet herbs and fruit salads, and are peaceful, disease-free, and indolent. Also, according to Theosophy, they are all twins, and their land marks a threshold between this world and the beyond, a zone of circumpolar twilight on the other side of which the lucky traveler emerges in a lucid region of invisibility such as the one I expected Nelligan would be bound to speak of, were I to insist.

Such expectations were more than borne out by a sonnet titled "Le Vaisseau d'Or" (The Golden Ship) in which this teenage denizen of the imagined northern paradise likened his mind to a light-filled hull on an ocean floor.

A basic issue in 19th-century Science that has again become a hot topic is that of mirror-imaging: from the right- and left-hand crystals studied by Pasteur to the whole situation as translated into fantasy by Lewis Carroll in *Through the Looking-Glass*. Mirror-imaging is also intrinsic to the mechanics of vision—the camera inside the eyeball—and of thinking itself: right lobe, left lobe, and so on. To move back and forth between the two is a matter of orientation. One must know where the sun comes up and where north is; and to become disoriented means to lose the north as well as the east.

The traveling itself is magical, because the gap between the two dimensions is empty and invisible. The spark crossing that gap is language. There are several ways to magnetize and potentiate the word. One is repetition; and another, sometimes even more powerful, is rhyme. To make two unrelated words vibrate in unison is to make two propositions mirror each other. Rhyme can make imagined configurations crystallize. To generate rhyme is to link the binary principle of mirror-imaging with the randomness basic to chaos, as in the *I Ching*. I am a pun, wrote Nijinsky after he went mad. Émile Nelligan could have said, I'm a rhyme. His whole world was double. The bilingual culture wherein, despite his name, he was French not Irish; the family in which his given name Émile, like his face, mirrored his mother Émilie's.

The real turn-of-the-century Montreal was a city of 360,000, one of the biggest seaports on earth, with as many churches as Warsaw and tens of thousands of spic-and-span maplewood interiors crowded with crucifixes and religious pictures, portraits of Napoleon Bonaparte and Pope Leo XIII, lamps with red globes, flower baskets upheld by porcelain cherubs, and samplers with mottos such as "No Rose Without a Thorn" in a reek of bergamot, camphor, and patent hair oil, where I am a fly on the wall this evening of May 26, 1899, looking at a room crowded with some two hundred poetry lovers lit up by a spectacular sunset flooding the windows in a rainbow of tropical colors. It's a reading, and the poet is Émile:

> *. . . I'm high! The crystal rings. Let May wine pour*
> *Bubbling out of the barrel! Bring me more!*
> *Let me forget how real life daily passes*
> *Me by, how I despise the sneering masses . . .*
>
> *Whether he gnash his teeth or flash a grin*
> *A man like me's an object of disdain*
> *And has no one to comfort his chagrin*
> *Save for a moonbeam or a hurricane . . .*
>
> *The stars are coming out and I am sorry,*
> *The dying day I rage against, uncouth,*
> *Out of step with the year's advancing glory,*
> *Staggering in the pitch-black night of youth . . .*

Émile finishes his poem "Romance of Wine" with blazing eyes and wildly exaggerated gestures. A thrill of emotion grips the hall. Frenzied ovation. The boy poet is carried in triumph on his comrades' shoulders through the twilight to his parents' house. The crowd includes his mother and 17-year-old sister Eva, as well as Anne-Marie Gleason, a family friend, and a handful of schoolmates who have never dreamed that Émile might win glory. Standing apart is a 35-year-old monk named Eugène Seers, who has copies of everything Émile has ever written and intends to publish Émile. He fears for Émile's sanity. Émile just told Seers that he has been staying in for weeks, and the objects in his room are coming to life, singing to him by day, and by night he is seeing things in the dark, visions of beautiful women, and then terrifying, horrible things that he cannot describe.

> *The big red ox with seagreen horns*
> *Mooing in a ghastly death-rattle*
> *Haunts the pastures where our cattle*
> *Graze in the sunset on the hill.*
>
> *Stop your singing, cease your prattle*
> *In the elms at dusk, boys and girls.*
> *The big red ox with seagreen horns*
> *Haunts the sunset in your curls.*
>
> *Beware, beware, he means you ill,*
> *You belles and bubs in lace and rags.*
> *Adjust your skirts, hike up your bags,*
> *Flee through the fields and trenchant thorns*
>
> *The big red ox with seagreen horns.*

Consider this photo of Émilie Nelligan, Émile's mother, taken sometime in the mid-1890s: a dramatic, sensuous, perverse, pre-Raphaelite gorgon in a pearl-gray silk dress embroidered with tiny black beads, her lustrous auburn hair heaped in serpentine coils round a seraphic face that is the face of her Émile. Both mother and son are beautiful. "A dreamy, tormented Apollo with very dark, shining eyes," Seers has noted of Émile. And Émilie's face has the dramatic beauty of a Medusa imagined by Oscar Wilde or painted by Burne-Jones. This 40-year-old mother of two girls and a boy is her teenage son's identical twin. Her face is a glass in which he gazes at himself.

Mother and children have long summered at Peek-à-boo Villa, the family's vacation home in the Saint Lawrence resort of Cacouna. (The place-name means Abode of Porcupines in Algonkian.) Émilie used to be in the habit of reading out loud to Émile: Lamartine, Hugo, Gautier. Émile prefers Baudelaire, Verlaine, Rollinat. Medusa hearkens, and her snakes uncurl.

The father is away in a remote universe. Postal Inspector General of Quebec Province, the 49-year-old David Nelligan speaks with an accent but is rarely heard. At least he is not English, but Irish Catholic. The Celtic strain is the only shared trait that Émile will ever be able to acknowledge. Émile has never exchanged a word of English with his mother, yet the inside cover of one of his poetic notebooks bears a rhyming self-description in English, in case his father opens the book:

> *He is a dreamer, for all the time*
> *His mind is wedded unto rhyme . . .*

At the Collège de Sainte-Marie in Montreal, Émile won first prizes in Latin and Greek and French composition, and a second prize in English, but failed at everything else. Last summer, after dropping out, he made a voyage as the bursar's assistant on a steamer bound for England, a berth his father had obtained for him. On returning to Montreal, Émile jumped ship. His father got him a job as a clerk in a countinghouse. He walked out after a few days. His father has not spoken to him since.

Émile did not lose his virginity either on shipboard or in the stews of Liverpool. Émile's is an innocence untainted by experience. But something happened to his head in mid-Atlantic:

> *There was a ship built all of solid gold;*
> *Her mast touched sky above an unknown sea;*
> *Her figurehead a naked Venus, she*
> *Ran in the excessive sun and danced and rolled.*
>
> *But one dark night she ran into a reef*
> *In that false ocean where the sirens sang;*
> *Horribly wrecked, she foundered and the deep*
> *Immutably entombed her as she sank.*
>
> *She was a golden ship. You could see through*
> *Her sides all the treasure that profane crew*
> *Disgust, Hate, Nerves disputed for their cut.*
>
> *What's left of her, now that it storms no more?*
> *Oh what became of my abandoned heart?*
> *Alas, she's dreaming on the ocean floor.*

An unquiet ocean, an ominous sky. Twenty crewmen remain on the raft, now weeks adrift on the open sea, but of them five are dead or dying. An old man weeps over an expired youth whose torso, fallen back from a last attempt to breathe, sprawls across his lap. The dead boy is naked, his exposed genitals occupying a midpoint in the left-hand foreground. Lugubrious seas and menacing clouds of a more than merely natural beauty frame the scene. Near the top of the composition's upper right-hand corner, two men have climbed onto the crates and barrels at the stern of the raft and are waving rags white and red as signals towards a patch of dimly sunlit clouds at the horizon, at the center of which a dot, the brig *Argus*, heaves into view. The tallest figure, a black man, is stripped to the waist, sunlight glistening on his muscular back as he waves his red rag. At the raft's edge an exhausted crewman tries to raise himself but is prevented by the death-grip of a man who has just died clutching at his legs. Next to the ship's surgeon, a bug-eyed sailor seems to be giggling.

Such was the raft of the *Medusa*. Such is the raft that will drift on with the tattered remnants of Émile's mind after his golden ship has gone to Davy Jones's locker, a scandalous event that Émile fears may happen any time now:

> *Oh what became of my abandoned heart?*
> *Alas, she dreams beneath the forest floor*
> *For nothing could have edified me more*
>
> *Than sea-chanties marooned on a far shore,*
> *Snakes dying on the captain's bridge alone:*
> *The world will not get better on its own.*

Here is a theory about the golden ship. One day a porthole opened in Émile's chest. He looked inside and saw his heart. It had turned into a chamber of pinkish quartz the size of a mountain, whose walls he found himself passing through as though they were of air instead of stone, expanding and contracting rhythmically, as rivers shot past, streaming down their sides. On a crag where the mountain broke off over a gulf beyond which he glimpsed a golden vista interrupted by an advancing rack of thunderheads, there was a sunlit spot where, as if looking down from above, he sees himself stark naked in his naked mother's embrace, swooning in the warmth of her smile. If only it could go on forever. The smile broadens. I was born on Christmas Eve 1879. At the moment of my birth, the heavens stopped turning. About to draw my first breath, I opened my eyes and glimpsed the mouth that was disgorging me from my sojourn in the dark just seconds past, and I screamed. The room began to turn. The ceiling opened to a night sky full of stars, in which sheets of colored lights moved to the beat of *In dulci jubilo*. Wavelike they swell and peak, only to crash back again into the petrific chaos of my mother's serpent-tressed, horribly gaping Gorgonian aegis of a . . . I can't say it.

> *At times she lays her clean hands on my head,*
> *And they are white as whitely rustling lace;*
>
> *Then murmuring in tones golden and sad,*
> *She leans over to kiss me on the face,*
>
> *With eyes the color of my dreams, no other—*
> *O poetry, O ecstasy, O Mother!*
>
> *Her feet I wet with tears, her flame I fan—*
> *I am her baby always, though a man.*

Émile confides to Seers: "I will die insane, like Baudelaire."

To claim poetry—that is, the invention of life through language—as one's sole occupation suffices in the Montreal of 1899 to ensure one's incarceration as a lunatic. Will Émile make it past the turn of the century and still be at large in 1900?

As shepherds in the red dusk went to hurry
Their big black goats with golden-wheezing flutes
And pressed on homewards from beyond the buttes
Along a hedgerow bristling with holly,

Schoolboy gypsies fresh from our study halls
With chalk dust in our hair, virginity,
Ink blotches, and unstained serenity,
We hunted nuts and laughed at waterfalls;

And, in the valley where a sheepdog ran
Yapping before the tranquil sons of Pan
Whose piping floated plaintive down the brae,

Although our coats were thin and rations sparse
Still radiant in our palaces of hay
We breakfasted on dawn and supped on stars.

Since the age of sixteen, Émile has written a hundred-odd poems and published twenty-three of them under pseudonyms. Recently he joined a writers' club, the École Littéraire de Montréal, that has organized a series of public readings. The École Littéraire declares itself independent of politics and religion, in other words, of the Church. Nelligan Senior considers it a subversive group. The École has twenty members. Émile enrolled under the pseudonym of E. Lennigan. Among these stylishly mustachioed and bearded worthies with their slicked-down hair amid potted palms, Émile is the angelic incongruity.

Émile is in love with a teenage German immigrant named Margaret. He has never got up the courage to speak to Margaret, but in his fantasies nicknames her Gretchen and has already written several poems to and about her. Aware that the relationship is purely imaginary, Émilie encourages Émile to develop the theme. In one text Émile pictures himself and his beloved living together as Bohemians in a garret, it is unclear whether in wedlock or in sin. Both conditions present equally breathtaking possibilities. They have acquired three parrots:

> *I had them up from Baton Rouge,*
> *With their eyes as clear as springwater*
> *And talk learnt from a gigolo:*

> *Three lamp-lit shadows wavering huge*
> *As Gretchen fed them from a saucer*
> *And I played on the piccolo . . .*

Seventy years from now a writer named Ducharme is going to reinvent the loves of Gretchen and Émile in a pair of teenage runaways (whose idol is Émile Nelligan) in a Montreal rooming house where they will, alas, end quite badly—in a novel, *Le nez qui vogue*, whose title might be translated "The Quivocal Shnozz."

Émile has no way of knowing it, but one Professor Freud in Vienna is even now preparing a bombshell which includes the revelation that in dream language the shnozz equals the shvantz (which some might consider to be yet another statement of the obvious).

Émile has a fear of turning into stone. He often feels himself starting to petrify, especially at moments when he wishes himself dead. If a statue gets mutilated, what parts will be the first to go? As the mind closes on itself, that stoniness increases. When the member rises in a boy's pants and will not go down, it feels hard as a rock.

Mount Royal Park, with its stone fauns and other sculptures, puts Émile in mind of the City of Statues in the *Thousand and One Nights*. Don Giovanni was pursued by his stone Commander; Émile is haunted by a voluptuous gorgon whose head of snaky hair Freud would say is a displacement upward of his fear of castration that stems from having glimpsed the female genitalia surrounded by hair and essentially those of his mother. Yet it is inconceivable that any such glimpse could ever have been afforded in fin-de-siècle middle class Montreal. Never mind, says Freud. The snakes both resemble and replace the penis, whose absence is the cause of the horror.

Herman Melville (1851): "Though in many of its aspects the visible world seems formed in love, the invisible spheres were formed in fright."

The gorgon face is indestructible. It is the face of lightning. Athena carries it—the aegis, magical goatskin—on her left shoulder. The word gorgon means horror. From her severed head is born Pegasus, the winged horse whose hoof striking the side of a mountain, Mount Helicon, causes the spring Hippocrene, source of poetic inspiration, to gush forth.

Émile is an adolescent Faust pursued by a phantom Gretchen with arms of an ethereal whiteness like the whiteness of Parian marble, looming tall as the beacon at Rhodes that was anciently one of the seven wonders of the world. The Gretchen poems can start on a note of chromolithographic porn—the theme of pale beauty is, after all, really about violation, bleeding 'em white, à la Sade—but when his female subject turns into "a polished tusk" and comes up out of the depths to get him, Nelligan begins to sound an authentically original, visionary note:

She looks like certain beauties by Rubens,
An even calmer majesty than theirs.
Her golden voice evokes soft mandolins
At balconies in Venice, mellow airs.

Her hair recalls a shower of light-filled rain,
Her step's a sigh of milk-white muslin, plain
And simple as an angel glimpsed at dusk;
Her skin is gleaming like a polished tusk.

That golden skin, that strange blond hair disguises
I know not what. Look at her there, she rises
(Is she from Eden or some black abyss?)

Like a young tree lifting its supple charms
Out of bottomless depths. Beware of this
Man-killing Pharos with its marble arms.

If priestcraft were not a primary strand in the weave of Émile's doom, a priest would have to be (like the God he serves) invented. Picture a cleric who not only excels in the imitation of Christ, but at dinners may range from droll impersonations of amusing little people to philippics against evil in high places, for instance, 10 Downing Street or the Rothschild bank, a man of rock-hard principles who is resolutely pro-Boer and above all, anti-Dreyfus. Some such figure looms large in the lace-curtain Catholicism of the background. Poems such as Émile's "Murderers of God" don't pop out of thin air.

More recently, Émile has composed a number of bawdily irreverent pieces—one, for instance, in which a fat-faced man of God fondles a servant girl. Copies of these he has given his friend Seers who is currently working as a typesetter for *The Little Messenger of the Holy Sacrament*, a Church newsletter.

Born in 1865, Seers is about to publish (anonymously) a volume of devotional poems, his first book. He has also been collecting Émile's work as long as they have known each other. He will be the first to engage in publishing Émile in book form. Working by night, he will set Émile's poetry in type, in defiance of a ban on outside jobs. He will have laid out page seventy when found out. In consequence of his disobedience, he is to be banished to Cambridge, Massachusetts, where he will break with the Church, live with a Black woman from Roxbury, and work as a printer for Harvard University Press. Upon leaving Montreal in 1903 he will turn the project over to Émilie, who will have the distinction of preserving Émile for posterity, his muse become his editor. She will avail herself of Seers's further help in seeing the book through the press, and even accept a study written by him under the pen name of Louis Dantin for its introduction. The book will appear in 1904. As the introduction puts it: "In his mother Émile found a delicate and sure literary sense capable of vibrating in unison with his own."

But to return to the summer of 1899. One day Émile refuses to read Émilie his latest work. Words are exchanged. Émilie screams: It is impossible that my son has written things his mother must not read!

Émile walks out.

Holding each other close without a sound
All through that flaming golden June day, we
Were dreaming on our feet, forever wound
In deep embrace. Night fell triumphantly.

We ambled up a flight of granite steps;
Young trees gave off an opiated scent;
A mottled group of misplaced marble shapes
Slouched haughtily, massively somnolent.

From inside of an old refreshment stand
We heard screams of a maniac crazed by bells
Clamoring till engulfed in silence, and

Imagining an empty sculptured eye
Was eyeing us, we cringed, ourselves mere shells.
We held each other close, my Pain and I.

Over the next few weeks Émile stays with various relatives and friends, a night here, a night there. He can wander through Montreal for days without sleeping. Fantasies about death predominate. He is turning into a triton. Pearls are his eyes. When the gorgon's face pressed his seaweed hair, it stood up in a coral tree. Underwater his limbs are still pliant, but in the wind they turn to stone. He has a dream in which an unnamed *she* is dead. The female other has left him behind with nothing but the funeral music ringing in his head. He awakens suddenly to a realization that it's not her funeral, but his:

. . . I always did love the funereal silence
Of a sacred parlor, abrim with violence
You can't hear, or music that's soundless save
For a tingling as of a gathering wave,
In which I seek the soul that I forsook,
A sad omission in a long-closed book . . .

On August 9, 1899 Émile is put in a Montreal asylum. Shame and silence surround the event. The most frequent visitor will be his sister Eva, who will bring writing materials. Several notebooks will survive. Many others will be confiscated and destroyed. Émile is never to see his father again.

After three years Émilie comes to the asylum on her first and last visit. Her reason for coming is to get Émile to retract a handful of scandalous anticlerical lampoons that Eugène Seers has been intending to put in the book. Émilie's friend Anne-Marie Gleason accompanies her. Anne-Marie's record of the scene appears in the Montreal newspaper *La Patrie* on November 14, 1902:

. . . Gasping next to the white bed where a part of her own life lies slumbering, she hugs her adored baby to her bosom so he will feel the pounding of a mother's heart. Do sons ever grow up for their mothers? Supporting the young poet's head on her breast, she whispers sublime endearments. He smiles from his fever as though dreaming of Paradise. She has reconquered the child in the man! He opens his eyes. He's going to speak. She trembles, fearing a repetition of earlier delirious mutterings. Alas, we've come a long way from the days when we breakfasted on dawn and supped on stars. The poetic steeplechase came to a brutal finish. He had got so far ahead of himself, poor child, he fell flat,

his face still turned toward the sun, his mind on fire from too much brilliance. He says, 'Mama, you know, those poems that made you cry? I'm sorry I ever wrote them. I repudiate them. Mama, please tell everyone I retracted them. Émile Nelligan wishes he never wrote those poems. This is my amends to you, Mama, I swear to God.' He closed his eyes. The boy poet's mind wandered away in a night of dreams. His mother turned and said to me, 'Please tell this to my son's friends, so the memory of Émile Nelligan can be as sweet and pure as his love for his mother.' I was moved to the bottom of my heart by the exquisite good sense of this mother who was able to forget her pain and smooth over her heartrending memories in order to save a sleeping poet's reputation from the faintest stain. She wished for her son to have written only the poetry his mother would read . . .

The foregoing is published under the headline: "Spiritual Testament to the Friends of Émile Nelligan."

Émilie's side of this story can only be surmised. But consider: it was Émilie who was the first to nurture Émile's genius, she who formed his juvenile taste and talent, she who encouraged his adolescent dreams. A beautiful and intelligent woman trapped in a marriage with a strait-laced, utterly unimaginative government official discovers that her little boy is not only as handsome as herself but, a mirror reflection of her own soul, specially gifted in ways that in this narrow milieu are for a long time visible to her alone. Small wonder that in her lonely isolation such a woman would develop an unusual bond with her son. Had Émile not succumbed so young, had he succeeded in separating himself and growing into an adult, what may have appeared monstrous and gorgonlike in Émilie might only seem rather amusingly reprehensible, at worst.

Émilie is the mute in this play. It is impossible to know why she turns her back on Émile in the end. She never gets to tell her woes. Once he has been hospitalized for good and she controls the publication project, it is within her power to suppress the book, or to bowdlerize it, and she does neither. Émilie and Émile are like an amoeba that gave off poetry while splitting apart. Once separated, the new cells no longer recognize each other.

Émile ages rapidly, seems prematurely old to visitors and curiosity seekers. Like Hölderlin before him, he receives with exquisite graciousness. After a decade, one visitor reports, "The literary obsession continues." Émile is not, however, allowed to have books, not even a copy of his own book. He fills the blank notebooks his sister brings with poems, his own and other poets', transcribed from memory.

In 1913 Émilie dies. In 1924, upon the decease of David Nelligan, Émile is transferred to a public asylum. The cost of maintaining a custodial patient in a public hospital is about $400 a year in the mid-1920s. For the past quarter-century up until his own death, Émile's father has been spending much more than that to provide Émile with a modicum of comfort and good treatment. Some friends obtain permission to take Émile out for a holiday excursion around the time of his father's death. The experiment fails. Émile is put back in.

One evening in 1932, Émile's poetry is recited on Radio Montreal. They bring him to the asylum wireless set to listen.

He listens but withholds any reaction.

> *As in a lyric by Verlaine*
> *With tears ad infinitum*
> *Finally to deflect their pain*
> *(Bat 'em, boot 'em, bite 'em)*

These days with flaming haloes rip
The vault of heaven asunder
Meanwhile Mr Frog may dip
One toe and keep it under

Time passes and the Cyclops year
Reflects equivoco
For Summer's mirror will outleer
The smirking sosieko

On various occasions Émile is persuaded to recite. Sometimes he gets a fellow patient, a violinist, to accompany. He tells them: Poetry minus music does not communicate. No one takes away the notebooks anymore. No one imagines anything is happening in the notebooks, either. Émile is tranquilly staring at the pale blue ocean of the sky. As Góngora put it:

Because Medusa's bound to petrify
The only nightingale that needs to cry,
His woe is neither published nor suppressed.

November 18, 1941. Émile has just received the last rites of the Church. For hours he has been gazing at a chromolithograph of the Mother of God, a wooden crucifix clasped to his chest.

A Basic Document

"Many works of the Ancients have become fragments.
Many works of the Moderns are fragments the moment
they come into being."
— Friedrich Schlegel (1798)

Friedrich Hölderlin's Pindaric Fragments (1803) have never been
seen for what they are—a basic and deeply important statement of
latter-day poetics. Harking back as they do to an obsession with
Greece extraordinary even for his time, Hölderlin's translations of
the celebrated ancient Theban bard Pindar, and his writings based
on them, make strange reading. They have been viewed as a document of psychosis when in fact they relate most cogently to poetic
theory and practice. In 1988 an American editor suggested that I
take my version of the Pindaric Fragments to a journal of German
studies. He didn't get it. Hölderlin's work on Pindar has nothing to
do with German studies, but with the future of discourse. In my
translation, the Hölderlin versions of the fragments are in italics and
his amplifications in roman. In translating them I have consulted
the Greek but followed Hölderlin's personal liberties. My friend the
art historian Gert Schiff helped me elucidate an often-difficult
German text.

The Faithlessness of Wisdom

Have a mind like the hide
of a rock-clinging octopus, my son.
Boost each city you are in, and
speak kindly of whatever is in front of you.
Then think another way another time.

Fitness of the lonesome school for the world. The innocence of
pure science as the soul of discretion. For discretion is the art of
keeping faith under varying circumstances, science the art of
being reliable in one's use of one's reason in spite of positive
errors. When the reason is intensively exercised, it maintains its
power even among the distracted; if it easily recognizes the alien
by virtue of its own fine-honed acuteness, it is all the less easily
led astray in situations of uncertainty. Thus Jason, a pupil of the
Centaur, confronted Pelias:

I believe I do have
Chiron's lore, for I come from the Centaur's
cave where his holy daughters
and wife and mother Chariclo and Philyra
raised me. Twenty years, though,
in which I never said or did them dirt
I spent in there
and come home now
to reclaim my father's kingship.

Of Truth

Mover of grand virtue, Queen Truth,
don't let my thinking run
into a crude lie.

Fear of truth because it gives pleasure. That is to say, the first vivid apprehension of it in the vivid sense is, like every pure feeling, prone to confusion; so that one errs out of no fault of one's own, or disturbance, either, but on account of the higher object, for which, in proportion to it, sense is too weak.

Of Peace

Let any who can calm the commons
discover the light-filled holiness of manly peace
and let him check that mutinous
hurricane in his heart. It
makes for woe, wars
on the educators of the young.

Before the laws (which are the light-filled holiness of manly peace) can be discovered, someone, a lawgiver or a prince, in line with a nation's particular destiny, whether precipitous or stable, and the degree of existing popular receptivity, must tranquilly apprehend the character of that destiny, whether it incline to a monarchy or a commonwealth in people's relations, to usurpation as the Greek sons of nature were wont to do, or to custom as among educated folk. For the laws are the means of fixing that destiny in its tranquility. What originally applied to the prince applies by imitation to the true citizen.

Of the Dolphin

of the dolphin
whom an irresistible piping of flutes made dance
in the ocean's motionless deep

Nature sings in the Muses' weather as clouds float by like fluff over a budding glaze of golden petals and at such a moment each living thing strikes up its own tune in fidelity to itself and its integrity. Only the differences in species make for division in Nature, so that the whole is more song and pure voice than accent of necessity, or, conversely, speech.

It is the motionless deep, where the Tritons' pipe echoes sap rising in the water's tender flora to stimulate this mutable fish.

The Supreme

Law,
Lord of mortals and
immortals all, which executes
with omnipotent
vigor the most righteous justice.

Rigorously speaking, the immediate is impossible for both mortals and immortals. The god must distinguish between worlds in accordance with divine nature. Heavenly grace means unadulterated holiness. A human acting as a cognitive subject must also distinguish between worlds because cognition is possible only through opposition. Hence, rigorously speaking, the immediate is impossible for both mortals and immortals.

However, rigorous indirection is the law.

Therefore it executes with omnipotent vigor the most righteous justice.

Discipline, as far as it represents that *imago* wherein each, whether man or god, comes face to face with himself, the law of church and state, and inherited rules (the holiness of a god, and, for humans, the possibility of a cognition, a flash of insight) all execute with omnipotent vigor the most righteous justice; more rigorous than art, they make permanent the viable conditions under which a nation has ever come face to face with itself and continues to do so. 'Lord' here stands for the superlative degree, which is merely the sign for the deepest ground of cognition, not for supreme power.

Age

If a man lives right
and fears God

sweet Hope goes with him
warming his heart, and
gives him long life, being a
mainstay
of changeful mortal purpose.

One of the loveliest images of living: how guiltless morals keep the heart lively, and then there is Hope; and this in turn imparts to simplicity a flowering-time for complex endeavors, and makes the mind changeful, thus lengthening life by dint of the deliberation of alacrity.

The Infinite

Whether to scale the lofty battlement of justice
or that of humped deceit
and so overstep my own boundaries
is a thing I am of two minds
about going into precise details on.

The sage will have his jest; one might almost say the riddle ought not be solved. The wavering, the struggle between justice and common sense can be resolved only on a continuum, 'a thing I am of two minds about going into precise details on.' That I should then uncover the link between justice and common sense, itself ascribable to neither of the latter but to a third factor by means of which they are connected by infinitely precise detail (the infinite) is a thing I am of two minds about.

The Asylums

First the celestial Seasons
whisked prudent Themis
on golden steeds
up and away past Ocean's salt

to Olympus'
ladder of holy ascent and
sparkling return, to be
Savior Zeus's
eldest girl,
but she gave birth and her offspring were
goodly gold-filleted
sparkling-fruited sanctuaries.

Sit as a man may (if, owing to a thirst for perfection, his mind found no peace on earth or in heaven until, face to face with his own destiny, the god and man knew himself anew by the marks of old discipline) in the memory of primal misery a son of Themis gladly stays wherever he can.

Themis, that lover of order, has given birth to the asylums of man, his silent retreats which no alien thing can harm, for the action and vitality of nature were concentrated in them, and whoever intuits their existence learns (as if through remembrance) what they learned long ago.

The Enlivener

Once the Centaurs discovered the
man-mastering
violence
of the honey-sweet wine
they shoved away
the white milk and the table
with their hands, and

guzzling uninvited from the silver horns
drank themselves silly.

The concept 'centaurs' is surely that of the spirit of a stream, in that the latter makes for itself a path and a boundary by doing violence to the pathless primeval flowering Earth.

This is why the centaur image occurs, in those localities where a riverbank is rich in rockface and caves, especially in spots where the primeval stream sought to leave the mountain chain, obliquely ripping out a path for itself. On that account, centaurs are also the originators of the natural sciences, for in the light of such primeval violence nature is most readily understandable.

In such regions, the stream must originally have meandered in oxbows before tearing open a straight path for itself. That is how wetlands and underground mammal dens like the ones next to ponds were formed. In those times, the centaur was a savage shepherd, like Cyclops in the *Odyssey*. The flooding water swelled with longing to discover a direction of its own. However, the more solid the dry land became on either bank, taking its orientation from securely rooted trees, shrubs, and vines, the more the stream, set in motion by the configuration of the bank, had to acquire its direction and, impelled by its very wellspring, break through at the weakest point in the mountain wall hemming it in.

Once the centaurs *discovered the violence of the honey-sweet wine,* they took their motion and direction from the solid, thickly forested bank. *And shoved away the white milk and table with their hands,* the cresting wave did violence to the peaceful pond. Also, the whole way of life on the riverbank underwent a change. The invasion of the wild woods, with the first settlers—those lords of the forest, raiders and reivers, in their lairs—threw the lazy life of the open heath into an uproar. The steep bluff held the stagnant flood water in check, till it grew arms, and so, on its own *guzzling uninvited from the silver horns*, made itself a path, acquired a destination.

The *Poems of Ossian* are, in particular, genuine Centaur poetry sung with the spirit of the stream and as though by the Greek Chiron, who taught Achilles how to play the lyre.

To Hölderlin, Pindar was the supreme poet, the highest model one could aspire to follow. In this, Hölderlin was only dilating on the view of Pindar that was universally held in his day. Blake for instance once did 116 watercolors illustrating poems of Thomas Gray including Gray's Pindaric odes "The Progress of Poesy" and "The Bard." The very first depicts, in Blake's own words, *The Pindaric Genius receiving his Lyre*. A rosy, well-muscled poetic mind astride a high-flying swan reaches for the instrument of art as it pops out of thin air quivering with Energy and Delight. This was in 1798. Hölderlin was to carry the same notion much further. When the centuries changed, from 1799 to 1800, he abandoned the classical meters for free verse—the bound for the boundless— via a translation of seventeen odes by Pindar. Two years later, while working on the *Antigone* of Sophocles for a publisher who had just issued his version of the *Oedipus*, Hölderlin returned to Pindar, but this time to the back-matter as it were, the Fragments, of which there were about two hundred. Fewer than a dozen of these short meditations on randomly chosen kernel-texts survive. As the critic I.A. Richards used to say, a book is a machine to think with. Work on the Pindaric fragments actually began one year after Hölderlin was struck (or imagined he was struck) by lightning on a mountain in France, and a strange philosophic afterglow filled the window of his room at home in Germany. He jotted down an insight: Fire = Tragedy. His "Note on Oedipus" was to enlarge on that: "The representation of the tragic consists primarily in that the monstrous fact that the divine and the human commingle and the power of nature and man's innermost self become one in boundless rage may be grasped as a boundless tendency to oneness purging itself through boundless separation." The pyrotechnic rarefies to the etheric, the heroic to the ideal, rajas to sattva. At the turn of the century, he'd done the seventeen victory odes into an idiom neither German nor Greek—German words in pseudo-Greek word-order chosen for their correspondences of sound, gender, number, and so forth. 150 years before, the English poet Abraham Cowley had said that if anybody ever attempted this with Pindar it would sound like one madman translating another. Starting with Pindar's First Olympian in 1799:

> *First Thing is Water of course; like Gold,*
> *Fire flaring*
> *Flashes in the Night, a*
> *Gift from Pluto.*
> *You're here, though, dear Heart,*
> *To sing of Victory*
> *And search no shining Face*
> *Of fresher glow*
> *Than noonday Sun*
> *Solo in Ether . . .*

Hölderlin had a scheme of correspondences:

Water = naive tone = Epic
Fire = heroic tone = Tragic
Ether = ideal tone = Hymnic

So (according to Hölderlin) the opening of Pindar's First Olympian is naming First Philosophers' First Principles:

Water (Thales)
Fire (Heraclitus)
Ether (Anaximander)

To make it work, Hölderlin turns Pindar's "Water is Best" line into "First Thing is Water of course" = seven syllables as in the original,

Ariston men to hudor = Das erste is wohl das Wasser

so that the words *erste* ("first") and *ariston* as well as the word-order in both lines approximate a perfect match. Also, Pindar actually wrote that "Gold like fire shines by night." This, however, Hölderlin reverses, the better to illustrate a shining Heraclitean darkness.

Pindarum quisquis studet aemulari . . .

People do keep trying to rival Pindar,
So they put on Daedalus' wings of wax and
Rise up, soaring, only to tumble head first
Splat in the ocean . . .

As a stream pouring down a mountain headlong
Overflows its regular banks in springtime,
Pindar's language, seething with boundless power,
Opens the floodgates

Whether gods or kings or the seed of Heaven,
Heroes, form his theme, or the Centaurs rightly
Quelled by them soon after Chimaera's dreadful
Flame was extinguished . . .

When Horace wrote these lines comparing Pindar's language to a seething mountain stream, he echoed lines in the *Aeneid* where Virgil likens the descent of the Centaurs from clouds to the birth of a river, poetic language as a white-water stream high in the mountains, and that in turn personified by the half-horse, half-human figure of Chiron, teacher of music and medicine to Aesclepius, Jason, and Achilles. To Max Jacob, Centaurs represented the primal Adam, and he wrote of meeting one in broad daylight on a road in France. To Kenneth Grahame, author of *Wind in the Willows*, the Centaur was an avatar that humanity could and maybe should have become, but did not. Hölderlin's take on Centaurs goes back to a greater psychic and chronological depth. At the Indo-European level, Centaurs were Hellenic equivalents of the Indian Gandharvas, the celestial musicians who imparted raga to the seers. To Hölderlin they were the Indo-Europeans in person. By creating a river of song, of forward motion both measured and unmeasured, of invasion and migration, the Centaurs of the Greeks link up with the horse-taming sky-adoring patriarchal conquerors of the prehistoric lands ruled by women. They represent the beginning of the 4,000-year binge that is recorded history. Their ancestor

Ixion fucked a cloud shaped in the image of Hera, Queen of Heaven, consort of the sky-father, who punishes Ixion by binding him to a forever-revolving wheel, where spread-eagled, he moves in the shape of a forward-leaping swastika representing history as reckoned by the solar calendar. Never mind the fact that late 20th-century scholarship has shot down this image of the hard-riding Aryans—to Hölderlin it was real.

Centaur = river of language. It both nurtures and destroys. It is a double thing, a divided state, psyche versus spirit, half rajas, half sattva. "A thing I am of two minds about."

Also: suspension of everyday law and order. Excess, violence. Drunkenness, lust, adultery. Centaurs are also teachers of music and medicine.

A Centaur guided Saint Antony when he was searching for Paul the Hermit in the Egyptian desert.

To quote Virgil:

Just as Centaurs born from a cloud crash down a mountain
Tearing a boisterous swath through all in the path of
their onrush . . .

As at the center, so at the remotest points along the periphery. In Ireland their king fucked a mare. In India their queen fucked a stallion. Concerning those hell-for-leather Indo-Europeans, Hölderlin was of two minds. The shock by lightning on a mountain in France in the spring of 1802 gave him a measure of distance. The Hymns to the Fatherland, the Pindaric Fragments, and the rhyming nature poems came after. His father had died when Hölderlin was two years old. His mother was an ordinary middle-class person who wanted to see her son settled down in a respectable profession, married to a good match. Instead, the young Hölderlin longed to breathe the high stratosphere, reunited with Father Helios, and at the same time yearned to lose himself in the dark caverns of Mother Earth. He had written a novel in which the love of his life *Diotima* (actually a banker's wife, Susette Gontard, with whom he had had an adulterous liaison while living in her home as tutor to the Gontard children) died when separated from him, and when this really happened blamed himself and imagined he had killed her because he had written it that way in the novel. Three years later, when Hölderlin was already settled in the tower on the Neckar at Tübingen where he was to spend the last forty years of his life, one of his many visitors reported in a letter dated July 11, 1805, "Hölderlin, half-crazed as ever, is also haruspicating Pindar." The Pindaric Fragments still preserved today date from the fall of 1803, however. The fruits of the haruspications mentioned in the letter of July 11, 1805 have never come to light.

When the Centaur-siring Titan Ixion fucked the cloud, he not only imagined he was possessing sky queen Hera but fooling sky father Zeus. Pindar drew the moral:

> *Poti kentron de toi laktizein*
> *Telethei olistheros oimos . . .*

> *To kick against the goad*
> *Is a slippery way . . .*

Hölderlin translated:

> *Gegen den Stachel zu lecken, wird ein*
> *Schlüpfriger Pfad . . .*

On a mountain road near Damascus, Pindar's words were quoted by Jesus when He appeared to the future Paul inside a blinding light:

It hurts you to kick against the goad.

Euripides in the *Bacchae* has Dionysus say the same thing to the raging Pentheus when the latter is about to be decapitated and devoured by his mother and her sister Maenads. Hölderlin identified with the rebellious Titan, and the obtuse king, as well as the recalcitrant receiver of the light which is a yoke (zugon, yoga) that Pindar says is best accepted and borne lightly:

Pherein d'elaphros epaukhomenon zugon aregei . . .

In Hölderlin's version:

Zu tragen aber leicht
Auf dem Nacken, wenn es einer empfangen hat
Das Joch, dies hilft ihm . . .

But to bear the yoke lightly
On his neck, when he has received it,
Helps . . .

Soon it will be exactly 200 years since Hölderlin was the first to jump the whole way into the nonlinear—that is, from the central-nervous mode into a nerve-net mode encompassing the fleeting whims of time like a self-propelled butterfly net. His discovery is the air we breathe. Each of his Pindaric fragments is a hologram, a chunk of shadow bonded with light. Note the urgent union of two pressures, systolic, diastolic, concentration and release; also, the present tense—in a space of extinct thoughts and actions—listening for an as yet unimaginable machine that will set forth the grammar of the Millennium.

In Nomine

"Ranging the symptoms separately, one beneath the other,
start a fresh line with each new circumstance mentioned
by the patient or friends."
— Samuel Hahnemann, *Organon of Medicine* (1833)

One July evening in 1989, while riding the Greyhound between
Hartford and Springfield, I covered a notebook page with question
marks, which I drew to look like things that hiss and crepitate: ears,
waves, conchs, swans, scorpions, a poised cobra. What was that
icecold tea doing in a can, and Planter's Peanuts in a plastic pouch
no bigger than a teabag? Is music the art of speaking extravagantly?
That's what Ives said it is.

Now it is late fall, and I notice steam on my breath. Hölderlin
makes snow untune a bell.

I am thinking about a certain ancient type of music, which the
musicologist Denis Stevens refers to as "that once mysterious
melange of plainsong and polyphony, the In Nomine . . . "

An exclusively English genre nowadays almost entirely forgotten,
In Nomine is a form that came into being during the reign of Henry
VIII and died out shortly before 1700. Although many of the
historical questions concerning it have been answered, the genre
remains (at least to me) deeply mysterious.

In Nomine gets its name from the fact that John Taverner (1490–1545) set one of his masses to a certain old plainchant tune, *Gloria tibi Trinitas,* and then he or one of his students rewrote the *In Nomine* section of that mass's Benedictus as an independent piece for four viols, later transcribed for keyboard at Oxford around 1530. This transcription was the first In Nomine. The Gregorian original:

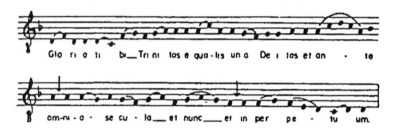

Translation: "Glory to Thee, O Trinity, One Equal Deity, both before the beginning, and now, and forevermore."

In this chantey from the voyage of medieval Christendom, past, present, and future revolve in a triune formula like that of the trident of Neptune seen upon crossing the Equator set between time and eternity.

The tune works as a cantus firmus against which other livelier musical lines are added to create a web of polyphony. A variety of ancient plainsong tunes were set in the same way at this time. It was a commonplace technique in compositions for instrumental ensemble or keyboard, but none ever developed to the same degree of fantastic elaboration as the In Nomine.

The words *in nomine* hark back to the Palm Sunday story. Riding in triumph into Jerusalem, Jesus was greeted as the Messiah by a cheering crowd: "Blessed is he who comes in the name of the Lord (*in nomine Domini*)."

When Taverner's first In Nomine appeared people were again looking for the Messiah, hoping for the new world that had been predicted for sometime after the year 1500. Other words associated with In Nomine, words of the *Gloria tibi Trinitas*, likewise indicate grand turning-points: " . . . before the beginning, and now, and forevermore." But from the plainsong skeleton of the In Nomine as performed in a keyboard setting, with voices flowing round it in ever-increasing rhythmic and figurative complexity, the words are absent, vanished. Only the tune that accompanied them for centuries lingers on, inaudible to any but the initiated. Still, a memory that words were once there haunts the music as it shimmers between major and minor. In Nomine does to plainsong what melismatic plainsong did to the words. It stretches beyond recognition. In In Nomine, the ghost of a word takes a shape and becomes the shape, and the shape becomes what the word means. Like an airfoil advancing over a vacuum and filled by an upward rush of air, the plainsong lifts.

In 1725 the music historian Roger North, who had heard In Nomine performances when a boy half a century earlier, confessed a distaste: "In the In Nomines I never could see a cadence complete, but proffers and balks innumerable . . . In Nomine is a sort of harmonious murmur, rather than music, not unlike a confused singing of birds in a grove." The very qualities that repelled in 1725 may attract today.

For cognoscenti of the 16th and early 17th centuries, In Nomine had cryptic political overtones. The tune on which it was based, *Gloria Tibi Trinitas*, had a long-standing association with the feast of Saint Thomas à Becket, the archbishop of Canterbury murdered at the behest of Henry II in 1170. Because of this link, use of the tune, semi-disguised in the In Nomine, became a code for Catholic and anti-regal sentiments.

John, also known as William, Blitheman (1525–91) was the first composer to write In Nomines purely for keyboard. His set of six defined the idiom.

Following his teacher's lead, Blitheman's pupil John Bull (1563–1628), who was to become the greatest keyboard player of the day, composed a series of twelve In Nomines in sets of three. Although a Catholic, Bull may also have had some distant affinities with the invisible order that sprang up at exactly that time, the Rosicrucians, whose members were said to share knowledge of occult and magical sciences, such as transmutation of metals, power over the elements and elemental spirits, and ultimately a vision of universal transformation. In his Great In Nomine (number 9) Bull lays out each note of the tune in the bass in long measures of eleven quarter-notes, or 22 eighths, which he changes proportionally to 33 in the concluding *tripla* section.

A wave: I think of a trill in which the notes blend and overlap *legatissimo.*

At Indian Wells, a six-inch-broad jellyfish, pink-rimmed with long scalloped arcs like pale green meringue. A choppy gray surf, wind northeast. Minutes ago, or so it seems, I saw wild roses still blooming behind the dunes, and it's winter.

"Snow untuned the supper bell." As Heidegger explicates this line by Hölderlin, *snow* means the winter of the soul. *Supper* stands for a banquet held in the evening of time, and the poet's voice is the *bell* that summons to this exalted repast, marking the end of one era and the onset of the next.

At a dinner party I meet a German writer on art and music, Jörg von Uthmann, who deplores the cult of Heidegger. An unpleasant, evil fellow, he explains. People do always find Mephisto more interesting than Faust. But there it's a fallen angel. Here, we have a fallen petit bourgeois. "Just look at the picture of him—a demented peasant!" Eileen Myles, sitting next to him, rejoins, "That could be something to shoot for."

The In Nomine flourished at a time when—in the words of a contemporary—"many chose rather to fiddle at home than go out and be knocked on the head abroad." A time similar to the present. Like Bull and his colleague Thomas Tomkins (1572–1656), we live in an age that fulfills Ezekiel 8, in which it is written that people are sitting in darkness, "each man in his room of pictures."

Imagine the octogenarian Tomkins in his tower room overlooking College Lane, Worcester, a dissident under Puritan occupation, living in retirement with a library of manuscripts and a keyboard, copying out old In Nomines and making a half-dozen new ones that were to be almost the last ever composed.

Each in a room of pictures in the illumined shell, globus mundi, or light-filled room in a seawave. Bull's 6th In Nomine is a wave. How to undress a wave.

Wilfred Mellers on Bull's Great In Nomine: "Sounds rather like Vaughan Williams, only more modern."

Bull's life involved alarums and excursions not at all surprising for a favorite of Elizabeth I. After the Queen's death in 1603, however, Bull was increasingly out of place in King James's court. In due course enemies obtained testimony concerning Bull's misdeeds, and he fled to Antwerp, there to spend the rest of his life as Cathedral organist, despite English attempts emanating from the King in person to extradite him.

He did steal out of England through the guilt of a corrupt conscience, to escape the punishment, which notoriously he had deserved, and was designed to have inflicted on him by the hand of justice, for his incontinence, fornication, adultery, and other grievous crimes. (William Trumbull, English Ambassador in Brussels, March 31, 1614.)

A portrait of Bull with an hourglass and skull at age 26 in 1589, now at Oxford, is framed in a rhyming motto: The bull by force in field doth Raigne But Bull by Skill Good will doth Gayne.

Domine quam admirabile est nomen tuum.

A hand raised in prayer is an upraised image of God.

In *Piers Plowman* the hand (fist, palm, fingers) is a figure of the Trinity. Wax, wick, flame.

Gloria tibi Trinitas. An orchestra of saints make a joyful noise on a mountain face to face with the Lamb and God the Father on a throne inside the cloud of the Holy Spirit. The keyboard player is in the center facing the Lamb. The instrument rests on the mountain's base. This illustration appears in the *Apocalypse of Margaret of York*, ca. 1475, now at the Morgan Library.

The Trinity: Sulfur (Nothingness, Father), Salt (Maya, Son), and Mercury (Prana, Spirit). Each of these is fundamentally androgynous. According to Wilhelm Reich, the segmented tube is a basic morphology encompassing all that lives, from jellyfish to man. Since the human form includes this, is the thing also part of the image of God mentioned in Genesis? Poe's "Conqueror Worm" comes to mind; also a line by Susie Timmons: "Love slave in tube sox . . . "

The notion that music was invented in heaven and descended to earth corresponds to the Platonic doctrine of the Ideas which in turn must ultimately go back to that Mesopotamian genealogy of kingship after the Flood echoed in *Gilgamesh*. Does the Chinese notion of celestial originals on which earthly counterparts are modeled have the same origin, Mesopotamia?

GOD = "the invoked one" derives from an Indo-European root meaning "call." Compare Germanic *gud-igaz*, possessed by a god (from which comes our word *giddy*).

To Palanc (the pastry cook outsider artist discovered by Jean Dubuffet in Vence about 1950) the square signified man and the circle woman. Man was straight lines, angles, "definition," "the constructed." Woman was curves, "the natural." Artemis versus Artificer.

Palanc's conception is astonishingly coincidental to that behind the famous Plate XXI in Michael Maier's *Atalanta Fugiens*: the Squaring of the Circle, with prototypical male and female figures at its center. Palanc's painting TOI DANS MA VIE shows the square and the circle separated on two inclined planes, then side by side on a single plane, and finally overlapping at the top of a vertical line, with a call-out label JOY.

Ancient China has the opposite scheme. There Woman is square and Man is circular. Woman was the housebuilder, the earth, the concrete; Man, the hunter-gatherer living in a yurt under the sky, standing for the abstract. This square-circle version of yin/yang appears in the ancillary literature of the *I Ching*.

When a Taoist sage achieved liberation, the pupils of his eyes sometimes turned into concentric squares. One of those old hermits with square eyes was said to be able to see life on other planets. (One of the most distressing sights I ever saw was the eye of a friend who was dying of cancer and the eye had been operated on to remove a fungus infection which if unchecked would have spread to the brain, and the result of the operation was that square-pupilled look, only it was just in one eye, not both.)

Snakes stand for either sex because they can become both straight (as in Aaron's rod) and circular (the *ouroboros*, or tail-devouring world serpent).

Bull constructed a circular canon titled *Sphaera Mundi.*

The phrase *in nomine* is reminiscent either of

> *in nomine Patris et Fili et Spiritus Sancti*

or

> *in nomine Domini.*

The former a Trinity invocation, the latter from the Benedictus of the mass. People always think the sing-song rhyme comical.

> What does *in the name of* really mean?

> "Open up, in the name of the law!"

> "What in the name of God do you think you're doing?"

For the Israelites, GOD had only one real name (despite many epithets) and that name was the taboo YHVH which moderns think may have been pronounced something like *Yahweh*. It may have meant "causes to exist." However, no one knows for sure.

When the priest says the words *in nomine* over the altar it is by way of a greeting to the angel that psychics have reported hovering there during the Benedictus, and if it is pronounced just right something like a wave rolls back over the priest into the congregation, and when it is sung (the purpose of putting it to music is to magnetize the words in such a way as to vastly amplify their power) the chant takes the words and stretches them out to where the listener's ear can't process them grammatically. In In Nomine the formula *in no-mi-ne* stretches itself into a string of phonemes with the vowel colors *i o i e*, which if you contracted them back into words would be *io, ie*, and this is precisely where the reality concealed in the Biblical words comes out of hiding and speaks to humans in the voice of angels, and the human voice responds with the kind of glossolalic cry that Saint Augustine, upon hearing someone freely improvise on a hymn tune, termed "a shout of happiness too great for words."

Among the Inuit, Larry Osgood informs me, each child receives, in addition to his or her Christian name, a private name, usually that of a recently deceased relative or close family friend whose qualities the parents would like the infant to acquire. They never reprimand a child younger than ten or eleven, for fear of insulting the spirit of the man or woman whose private name the child bears. Older children are assumed to have learned all that their tutelary spirits had to teach them. If they err, they have either failed to learn properly or have deliberately chosen to do the wrong thing. One may rebuke them without fear of offending the spirits. A linguist worked for four years with an old man who was one of the only speakers of a nearly extinct Inuit dialect. One day, after hundreds of hours of working together and an increasingly warm friendship, the Inuit asked the linguist if he might impose upon him with a very personal question. The linguist assured him that he was welcome to do so. Whispering in the younger man's ear, the old man inquired, "What is your name?"

I have discovered a hidden connection between the concept of Name and that of the so-called "triple image of perfection." In

Matthew 28.19 the singular *in the name of* is used with reference to the Three Persons, each linked with the other by *and*, indicating Unity in Trinity: "Baptize them in the name of the Father and of the Son and of the Holy Spirit." It does not say "in the *names* of . . . " The next sentence says: "I am with you always until the end of the age." Passages of this type, and there are many, imply presence behind seeming absence (or absence behind seeming presence: "I am no longer in the world," John 17.11). They also seem to say that the invisible is better than the visible, the unheard better than the heard.

"Unheard music is better than heard." (Greek proverb of late antiquity).

"That music must be heard is not essential—what it *sounds* like may not be what it is." (Charles Ives, *Essays Before a Sonata.*)

The proposition of Jacques Attali's *Noise* is different. He says that while noise is a deadly weapon, silence is death.

Physical law = a passing ripple in a vaster chaos.

In Nomine flourished in the last decades when the learned could openly profess natural magic. It vanished with the scientific revolution, whose theological foundation is in the system of control that is monotheism.

Pagans saw the monotheism of the Jews and Christians as a *malefica superstitio*. They were right.

Love is drunk on the wine of music, James Thomson wrote. "He reeleth with his own heart, that great rich vine."

The Name has got to contain as much female as male. Obviously, the Holy Spirit is female, something female in the air.

The dying swan witnessed by James Nares in Sagaponack last summer writhed like a white Hercules in the shirt of Nessus. The other swans formed a cortege and escorted it to shelter out of sight behind a clump of reeds. Its contortions having swallowed something it could neither get down nor get up seemed an allegory of the predicament of one whose business, pleasure, and religion it is to make art.

James has been nailing tuning forks (x and y chromosomes) to a steel door in consonance with *aurea proportio*.

His family name in Latin means 'power of observation.' *Nares acutae*, a sharp nose.

The other day he told me about the part of Ireland he is from, where cattle and sheep make paths over the downs to stone circles in order to huddle inside, rub up against the standing stones, and shit.

The Spanish term for a dissonance was *un punto intenso*. To chromatic inflection there was a pungency suggesting that of brimstone.

From the very last paragraph of Hölderlin's *Hyperion*: "Like lovers' quarrels are the universe's dissonances. Resolution is in mid-conflict. All that was sundered reconciles. The heart's veins fork and converge."

Nomen omen est. Omina nomina sunt.

"*Nomos* and *onoma* (order, name) are related terms in many languages for the obvious reason that by their names leaders imparted order to time." (Eugen Rosenstock-Huessy, *The Origin of Speech*, 1981.)

Inscribed in Phoenician lettering on the temple of Astarte at Sidon: SHEM BA'AL = "in the name of the Lord."

Dissonances "sting" the listener. Harmony brings happy relief.

In Nomine's very name situates it in the zone between what can and can't be said, in the sphere where apparently contradictory theologies harmonize point for point:

"That Thy Name is near, Thy wondrous works declare." (Psalm 74.)

"I am the speech that cannot be grasped. I am the name of the sound. I am the sound of the name." (*Thunder, Perfect Mind*.)

"Thou hast no name or form, even to the extent of allusion." (*Avadhuta Gita*.)

According to *The Cloud of Unknowing*, the division of the nostrils (*nares*) stands for spiritual discrimination. The Devil's nose is just a hole with no division into nostrils. It is possible to look up it all the way to the Devil's brain, which is hellfire and nothing else, but all who look go mad forever.

Gregory the Great's codification of plainchant institutionalizes glossolalia, or the materialization of the angelic tongue that was a disarticulation of human language.

I was practicing one of the Bull In Nomines, a long fast section in running thirds, when I recalled the gruesome climax of Kafka's *Penal Colony* wherein the parallel styluses (like musical staves with running figures pricking an arabesque of tattoos) incise the Court's sentence ever more deeply into the condemned prisoner's flesh. The Elizabethans had a six-line staff instead of the five-line one that has been universal ever since the mid 1600s—except in the drawings of Adolf Wölffli, who reinvented the six-line staff and filled thousands of drawings with his own music—marches, waltzes, polkas—written out in this unwittingly anachronistic style.

I had to learn the old notation because there are manuscripts now available on microfilm that have never been published. I taught myself, using a facsimile of *Parthenia Inviolata*, the first book of keyboard music ever printed in England (1611). Long ago I read an article by the musicologist Joscelyn Godwin on playing from original notation, in which he asserted, "A mere pianist who can play from the original score of *Parthenia* has penetrated further into the Jacobean musical world than someone who plays from a transcription on a Ruckers-type virginal."

The handwritten scores, of which I have photocopied dozens by this time, are often very hard to follow, even after one has mastered the old-time notation. Some are "pricked out" with the utmost calligraphic elegance while others are downright sloppy. (Nevertheless, no matter how messy they get, there is always a saving grace, a flourish). It's been several years since I began, and now I can play from them, yet not with any ease.

In Nomine is resistance between two efforts, the effort to hear and the effort to make sense.

The purer the Spirit the scarier.

Who wants to be possessed?

Who wants to lose

It, meaning Me?

To let go of the difference between Me and What I See?

Between being alive and being dead?

Between Me and God?

Who wants to overflow with a joy too great for words?

In Nomine does to plainsong what plainsong did to the words—in visual terms, it's equivalent to painting a sign on a skyscraper or sitting at the foot of a wide-angle screen to watch a film.

"The abyss of music is at the body's core." (Antonin Artaud.)

In Nomine has to come out of the player. To put the whole body into it. To become the crystal it vibrates in, while at the same time allowing it to become a crystal inside which one's own self may crack.

I got a letter from Joscelyn Godwin confirming my hunch that he is a fellow admirer of In Nomine: "I recall the words of Marco Pallis and Richard Nicholson, founders of the English Consort of Viols, Buddhists, and pupils of Arnold Dolmetsch—that the *In Nomine* was a contemplative form, and that the plainsong, while being a useful part for beginners to play (speaking of viol consorts), was analogous to the drone of oriental music that symbolizes the unchanging Self behind appearances."

Blitheman was to Bull as Chiron to Achilles, a centaur teaching a hero music and medicine.

"Each illness is a musical problem, each cure a musical solution. The shorter and more complete the solution, the greater the talent of the physician." (Novalis, *Encyclopedia.*)

"Musical instruments are only a means to replace the work of the voice and the body with tricks discovered by an ungifted race. I am not particularly astute, but I ought to know how to play music in a certain fashion with my voice, my hands, and my feet, *on the earth* and not in the clouds, never, though that can be heard from very far away." (Antonin Artaud.)

"Music has always had but one subject—the body. Noise is a weapon. Music, by domesticating the weapon, becomes a simulacrum of ritual murder. To compose is to commit a murder, to perform a sacrifice, to be both sacrificer and victim." (Jacques Attali.)

"Of all the evils that plague medicine, the worst is the practice of imposing generic names on illnesses in order to deduce from them generic remedies." (. . . *generalia quaedam nomina morbis imponere iisque aptare velle generalem quondom medicinam.*) (John Huxham, 1764.)

"The gods have become diseases." (C. G. Jung.)

"What they call GOD is germs." (Artaud.)

Even as I have been discovering this musical genre that seems to me a Western equivalent of raga, many people I know have fallen ill with the new plague, AIDS. The *Gloria tibi Trinitas* tune behind In Nomine was originally associated with the feast of Thomas à Becket, a patron saint of the sick. I sometimes picture In Nomine as the kind of music that Prospero might have played in his cell on the enchanted island. In Nomine becomes a country of the mind, one that is all the more inviting in that it has not yet become an officially recommended object of pilgrimage.

"Let us flee to our own country!" Plotinus turned this tag from Homer (*Iliad* 2.140) into a slogan calling for retreat from the world as it is.

The main accusation against Bull in 1613 was of adultery "notable and impudent." No less than the Archbishop of Canterbury wrote a letter detailing the charges:

> *Himself and his wife lay in the upper bed, and in a truckle bed under him lay two of his maid servants. Bull, in a summer morning when it was very light, riseth from his wife's side, goeth to the other bed, raising up one of his maidens, biddeth her to lie by her mistress, he taking her place committeth adultery with the other, which the maid beholding awaketh her mistress, and biddeth her see what her master is doing. His wife beholdeth it and telleth her servant that this was no news to her, for her husband had long and often been a dealer that way, which indeed is since verified by common report. Again he was charged to come into a church a little before the beginning of prayer, and there as the minister was entering into service, in the sight of the*

congregation Bull pulled him violently out of his seat and despitefully entreated him. The man hath more music than honesty and is as famous for marring virginity as he is for fingering of organs and virginals.

After escaping to Antwerp Bull led a quiet life. His grave is beneath a traffic island in the middle of one of present-day Antwerp's busiest thoroughfares. "He remained until his death—his music tells us—a passionate and sensuous man; yet the outward shows of the world affected him less. The intimate plainsong fancies of these years contain the essence of his personality; and it is perhaps not fortuitous that the pieces in which his spirit seems to find its ultimate sweetness and light are those that are most strictly scholastic and canonic." (Wilfred Mellers.)

To repent, to get religion, to return to the straight and narrow, is first and foremost to betray one's companions in misery; it is to turn oneself in, to turn oneself and one's friends over to the cops who are everywhere the same, be they the real ones or the imaginary One, cops in flesh and blood, specialists in roughing up suspects, or the great fog-skinned cop Himself, God, whose name is never invoked except to neutralize the people's anger, to pulverize our fists of rock, to quench our eyes of flame. (René Crevel.)

Sound is the substance of life. It comes out of the insides via the mouth. Passage through the mouth is entry back into the world before birth (which is the same as the world of the dead). Sound represents exchange between night and light. But it comes out of night. Its power is in darkness. As I write this, Sagittarius is in mid-heaven. Glimpsing the constellation through my window, I picture the Archer firing off a song. I once helped pack drumsticks in an amp that was about to travel. The thought crossed my mind: Arrows. Musical beats keen as darts, sharp as nails, the pins that hold everything together. I read about this tribe that call singing through the nose sniffing the honeypot. The best drum is one whose head has been dipped in a suicide's blood. The basic sound is an oscillation of thirds that matches the flickering balance between speech and song, a fluctuation that is the fundamental rise and fall in In Nomine and also the motif governing the whole of Beethoven's Hammerklavier. A basic dynamic fluctuation—call it talk-song— that connects the visible and the invisible, the past and the future, the living and the dead.

Why does the Name of God sound like that of Poe's "King Pest" nowadays? If I could only enjoy that serenity without worship, without object whose simple truth has seemed implicit in many of the good lives that I have witnessed, I might excuse the universe for taking no interest in me or mine as individuals. I might accept the rise and fall of historical cycles with some equanimity. I might even remain undaunted by the prospect of this new pestilence that is ever so slowly eating out my friends' immune systems and brains and leaving them prey to fantastic, hitherto unimaginable ailments, as a civilization I feel I am not really a part of moves into its third if not terminal millennium.

With the triadic style, the development of polyphony at the keyboard, and equal temperament, Plato's musical theory becomes a reality exactly 2,000 years after the *Republic*. (Ernest G. McClain, *The Pythagorean Plato*.)

In Heidegger's lecture on Hölderlin is a statement to the effect that to set measure before that which is amorphous and to winkle simplicity out of chaos is at once the most criminally reckless work there is, and the innocentest of pastimes.

Stravinsky once said that he owned more Old English church music than any other.

I must handle this like something very delicate (and precious) that can neither be dropped nor squeezed.

Transcript of a Talk on Translating Artaud

*Working up from the cellar to the roof cesspool to asthmatic nose,
there goes, there he goes, who is it, that hired hand, or the monkey
hand?*

the working man, you filthy old monkey . . .

*who'll wear hipboots to climb clear of this
shit from cesspool anus to the roof*
> *who'll sweat then*
> *sweat some more, writhing*

*in all that clay you thought you created him out of
(you did force him, when you thought you'd force him
to be*

> *born*

*again
to be born again in your plagiary of innate essence
your Being innate by presupposition at the bottom of your
innateness supposedly above all creatures you
get your creature comforts forked to you with your fecal
monkey hand) dirty old punk
monkey that would lend yourself to anything at all
but never made anything alone*

> *ever*

and didn't even know how to make yourself be born
with the tonsure of your hole

                              god

                                        you filthy old
monkey
where did your hand plunge into the mildewed
pus of that being who
was fucked by the crime you committed
when he tried to resemble you

                              god?
but WHEN *did your hand ever bleed where the prisoners are*
                                        being flayed
alive?

                              god?
who was it gnashed his shoulderbones as if
to crawl on all fours
over his own gangrened skeleton

                              god?
you lousy faggot you crotch
full of stars (who
made the lice you're infested with

                                              shine?

Your old man Man or was it you the
Ancient of Days you filthy old cocksucker?)
who ever could earn a human hand
over the shadow of your innate hand
workman or chimpanzee?
the workman I'd rather guess

                              god?

oh god

who is it knows his own hands
from the bottom of his well-proportioned toes
to the sinus of the fingers of his nose?
you, or he who sweated it out
long before your eternity

god?

and it was hard labor made him human

yes it was almost the perfect crime
you perpetrated against him
who digged in the earth for you and let
you grope all around in his funky sweat
with a withered fecal hand
that monkey hand amputated from the human

who ever shared his hatred
of that cross you've
always wanted to fuck me in the ass with

god?

and the stale donut of your ass
you cornhole punk
you old shit ass
you tonsured hole

you tonsured old punkhole
and the stale donut of your ass
and the circle of your bungsoul
you corny old bunghole
and the circle of your grunting

bunghole soul
that soul
you wanted to slip into me
from the bottom of your bunghole
you tonsured old fuckhole
and the stale donut of your ass

and the circle of your grunting
                                    soul
you wanted to slip into me
from the bottom of your bunghole
you tonsured old fuckhole
and monkey hand with the hairy wrist

when your
monkey hand with the fairy wrist
was gathering all the filth you had
hung in clusters
down your ass
in order to make me
throw it up
whole

Artaud's "Workman's hand, monkey hand"—the poem I just read—first appeared in the Paris avant-garde magazine "K" in 1947. I translated it in the summer of 1962 at a kitchen window on the Lower East Side, overlooking a mean little back court, just the right environment to be recasting a modern Gnostic canticle to the deific dingle-berry.

My earliest translations of Artaud were for my friend the poet Alden Van Buskirk, who had given me a copy of the Grove Press edition of *The Theatre and Its Double* in 1960. He didn't know French and asked me what Artaud's poems were like. The first I located was a wild rant about Popocatepetl, the Mexican holy mountain. This had just been published as a "document" in Sartre's magazine *Les Temps Modernes*. I translated it and mailed it to Van Buskirk. "Send more!" he wrote back.

Another friend, Jack Hirschman, was commissioned by City Lights around this time to do an ARTAUD ANTHOLOGY. He saw my translation of the Mexico fragment and asked me to help with the book. I ended up translating roughly two-thirds of the whole thing, during the years 1962–63.

I was living on East 12th Street. At that time amphetamine could be obtained semi-legally in New Jersey. I ordered about a ton of so-called crystals that had been purchased or purloined from a pharmaceutical factory over there. It was delivered to me by a guy named Jake Mark who wore a Russian-style greatcoat dating back to Czarist times. He wore it even in hot weather with the collar turned up. It reached down to his ankles. He was so spaced out from many months of repeatedly injecting himself with amphetamine hydrochloride solution—or "soloosh" as we called it—that he couldn't talk anymore. This wasn't unusual. It happened to the poet Bob Kaufman, too, a couple of years later. Like many people I knew at the time, Jake carried a tote bag full of magical trinkets—a flute, a box of watercolors and crayons, a notebook with esoteric diagrams. In addition to this standard equipment, Jake had another book in which (like the late Beethoven) he conversed with you. You said something to him, and he wrote in his reply.

Anyhow, I used a lot of amphetamine, plenty of other drugs, too. This was to speed myself up so I could do my Artaud translations in record time. Ferlinghetti wanted the manuscript within a few months. I worked very hard and put myself into it in a way that I think absolutely indispensable for somebody translating a writer like Artaud.

You have to identify with the man or the woman. You have to identify with their work. If you don't, you shouldn't be translating it. Why would you translate something that you didn't think had an important message for others?

I wanted to turn my friends on to Artaud and pass a message that had relevance to our lives. That's why I did it. Not to get a grant, or be hired by an English department.

Maybe I did end up in a black hole of sorts from identifying with Artaud in ways that I had no business doing. I think that's an occupational hazard. Artaud himself identified with role models from the past, starting with Gérard de Nerval.

You guys have probably seen the complete Rimbaud published by Harper Torchbooks. It was translated by Paul Schmidt. Schmidt writes in his preface about having had the same experience as a translator—highly personal self-identification with the original author to the point of near self-destruction. Schmidt's account of this is very interesting to read. Read it. It dispenses me from the necessity of having to explain what happened to me with Artaud.

Now, why don't you ask me anything you'd like to ask, and I'll answer the best way I can.

Q: What part of your own personality is closest to Artaud?

A: It is the same as what motivated me to translate him—an anger deep inside of me. Like every one of us, I think there's a lot in reading a text like this, and I wanted the most eloquent English idiom that could correspond to the French original. It's that anger that I would say is almost like a force of nature, but beyond that. What was it that I identified with in him? Within him it was this sense of displacement, of not being your own person in your own skin, of not belonging where you were. And of course I was a drug addict and an alcoholic too, which didn't help matters. And I was crazy, and I didn't know what was wrong with me, and I didn't know what was wrong with the world. But I DID know something very serious was wrong with it, and I was in terrible pain and terrible confusion. And it seemed to me that Artaud had made some spiritual discoveries, ones of real importance, not just to sick people like himself and me, but to all of humanity. And these discoveries, how could I say? It's like the rediscovery of the truths of Gnosticism, of the notion that this universe is crazy. It's crazily defective. Perhaps the forces that threw these defects into motion are crazy themselves. Maybe there's a strong element of irrationality right at the heart of things.

Q: Did you get pleasure from this sickness?

A: Certainly not! I wanted to be well. And so did Artaud want to be well. If he was using drugs, it was to cut the pain in order to be able to open his eyes and see. If you are in terrible pain, you can't see things clearly. You can't think or see clearly. You can't articulate your thoughts clearly. If you're in terrible pain, all you can do is scream. So the idea of drugs was in no way a self-administration of pleasure, but I can't deny that pleasure was often involved . . .

How I Became One of the Invisible

In order to become one of the invisible, I had to go through an ordeal technically known as throwing oneself in the arms of God. This consisted of going out in the empty desert with nothing but the clothes that one was wearing and a bag containing certain things. Some of us stayed there for months, others years, many forever.

One night I made up my mind. Pedro, who had already gone, walked out a ways with me in the moonlight.

"Keep on until dawn," he advised. "Then dig a hole just big enough to lie down in. Watch out for snakes and bugs. Wrap up. Try to sleep. Whatever you do, stay out of the sun. There is a cloth in your bag. Put it over your nose and mouth. The air out there is very clean but too hot to breathe. Travel at night. Locate plants; stay with them. Never leave one until you have figured out where the next one will be. Make a slit to suck out the moisture. Eat whatever you can chew, and pretty soon the plants will start coming out, just like stars. Follow them. If a plant makes you nervous, eat just a bit. Find out what it does. You will run into some that give strength, more than you ever dreamed of. At first you are going to feel miserable. You will want to die. Sand sticking to your clothes will rub your skin raw, get in your mouth and down your throat. You will be half blind. You'll think all the time; your mind will race. You will have strange dreams. You will find yourself doing things you would never think of doing anywhere else. You will imagine you are going crazy.

All this for a little walk in the sand. There are many animals. Start with the iguana. By the time you learn to get an iguana out of a hole you'll also know how to keep him fresh. Break his back, tie the legs, block the jaws, drop him in the bag. Two days later, still fresh. You will find the desert as crowded as any habitat on earth. After the reptiles, animals and birds, you will meet a few other things. Devils, actually. When you tame your first devil you can eat scorpions if you choose. At that point you can also start going out in broad daylight. You'll get tanned black all over, no matter what you wear. Lions and tigers will sit at your knees. Crocodiles, elephants, hippopotami will ferry you across the river that sometimes rushes through the center of this desert for a day and then vanishes as suddenly as it appeared. When it's time for you to leave, there will be a sign in the sky. All of us witness it. You will feel something like a sudden draft of air. Turn round and face it and you'll see a cloud of white dust pouring out of the sun. An iridescent arc will appear to the east. Within a few seconds the whole sky will glow with luminous crescent-shaped figures, the biggest of which will form itself into a circle round the sun. This will in turn be intersected by a second ring centered on the zenith, its circumference coinciding also with the sun's position. The smaller arcs will fall into concentric patterns about these two grand rings, filling the whole sky with lights. Then you will imagine yourself inside a prism that is vibrating like a gong. You will long to vanish in thin air, to disappear in that sound.

"Then, at the points, three of them, where the two grand circles intersect (east, north, west) you will witness something truly extraordinary: an extra sun at each. Four suns and a whole sky on fire. When you have seen those four suns, turn around and tell your devils to pull their pants up and point you straight to the nearest town."

Four years later, Pedro and I found ourselves together again for the first time, sitting at a table by a mirror in the Café Estrella in Pochutla. The cafe faced out on the marketplace, opposite the jail. Glancing in the mirror, I could see that both of us were skeletally thin, and our eyes bright and bloodshot. In my hair and beard there were traces of gray that I had never seen before. Pedro was beardless still. Both of us wore the crazy-quilt of rags known in that part of the world as *la túnica polimita de Joselito* ("Little Joseph's coat of many colors").

I found myself staring into a bowl of black coffee, breathless with rapture. Oblivious to me, Pedro worked at carving a pipestem, shaping it from a stick of wood known as jewelwood. Having roughed out a pentagonal star at one end of the pipe, Pedro took up an ice pick and hollowed out the inside a bit farther, then resumed where he had left off on the star.

Not even the most flagrant of the invisible had ever yet had any serious trouble in Pochutla, so the town was a favorite stopping place. There was what we called a supervisor there, an old man who could if need be go to the authorities on our behalf. But the local Commander's friendliness to us had always been so genuine, though distant, that none of us had ever needed help from the Pochutla supervisor since the previous Commander's day. (The present incumbent was his nephew.) Not that the old Commander had been harsh, only his role in those times had been a much more serious one than that of his successor, or at least he had taken it more seriously.

A generation earlier, the town had been invaded by a group of wandering midgets who were tinkers and bootleggers by trade. They sold and also drank absinthe in enormous quantities. The reason they had come to Pochutla was that the tomb of a long-dead saint named

Pepe was there. During his lifetime some two generations before that, the midgets' forebears had frequented and revered him. Now their tribe was dying out, and they decided to camp next to his tomb, having long claimed him as their patron and protector. Pepe was always said to be the wormwood-eater's friend. Once settled in, next door to the tomb, they set up shop as repairmen and traffickers as usual.

Late one night, the old Commander decided to get rid of them. Soldiers roused the midgets at bayonet point; they were given one hour to pack and leave. That same night the old Commander had a dream in which Pepe rebuked him. The saint looked just as he had in life, except in the dream his white beard reached all the way down to the ground. When Pepe finished, the old Commander noticed that a crack had opened at his feet and smoke was rising from it. He leaped out of bed, shouting.

Soldiers went after the midgets. When they were overtaken and persuaded, with much kindness, to come back, the old Commander entertained them in the street in front of his house and (remembering the dream) said over and over:

"Pepe is your friend. He loves you . . . "

We invisibles encountered real trouble only when we allowed ourselves to be seduced by the attractions of the city. There we were viewed as untouchables.

In the capital, for instance, because a newspaper publisher whose brother was a senator had denounced our order as an anachronistic and malodorous impropriety, policemen kicked and punched those of us they had arrested until they were themselves exhausted. Then in the middle of the night the victims would be pushed, more dead than alive, into the back of a truck and driven out to an empty spot on the highway to be discharged with warnings never to return.

For his part, Pedro had long since resolved never again to visit the big city. We were now staying at a settlement in the salt swamps south of Pochutla, some ten miles inland from the sea, an area so flat that from the top of a stepladder placed anywhere one saw the ocean glistening in the distance like a curved blade. Between oneself and it, there was an unending expanse of reeds running in all directions, billowy yellow, and bounded on the east by the snaky brown, blue and white outlines of the mountains which defined the approaches to the Wilderness bordering Pochutla to the south.

The swamp settlement served only as a rest stop for transients, and as in all such places there were only a few permanent visitors, a supervisor, and a handful of old men who had decided to remain until their death.

Built on an island of dry ground, the red mud huts we were living in formed a circle round an inner square at the center of which there was an immense and ancient olive tree, its trunk and branches forming an umbrella beneath which we spent long days outdoors in dry weather.

Squatting in two parallel rows facing one another, we played the pebble game. As the game proceeded, both spectators and players kept up a continuous nasal drone the whole time, punctuated only by the click of the pebbles and the beat of a drum played by an aged resident.

The purpose of this game was twofold: it could be used for gambling or as a method of divination, thus resembling almost any other game. However, we set no store by material possessions and had no interest at all in predicting future events. Nevertheless, we surrendered ourselves body and soul to this game of nonexistent stakes and meaningless prognostications. Quitting for the day, an hour or so before sunset, one of us might tell his brothers how he had been to the bottom of a sea teeming with luminous fishes and plants, while another, who could have told how his soul had been ravished into the center of a rainbow, said nothing. At other times, the lives of various paragons of preceding generations were related. One whose name was Serafín I often heard cited as a prodigy.

Serafín had worn woolen clothes exclusively. He refused to put on any garment that was not one hundred percent wool. He wore his hair long, never married and renounced worldly things. All that he had was his mother. Her he honored with absolute obedience. Serafín traveled constantly, but never set out without his mother's permission, and he always returned on the exact date set by her. He smoked tobacco mixed with rifa, was afraid of the dark and could not sleep by himself. Nor could he endure the neighing of horses or the braying of donkeys. He had the gift of second sight. When an inhabitant of any of the villages through which he passed in his wanderings was about to die, Serafín was likely to appear briefly and then, wraithlike, vanish. This always happened at dawn, so that the mere sight of him at that hour came to be taken as a sign that someone must die within the day.

Serafín had a prodigious memory. It was said that he had spent some months in a flying saucer where he met with scientists from another planet who taught him their language, their names and the names of their cities.

The evening meal was the only meal of the day in our settlements. The fare varied according to season and the number of people on hand. Sometimes it consisted of nothing more than a pot of boiled mallow root. We were not prevented by this diet, however, from enjoying happy dreams during the hours of darkness. Each night we gathered round the fire with our pipes, some in small groups round a waterpipe, others sitting alone or in pairs with the smaller pocket pipes. We filled the pipes with the ground-up leaves and flowers of the rifa plant (sometimes mixed with a pinch of Mixtec tobacco) and thus made up for our indifference to the pleasures of eating with an unbounded appetite for the joys of smoking rifa, so much so that the inhabitants of the region had a saying to the effect that if there were no more rifa left on the face of the earth, the invisibles would nonetheless have a little something left over.

On the question of how this plant first came to be discovered, we used to tell the story of a king of old who was out walking one day with his top adviser and noticed a plant whose distinctive odor aroused his curiosity. Uprooting it, he dried the stems, flowers and leaves, then ground them up. Later, after taking them in a mixture of cloves and honey, he was filled with a mysterious bright, warm feeling. When the adviser asked whether he was satisfied with the experiment, the king replied:

"*ana h'tloc a rifa*" (I was looking for precisely this!).

Thus both the name of rifa ("precisely this!") and rifa itself were discovered on the same day.

Mixtec tobacco, which we not only sometimes mixed in pipes with rifa for smoking but often chewed while trekking cross-country, was the only kind we ever used. This tobacco was endowed with the most energetic properties, twenty to thirty times more powerful than the ordinary leaf. Our order had used it for the past thousand years, ever since one of the invisible was initiated by a hermit who made him a gift of some cured leaves, together with the following charm:

> *Chew me and be strong,*
> *Drink my juice, your every member*
> *Will tingle all day long;*
> *Smoke me and remember.*

Not that the introduction of tobacco was without serious consequences for us. Because of it, a number of heterodox brethren withdrew to hermitages near or actually within the Wilderness, where—typically—each would build himself a hut, live by fruit-gathering and clear a patch of ground, with his sole object to grow tobacco plants, to live in their midst and to chew and smoke them day and night.

All of us without exception had two pipes, one pocket and one water. The waterpipe consisted of a long stem inserted in a fat earthenware bowl, which rested on the ground, with a hollowed-out smoke-hole of conventional type, whereas the pocket pipe was simply a length of hollowed wood with a small metal bowl.

We thought of these two pipes as a pair of demons, the water-pipe a female and the pocket pipe a male. This demonic couple we imagined to be in league to bewitch their owner and keep him in a state of enslavement, for the pocket pipe was forever glued to its owner's lips while on the road or otherwise employed, and the water-pipe was the companion of our nights next to the embers of a lone campfire or with our brothers in the darkness of a cave, smokehut or hostelry.

So important were these pipes that nobody ever willingly traveled without both male and female. One of us, an aged man named Dáfnis, whose twofold beard overspread his weathered chest as whitely as the wings of the Pentecostal dove, losing his male pipe in the neighborhood of Candelárias, even went so far as to declare that he would not proceed one step farther, but built himself a hut where he kept a black she-goat which he named Lucky.

On market days, Dáfnis would appear in the center of Candelárias, accompanied by the black goat. Setting up his water-pipe he would hold forth for hours, surrounded by a crowd of locals who listened attentively to everything he said. Snapping his fingers at the end of a peroration, Dáfnis would send the pipe circulating from mouth to mouth. He would then point out, for the general edification, that Lucky the goat was perfectly clean, and above all not covered with flies:

"This," he would affirm, pointing to the pipeful of rifa, "knocks them out of the air!"

Dáfnis concluded by forcing the goat to eat a large bolus of concentrated rifa. He then also put the mouthpiece of the pipe to the animal's lips, shouting:

"Find me a husband for this woman!"

The goat endured all this with perfect docility but soon exhibited signs of agitation, at which bystanders would nudge one another and grin.

After a few years Dáfnis and Lucky disappeared, leaving an empty hut behind. It was generally assumed that the black goat had at last presented her master with a compatible mate for the widowed waterpipe.

We all lavished particular fantasy on the embellishment of our female pipes, tying colored rags of every description round the bowls—ribbons, bits of coral and cowrie shells, snailshells, brass buttons, picture buttons and likenesses of the Virgin Mary and the saints, pearls of every grade, policeman's whistles, bells, little mirrors, locks of hair tied up at one end with a length of scarlet thread, pierced coins, scapularies, tin soldiers, Maltese crosses, holy medals, gold watchbands; and yet none of this ostentation ever led us into vanity or an infatuation with physical beauty. We never forgot that by the very act of dressing up the female pipe we were channeling away from ourselves the energies of an ogress who delighted not only in enslaving her owner but in obliging him go to work in order to fit her out in finery—"ogre brocade" we called it.

"A bonfire smothered in ashes" is what a famous recluse of our order once called the settlement where Pedro and I were staying. It maintained a close bond with another, identical in organization but high in the mountains some forty miles to the southeast, close to the Wilderness. One could reach the mountain settlement by a trail running straight, and it did run straight as the proverbial die, from Candelárias. It was said of the two that their fates were joined and that whatever happened, good or bad, to either must infallibly happen to the other. Both were wide open, their rule being absolute hospitality with no distinction being made between good, bad, rich, poor, visible, or invisible. Thieves, robbers, even murderers had more than once enjoyed the enigmatic privilege of our welcome. On one occasion within living memory, our swamp settlement had gone so far as to harbor an escaped mass murderer for a little more than a year before he finally vanished.

It was a well known fact that in both places our gardens had never been molested by birds or insects, our pantries had never seen rats, mice or cockroaches; there were no flies anywhere; and the cats never took anything but what was set before them.

Additional Prose

Edited by Robert Dewhurst

Note on the Texts

In selecting texts to add to this expanded second edition of *How I Became One of the Invisible*, I have not sought to gather all of David Rattray's remaining uncollected prose, but to present texts that seem sufficiently of a piece with the original edition—keeping its wonderful heterogeneity intact—and which especially extend or amplify his late conception of *Invisible* as a "poetic autobiography."

"Weekend with Ezra Pound" first appeared in the *Nation* on November 16, 1957, and was later collected in *A Casebook on Ezra Pound*, edited by William Van O'Connor and Edward Stone (New York: Thomas Y. Crowell Company, 1959). Its circumstances are described in my introduction to this edition.

"Yoga of Anger" appeared in *Just Another Asshole*, no. 6 (1983). A holograph manuscript of "Yoga," extant in the poet Gerrit Lansing's papers, describes itself as a "sermon preached at Tina Lhotsky's White Trash Southern Funk Night at the Pyramid, June 28, 1983."

"A Revelation," "Max," and "In the Hand of Wind" are three of the last texts Rattray published, all appearing after the publication of *How I Became One of the Invisible*. "A Revelation" appeared in *Long News: In the Short Century*, no. 4 (1993); "Max" appeared in BOMB, no. 43 (Spring 1993); and "In the Hand of the Wind" appeared posthumously in BOMB, no. 49 (Fall 1994). Rattray intended for "Wind" to be the final text in his manuscript of "collected poetry and prose," *The Curve*, left uncompleted when he died.

Ken Jordan's interview with Rattray, "Taking Risks Seriously," was conducted in late 1992 when *Invisible* was published, and first appeared in the February/March 1993 issue of the *Poetry Project Newsletter*. More recently, it has reappeared in *What Is Poetry? (Just Kidding, I Know You Know): Interviews from the Poetry Project*

Newsletter (1983–2009), edited by Anselm Berrigan (Seattle: Wave Books, 2017). An unabridged transcript of Jordan and Rattray's conversation is extant in the Sylvère Lotringer Papers and Semiotext(e) Archive, 1960–2004, at New York University's Fales Library.

Finally, three texts are being published for the first time here.

"Letter to a Young Poet," my title for its publication here, is an item of private correspondence, whose occasion is self-evident. A copy of the original letter was given by Rattray to David Abel, publisher of Rattray's *Opening the Eyelid*. My thanks to Abel for bringing it to light.

"On Spirals" was found in the papers of Gerrit Lansing, as an undated holograph. It has been lightly edited for typographic consistency and for the accuracy of its quotations, some of which I imagine Rattray transcribed in haste or even from memory. While "On Spirals" should not be considered something that Rattray saw as a finished work, it was clearly composed as an essay and shines a revealing light on his wide reading of esoteric and literary sources. Thanks to David Rich, Lansing's literary executor, for helping to facilitate its publication here.

Photocopied excerpts from Rattray's late journals, written during the period of his illness in early 1993, circulated among some of his friends after his death. Thanks to the poet George Green for sharing the copy from which this transcription has been made. As with "On Spirals," it has been lightly edited, for grammar and accuracy, to create a clear-text version for publication.

The best point of departure for any reader intent on discovering still more of David Rattray's uncollected work—poetry, prose, and translations alike—is the East Hampton Public Library, which maintains an archive of his publications and papers within its Long Island Collection.

Weekend with Ezra Pound

It was raining in Washington when I arrived, and the dull red building of St. Elizabeth's seemed particularly discouraging. After checking in at the main office, I climbed the spiral stairs, all steel and dirty enamel, chipped and peeling walls, to the heavy black door of Ezra Pound's ward, and rang the bell. I could hear radio music inside.

A Negro attendant with a great jingling ring of keys let me in. Half a dozen patients gathered round a TV set next to the door. The hall was very wide and dark as a subway station. There were benches on either side, and patients were sitting or lying on them. Doors opened on rooms for two or three, and there were several alcoves where rooms might have been, with tables for games, and chairs. Pound and his wife, with a young novelist named Jean Marie Châtel, and a painter, Miss Martinelli, were sitting in one of these alcoves when I arrived.

Pound sprang up from the canvas lawn-chair and shook my hand. "You're Rattray? How fortunate you got here at this moment—John here was just beginning to be tiresome, and so now," and he laid his hand on the chair in which Châtel was still sitting, next to his own, "*he* will sit over there, and you may sit here." Châtel, looking a little embarrassed, took a seat in the corner on the other side of the round game table. Pound picked up his overcoat from the arm of my chair and flung it across the table after him.

He sat back down, in a reclining position with his legs crossed, eyes half closed, looking exactly as he did in the Wyndham Lewis portrait made many years ago. His hair is now white all over and he is getting bald. He was dressed in tan shorts too big for him, tennis shoes and a loose plaid shirt. His face looks weathered, like that of a man who has worked outdoors all his life. His heavy-wristed hands are coarse and calloused, but the fingernails neatly cut short and square. I was surprised by the appearance of his arms and legs. There was no sign of that flabbiness that comes even to some of the strongest men in their forties and fifties. The Greeks spoke of "old age that unstrings men's knees," but as I watched Pound stride up and down, his knees strung taut, his calves bulging like an athlete's, I thought of some lines from Ramon Guthrie's poem, "E. P. in Paris and Elsewhere":

> This is not walking.
> This is stalking, pacing
> as done by jaguar or ounce
> in Zagreus' days, tracing
> the lay-out for the Labyrinth . . .

Before we had a chance to talk about anything, Pound jumped up again: "You'll have tea, won't you?"

I said that I would, and immediately he was everywhere at once, in a frenzy of activity, loading himself with jars of various sizes, tin boxes of sugar and tea, spoons and a saucer. I stood up in embarrassment, not knowing what I ought to do, but Mrs. Pound beckoned me from her corner: "Let's sit here and talk while he makes the tea." She was sitting behind a ramshackle old upright piano, so as not to see the people in the hall or be seen by them. Miss Martinelli was making sketches for a portrait of her.

Suddenly Pound was standing before me, holding out a peanut butter jar filled with hot tea. When we got settled again, he glared up at me and said, "Well, what specific questions have you? Or did you just come to talk? I'd just as soon talk."

So we talked quietly. Pound took a sip of his tea and sat back with his eyes closed. I sipped nervously at mine. Miss Martinelli went on sketching Mrs. Pound, the two seated next to the barred windows, in which the gray day peered uncertainly, through a tangle of wet vines laced over the trellis-work of the bars. It was dark in the alcove, but a bare electric bulb blazed from the high ceiling of the hall. Châtel, with his back to it, was reading, his face concealed from us by a huge newspaper, *Truth*. I hitched my chair over out of the light.

"D. P. has a beautiful face," said Miss Martinelli, "I think she has a beautiful profile, but it is so *difficult* . . . yes, of course, that's why. Maestro . . ."

"Yes Ma'am," said Pound, jerking around to sit on the edge of his chair.

"Will you look at this drawing?" Pound looked at it, squinting in the light, then said, "It's a likeness," and swung himself violently back into the reclining position.

I told him I was planning to spend a few weeks in Dalmatia.

"So you're going to the Damnation Coast? Don't know what the Hell you'll see there, do you?" I said that I had friends in Split and Dubrovnik. One of them was a painter, who wanted to show me the medieval frescoes.

"If I were you, then, I should get to the heart of the matter, and see them in Turkey. I hear they've done a lot of work there recently, restoring them where the Turks had painted 'em over." He told me about a Professor Pearson of Yale, who is an adviser on the selection of Square Dollar Books ("American textbooks for students who want first things first") and who is very interested in

Byzantine frescoes. He jumped up and rushed to his room to type Pearson's address.

"You could make an appointment with him if you happen to be passing through there any time. He'd confirm what I told you about medieval Greek. Now there's something that's wide open, plenty there's not even published yet, not chewed and hashed. . . . Now you're talking to an old man that never learned his Greek properly, but you, you're lucky, to know it at the beginning of the game. But I know it well enough to recognize style when I see it, and Psellus's style, he's seventh or eighth century, Psellus in the Chronographia, he writes with the precision and economy of Flaubert or the Goncourts. And Psellus had enough perception to see 'em fall into just about the same categories they do today. He knows the difference between true credit and *creatio ex nihil*. . . . So you're going to southern France next year. Well, I've been trying to make some people wake up to a number of simple facts, and they'd better hurry up, if they don't want to wake up too late to *do* anything. Now if you want to *do* some really live historical research, something that hasn't been chewed over, look into Bertran, Bertran de Born I mean, '*Baros mettez en gatge . . .*' you know the one I mean, 'Barons, hock your castles.' You'll probably walk that country a lot, and see those castles, the ones he was talking about, the ones they *hocked*. Bertran knew a usurer when he saw one—they hocked 'em to go on crusade, you know. That would be some *useful* research, what you told your reader, your reader could put to use—the area still suffers from when they put their lands *en gatge*—you could find out for yourself, and tell your reader what happens when you hock your castles to the Jews."

Mrs. Pound interrupted this tirade by telling about the walks they took together in southern France.

"We always used Toulouse as our base. Toulouse itself is a mediocre town, but one comes to grow fond of it, and the country all around is as beautiful and full of Provence as any place else in the South. I went with him on his last two walks. We had been married only a short time, and we went all over with rucksacks, and slept outdoors, but then the war interrupted all that."

"I don't suppose," said Pound, "that the old cupboard is still there, the one that was bulging with pornographic books. And old Pere—is dead. Now let me see who *is* still alive." Then he slowly unraveled the number of his acquaintances now living in France, who were interested in Provençal literature: Laubies, Vanderply, Pellizzi ("a civilized wop") and Brancusi ("probably gaga by now, if alive at all"), and told an anecdote about each.

"And you *could* go see old Aldington as to Greek or Provençal, but better not as from E. P.; you'd better just be the *jeune homme modeste*. He lives in Montpellier now, I believe."

Mrs. Pound repeated the list of poets and scholars back to him, counting them off on her fingers, and he went to his room and typed their names and addresses for me.

When he came back, we sat for a while in silence. It was late afternoon. Miss Martinelli was perched like a bird at dusk, her feet planted on the rung of the wooden chair. She was still at work on her sketch. Looking at her, with her golden hair falling down round her thin shoulders, I thought of Pound's line,

In the gloom the gold gathers the light against it.

She was dressed in blue jeans and a checkered blouse. Her appearance suggested a frayed and faded survivor of the early bobby-sox days. She had huge eyes like a cat. They bulged in a flushed face that tapered down from an enormous forehead to a tiny chin and tinier double chin. Her lips were tight and pale, but sometimes relaxed and parted into a naïve smile. I assumed that she was a patient from another ward.

Pound jumped up and strode across the hall to his room, making a sign for me to follow him. He give me one of the Square Dollar books, *Roman and Moslem Moneys* by Alexander Del Mar. The notice on the jacket informed me that Del Mar was among those "American writers who can hold their own, either as stylists or historians, against any foreign competition whatsoever," who are being printed by the Square Dollar Series. I was further impressed by the following paragraph on the opposite cover:

> The sheer incompetence, triviality and worthlessness of our universities is nowhere more blatantly exposed than in their ignorance of Del Mar's writings, published from 1862 onwards in both London and the U.S. Had one not met some of the low-grade personnel of the faculties, one would be unable to attribute the historical blackout to anything save the great conspiracy which some fanatics claim to be at the root of it.

Pound's room was strewn with wadded papers, bits of envelopes, trampled books, pencils, lengths of string, cardboard files, trunks, old paint cans, jars filled with teabags or scraps of food. The walls were hung with paintings, some by Miss Martinelli. There was a dressing table with a huge mirror which reflected the glow of sunset, and filled the room with it. The old man dove under the table looking for a couple of large tin paint cans. I noticed again how strong his bare legs looked. A person who saw him that afternoon might have had the impression, not of a poet who had lived ten years in the sordid prison described by MacLeish, but of an old-time seaman, aged but still spry from climbing the rigging every day, sitting at his ease in a coffee-house or tavern between voyages of exploration or privateering on the Spanish Main. He pulled out the tins and pried them open. They were filled with doughnuts and bread. He put some into a paper bag and tossed it to Miss Martinelli, who was standing at the door. Then he poked around under the bed until he found a box filled with boiled eggs and salami. This he handed to me to give to Châtel. It was marked *Books*, sent by Witter Bynner.

When we reached the big black door at the other end of the hall, near the TV set, Miss Martinelli saw a pair of singing comedians on the screen,

"Look at those fairies! Isn't it disgusting?"

Pound threw his arms around her, hugged her, and kissed her goodbye. He turned and asked me to come the next day. The attendant unlocked the door while we made our farewells. I was a little surprised to see that Châtel and Miss Martinelli were only visitors.

Châtel put me up for the night on a couch. We had the food Pound had given him for supper, and talked about literature and politics for several hours. He told me that he and Miss Martinelli were supplied with almost all their food by Pound, who gets it from the hospital cafeteria. In our conversation he revealed himself as a fanatic disciple of the "Maestro"; he apes his every like and dislike, even imitates his nervous tics and manner of speaking, and way of jumping up and stalking around. Next morning his father invited us to lunch.

Châtel's father, now a modest insurance man, was before the war a *colon* in Algeria; then joined the Free French and emigrated after the war. While we were at lunch, Châtel showed his father the copy of *Truth* which Pound had lent him, and which was filled with financiers, munitions manufacturers, a McFadden speech of 1932, and a "recently uncovered" Rothschild letter of 1862, "when America was sold to the Jews." M. Châtel read page after page, murmuring "*Très intéressant, très intéressant. . . .*"

While we were on the way from his father's to St. Elizabeth's, I asked my young companion if there might be some connection between the Kasper of Kasper & Horton Square Dollar Books, and the Kasper of Clinton, Tennessee. He laughed loudly and slapped his gloved hand on the steering wheel: "Ah! at last, the Great Dawning . . . why yes, of course, they're one and the same."

Kasper had recently opened a bookshop in Georgetown, D.C., organized the Seaboard White Citizens' Council and affiliated it to similar councils in the Deep South.

The group aimed to end "integration" in Washington, put the NAACP on the Attorney General's "subversive list" and abolish "rock-and-roll." Membership was open to anyone eighteen and white, who "believes in the divinity of Jesus Christ." Jews were not allowed. The *New York Times* quotes from a pamphlet sent out by the Council. It condemns "pink punks . . . freaks, golf players, poodle dogs, hot-eyed Socialists, Fabians, scum, mold on top of the omelette . . . liars for hire, the press gang, degenerate liberals crying for the petrefaction of putrefaction."

The phrase "petrefaction of putrefaction" had rung a familiar note, and I must have suspected what Châtel's answer would be, but it wasn't till then that my mind began to work, and the passage quoted above came to me, together with Cantos XIV and XV, Pound's Inferno, and the following phrases from them:

> *n and the press gang*
> *And those who had lied for hire . . .*
> *. . . a circle of lady golfers . . .*

and the fabians crying for the petre-
faction of putrefaction. . .

I mentioned this to Châtel. The sun had just broken through the clouds and was kindling a fire in his stiff brown bush of hair, lighting up his pale unshaven face, marred by pimples and a huge insect bite on the forehead, while his coarse features labored with excitement.

"Of course, of course," he said with a wave of his hand, and stepped on the gas. "And you know what else was in that proclamation . . . no, you could never guess, because the book he took it from was burned up by order of the International Jews after the war, every copy they could lay hands on. The important part, where he sets forth the economic program, is straight from Feder . . . Gottfried Feder, do you know who he was?"

I indicated by a smiling nod and a properly righteous shudder that I did.

"Feder's book on the Nazi Economics. That's the important thing, the Negro business is just a front, he knows it's the only way he can get the Southern farmers to vote for him, but *then*, when he gets the power (and they've already won here and there, Charlottesville is one place) then, he can get to work on the economic program."

I wondered, as we turned up the road to St. Elizabeth's, if Pound might not have turned out that "Seaboard" pamphlet, and had a hand in *Truth* as well. As it happened, I came away convinced of it, having met the Maestro in an Economic Mood that afternoon, and also made the acquaintance of Mr. Horton of Kasper & Horton.

When Châtel and I arrived, Mrs. Pound was already sitting in her corner. Pound said:

(335)

"Glad you could come again. Hell of a lot better company than what he brought with him yesterday, I'm sure. Sit down and I'll make you some tea."

Mrs. Pound explained that an uninvited caller had made his way into the ward with Châtel, having given him to understand that he was invited by Pound and authorized by the hospital. I asked who he was.

"He is a journalist and we don't like him. In fact, E. P. has a violent aversion to him, and so we got the attendant and had the man ejected."

I started to question Pound about Provençal music, and he said he had heard that more than 250 tunes survive, but he didn't know where they were published.

"Oh yes, it seems to me that one of those old fellows, the ones I told you about yesterday—could it have been Pellizzi?—one of them told me something about a facsimile edition being printed in Barcelona. Of course you know that most of those old manuscripts are just *motz* without *sons*. I've seen 'em with the staves carefully drawn on, but no *sons*, just the verses underneath, an entirely understandable bit of laziness: the fellow knew how it went, a perfectly simple tune, why waste time writing it all out? And as you know, transcribing these songs from the original to the modern notation is a job for a musicologist. Maybe that's why so few have been published. But you know, that old notation, it's just a kind of musical shorthand, an aid to memory, to be used only by someone who had already heard the tune at least once."

I told him about the record of Provençal songs made by Yves Tessier, who in addition to being a musicologist was an excellent singer. He waved his hand impatiently.

"Don't expect Grandpa to know anything about Provençal after 1920. That's all after my time. You have my *Spirit of Romance*? You do? All right, I cover all that in there."

I had noticed several times before Pound's unwillingness to be told anything that he hadn't already found out for himself; and yet, he declares that he never reads anything unless it's going to teach him something.

"At my age I can't waste the time. I read for information. I am not on the examination board to determine whether a young fellow's past the sophomore level in writing, or whether he should graduate with senior honors. I used to do it when I was young, but now I leave it to the young men . . . But speaking of notation as an aid to memory, that's the way I did my opera *Villon*. I have the only copy in existence over there in my room. BBC put it on in 1932 and they had some copies, but lost them. Too bad they didn't make a record of it, because I wrote out the *motz el sons* just the way the old troubadours did, just as an aid to memory. I used the modern notation in the old simple shorthand way, and I can read it, but nobody else can without hearing it first—I could hum it or whistle it to 'em. I don't have much of a voice to carry a tune, singing, but whistling or humming, I could make it clear to the musicians. They wanted to do it again, and get the tunes from me here, with a tape recorder. No, that wouldn't be any good, I'd have to rehearse it with 'em the way I did before. Imagine, recording engineers, singers, all swarming around in *here*—it would be a madhouse. . . ."

His eyes were shining with good humor, and we laughed.

"No, that's one project'll have to wait till I get out of pokey. I guess I'll have some more tea; how about you?"

Miss Martinelli appeared just as Pound was gathering up the jars and tins for tea-making. She was wrapped in a heavy wool overcoat and a long winding scarf, and was flushed and winded. Pound embraced her and ran his hands through her hair, and they talked excitedly, each interrupting the other. I turned and talked with Mrs. Pound. Miss Martinelli sat down in her chair and piled her things on the floor, announcing to us that she had been working since five o'clock that morning.

"At this time last Sunday," said Mrs. Pound, "he was making a record of his own readings. An old friend of his from BBC, a man we knew we could trust, brought one of those tape machines. He's never consented to have a record of his reading hawked in the market place, turned out by one of the great American nonsense factories. But he's known this man for years, and we know he's honest."

"What did you read?" I asked him.

"Well, it wasn't anything really serious. I just wanted to get something on record. I conceived the whole thing more or less as a ribbing for Eliot. Eliot is like that old mule, you light a fire under his tail to get him started, and he goes forward just far enough to burn up the wagon. That's neither here nor there. Anyway I read 'l'Homme Moyen Sensuel' (first time I'd looked at the damned thing for years), the *Usura* Canto, one of the John Adams, a couple of the Alfred Venison poems, and the preface I did for her book."

He made a gesture toward Miss Martinelli.

"I just wanted to give the old boy a jolt, some time when he's settling down for a nice cozy evening, if he turns on the Third Programme and hears E. P. reading Alfred Venison—I chose the ones he likes the least . . . As for her preface, I wanted to give her a boost. She's one of the few American painters of any promise, that I know of. The Esperia people in Milano did a book, in color, of her paintings last year, and I wrote the preface."

A dark hulking man, dressed in a black overcoat, appeared.

"Hello, Dave," said Pound. It was Mr. Horton.

In the gloom of the alcove his wavy hair and clothing were black, but Horton's face shone white, soft and slippery, as if crudely modeled in soap. I grasped his huge, soft hand. His eyes narrowing suspiciously, he smiled, parting lubber lips to reveal a pair of fang-like eyeteeth.

He sat down on the piano stool, opposite Pound and me, and produced a letter from his coat pocket.

"It seems that Wang has lost an important address book.* He's been staying at the Dartmouth Club in N.Y., and says there's a Jew been hanging around his room, hasn't been able to get rid of him. Says he suspects him of stealing the address book. Here, he says, '. . . contains names of all our nationalist friends and those working for our cause . . .' What the Hell do you think he's done with it? He enclosed this example of the Jew's handwriting."

He handed Pound a creased slip of paper with the following words crudely penciled in a large hand: "The home of the Jews is Israel."

Pound held it up to the light. "So this is a specimen of the Hebe's calligraphy. Strange thing for him to be writing."

"And the funny thing," continued Horton, "is that it looked exactly like Kasper's hand to me."

At this comment, I had to hold my mouth just right to keep from laughing.

---

* David R. Wang, a member of the Dartmouth class of 1955, is distinguished as being the only Chinese poet of record who devotes himself to the cause of white supremacy. Since graduation, the *Dartmouth* reports, Wang has been touring the Ivy league colleges with the purpose of setting up White Citizens' councils on the campuses. He has characterized Secretary of State Dulles as a "wishy-washy Socialist."

I had known Wang fairly well while he was at college, and besides finding him personally repellent, I had concluded that he didn't amount to much, as a poet, or anything else. He has become a legend on campus, an object of ridicule for both teachers and students. But I'd never suspected *how* stupid and conceited he was till Pound showed me a letter Wang had written him.

"Remarkably sensitive to the language for a young Chink," said Pound, looking at me sharply and grinning, as he handed me the letter.

I wondered as I read if Pound really meant it, or was just baiting me. In it Wang referred to himself in the third person, as "Hsin"—his Chinese given name for all I know; it means "Heart-mind." His letter was filled with phrases such as "the Cause which alone keeps body and soul together, in this horrible city where all stinks of Jewry." The last sentence was "P.S. Hsin has learned, from a reliable source, that *Hudson* has been selling E. P.'s typescripts to the Jews."

"How ridiculous," said Mrs. Pound.

"What difference would it make if they were, because at least they're publishing them."

"I don't think they would," said Pound, "I know the editor and he's honest. I think *Hudson* is honest. Now that's the kind of monkeyshine I wouldn't put past Laughlin, you know, Laughlin of 'No Directions.'"

"There are very powerful elements opposed to the publication of the Cantos, you know," said Châtel.

"It was 'No Directions' that suppressed that passage about the Rothschilds in *The Pisan Cantos*," said Pound. "They wanted to leave the whole thing out without any indication of the omission, and I said, 'Black lines or nothing' and so in went the black lines, so all my readers could see the censorship. I guess they were afraid of losing the support of the New York banks, if they published the truth about international finance."

"And so," said Miss Martinelli, "Grandpa's got to do it with suicide troops. Like Kasper. Kasper is your suicide troops. I have a strange feeling about him. I have a feeling that he is going to die very soon. And Horton is our coming President."

Horton laughed, "No, no, don't say that. That's looking too far ahead."

"But has one of my prophecies ever failed?" said Miss Martinelli. "You know perfectly well that every one of them has come true. Grandpa says I know intuitively what it takes a great genius years of study to learn."

During the rest of the afternoon Pound and Horton discussed their mutual political acquaintances. Pound was continually shuffling in his recent mail, and pulling out letters and pamphlets which he would hand to Horton. Horton tried to keep up with these, pursing his lips and murmuring as he scanned each one, before Pound thrust another at him.

I noticed two Negros sitting at a game table in a similar alcove just across the hall, both of them dressed in rumpled baggy suits and wearing pushed-in felt hats. They were playing checkers, but each seemed oblivious of the other. Once they pushed the checker board aside and talked loudly a minute in some unintelligible dialect. Then hitching their chairs over, they faced the checker board again. After a long pause, one of them carefully reached out both hands and moved two pieces at once. In a moment both men were moving pieces at random all over the board. When they stopped, one of the Negroes shuffled over to our alcove and stood in front of Pound, staring out the window, and extending an upturned palm. Without hesitation Pound reached into the pockets of his outsized drawers and fished up a handful of small change. With an abstracted air he selected a dime and a nickel and dropped them into the pink palm, then turned back to the stack of papers in his lap. The Negro stood there a moment, then turned without a word or even a glance at Pound, and stuffing the coins into his coat pocket, he went back across the hall. No one else had paid any attention to this little scene.

Pound pulled out a proofsheet of his biography which will appear in the next *Who's Who*, in which he pointed to a sentence vindicating his war-time actions.

"I had a Hell of a time with 'em over that, and told 'em they couldn't print the thing without that sentence, so they put it in."

It was time to leave, and Pound embraced Miss Martinelli as on the day before. As we went down the stairs, she said, "Grandpa loves me. It's because I symbolize the spirit of Love to him, I guess."

"It's true," said Châtel. "He wrote a whole passage in the 'Rock-Drill' about her."

I didn't have a chance to find out where that passage was.

We stood talking in front of Horton's shabby black car. A middle-aged Jewish couple walked down a nearby path, both of them extremely short and fat.

"Just look at those twin spheres!" said Miss Martinelli, giggling delightedly, "Isn't it too disgusting for words!"

Horton pulled a portrait of himself from the back seat of his car. He said his wife had done it, and it was just about her first painting.

"Oh, what a wonderful job for an amateur," said Miss Martinelli, "I can hardly believe it. Just think of it, her first painting."

I have seen portraits of great dictators, the kind that are printed in color and hung on every wall. Whether of Stalin, Hitler or Tito, they seem to run to a type, and his portrait of Horton was a crude imitation of that type. It was Horton conceived as Our Leader, the Square Dollar President. The painter had given him a hearty complexion, removed his double chin, remodeled his burly chest and shoulders, straightened his nose, lightened his lips, taken the heaviness from his eyelids and contrived to give him a calm and determined gaze.

I was taking leave of Mrs. Pound when the door of the building we'd just left flew open, and there stood Pound on the doorstep waving a sheaf of paper in his hand.

"Hey John, come back here and take your god-damned manuscript! How the Hell are you going to become a novelist if you leave your work all over the place? Goodbye Dave, you'll come over Christmas Day, won't you?"

He nodded smilingly at us, and disappeared in the door with a little wave.

Châtel and Miss Martinelli gave me a ride to the railroad station.*

---

* Ezra Pound published the following letter in the *London Times Literary Supplement* on December 6, 1957:

Sir: The techniques of contemporary defamation are perhaps a matter of more than personal interest, and in view of a recent spate of attempts to stir enmity between me and several of my friends, in the columns of papers which do not print rectification of their "errors," might I ask the courtesy of your office and the patience of your readers to state that I have not accused Mr. Hemingway of dishonesty, though maintaining my reservation as to the activity of some reds in Spain. I have not accused Mr. Laughlin of selling my manuscripts but did mention that he had detected someone else doing so.

Ezra Pound

Yoga of Anger

I didn't come in here tonight to talk about love and sex. God doesn't love a single person in this place. Who cares for the love of God anyhow. I don't. I'd rather deal with something more tangible like a pair of breasts for instance; and I don't believe God has breasts. Now my friend here has called me "the Mad Preacher." But that has nothing to do with mad-insane. What we are dealing with at this point is anger. Anger is more than the name of a filmmaker, it's universal. Anger is all over the place and rightly so. Did you know there was a yoga of anger? Right. All these swamis coming over here with a message of sweetness and light. What we haven't yet seen is the yoga of anger. They were the true mad preachers. These guys sitting up on Kailash in full lotus, screaming with rage, perfecting a glare that could zap anything at any range. Telling the sirenlike demonesses flitting in front of their eyes to fuck off, female spirits that were always making other lesser men have an involuntary ejaculation into the nearest river and it would get carried downstream where a doe would swallow it and a child with antlers would be born, or fish would get it and so, mermaids and mermen. Well since all of the above are nothing but figments of the collective unconscious, the yoga of anger would have nothing to do with them, it correctly rejected them, chased them into the woodwork where they belong without exception. You don't need ups, downs, goofers, speed,

Sermon at the Pyramid as "the Mad Preacher"

alcohol, psychedelics, or any of that shit. Just go for the pure nerve, adrenaline. Anger. Anger is the name of the game. Fuck peace. Fuck quiet. Go for anger. Be like the headlight of an oncoming freight train. Climb down the world's throat like a locomotive. Freedom from anxiety was one of the Four Freedoms spelled out by FDR. It turned out to be a fraud. You have a constitutional right, a duty even to get angry, vent your rage, act out any fucking way you please. When I heard the entire poetry establishment was gathered under one roof at John the Divine, the whole lot, Church, non-Church, Academe, Naropa, together with the Dalai Lama, an assembly worthy of the Questions of Milinda, 400 pederastic philosophers in league with Nagasena and the emerald Buddha of Bangkok, I had the power to strike that roof like a giant laser and bring the whole fucking building down on those people, let God recognize his own, and I might have done just that, except for the fact Eileen Myles and a couple of others could have been in there too, and there are places where legitimate anger does and does not apply. I realize that for me to merely mention I would prefer to deal with something more tangible like a pair of tits could be construed in some quarters as sexist. Now if I were to talk about kneeling down over in the trucks and getting reamed in the rumbleseat while sucking on a dirty exhaust pipe that would be okay because gay and the male homosexual is above criticism to anybody except angry women. Well let me tell you kids I couldn't care less what position any one of you may take on this, I've got my own. As a matter of fact I think about 90 percent of any given crowd is like Mechanical Man, bionically constituted of drugs, 3–4 veins on each limb, nostrils, lungs, a mouth, and a well greased anus for the insertion of toxic suppositories. A couple of orgasms and maybe one good shit a day. Eardrums shattered, thinking processes totally fried, and most of you not even half my age. How a man of seventy can find himself attractive and talk about jerking off in front of a mirror with a movie camera rolling, trained on him, till he "shoots," is beyond me. It is something I'll never understand until I reach that age myself. How would I know? I don't go around fucking sixty-year-olds. "Shoot" indeed. Every shot I ever fired was in anger. I killed a man in Mexico. Shot the motherfucker dead. Watched him bounce in the moonlight. This town on a plateau, volcanic fault lines, gaps bridged by rotten planks, and the son of a bitch was out to get me so I killed him, and I have never lost an hour of sleep over it because I was angry then, when I was twenty-five, and I am angry now. There's a line by Bessie Smith, Nobody knows my name, nobody knows what I done. That line applies to me. Every shot fired in anger. I shot my life and several other people's full of holes and never will forget John Wieners, "If a man were to die with the needle plunged in his vein he would not have died in vain." If you can believe in anything it's a volcanic fault. Eruptions happen when the sulphur sleeping underground has a dream and this swells into a mountain bringing it closer to the heat of the sun causing the sulphur to explode, "shoot" if you will. As for gaps, I think people ought to stay in their own age bracket. Want to play around outside your age? Why not just kill 'em, that would be the angry way, the correct way. If you think I have an ax to grind you're right, I do, and fuck you, I mean you, you know who I mean, you know who you are and what you are. Fuck you. Why anybody should be turned on by a person twenty years their senior is a mystery, a superstition. It doesn't fit, I distrust it, I reject it, I spit on it. Anybody hangs you up, you have a duty to get angry. Go for the jugular if it's within reach. I'll never forget this conversation between Vaccaro and Jackie Curtis bickering over who wrote this play and Vaccaro suddenly said, I'm gonna kill you Jackie, hang me up a whole fuckin summer over a fuckin play (and I wrote it) I'm gonna rip your eyes out, I'm gonna tear your tongue out of your head, go in Max's Kansas City. I'll get Mickey to really fix your ass, I'll kill you I'll kill you I'll kill you you'll never act again . . . Right fuckin on was my reaction and I like Jackie too but that was the spirit. Or when Valerie Solanas took that gun and went after Warhol's ass. This is what we need more of. Anger. That's my message. Dare to dream like a volcano dreams. Blow your stack. Kill. Smash 'em through the floor.

A Revelation

I once passed through Saint Louis in 1954 at age eighteen en route to a summer job in an iron mill in Pueblo, Colorado. The train stopped for an hour. It was eight o'clock on a Saturday night. Everyone detrained and drifted about under the art nouveau ironwork of the depot, which had been specially built for the Exposition of 1904, turn-of-the-century Saint Louis having been a great city, or at least a big dusty town on a prairie. Mark Twain was still alive.

I had known someone who knew Mark Twain. Mrs. John Adams Mayer, better known by her pen name of Dorothy Quick, was the author of a weekly column in my parents' newspaper the *East Hampton Star*. She had published several books of verse and was undoubtedly one of the worst poets in the history of American letters. She had a framed snapshot of Mark Twain holding her, a toddler, in his arms on a deckchair aboard a transatlantic steamer around 1900. Since that unforgotten day, Dorothy had lived a long and happy life in a penthouse at 1050 Fifth Avenue with her companion Miss Voorhees, housekeeper Edith, and chauffeur Lincoln who drove her around town in a 1932 Rolls with a silver elephant (her totem animal) on the hood, and a round porthole for a rear window, as well as two miniature poodles, Victory and Quickie. They were both males and frequently engaged in bestial acts until Dorothy cried, Oh do stop, Victory! Down, Quickie! as she rang for Edith and the maid to separate the animals and carry them off, squirming and snapping, to the kitchen.

Outside the station or depot was a long line of moviegoers waiting to get in under a marquee proclaiming *Intruder in the Dust.* The roofs of the theater and the depot glowed like orange sherbet in the setting sun.

To this day I have no idea whether the Saint Louis station was properly or originally termed a depot. At that age I referred to all US railroad stations, except for Union, South, Grand Central, and Pennsylvania Stations, as depots. This was what my Uncle Daniel Huntting had taught me to call them.

A lifelong horseman and painter of horses, my Uncle Dan had attempted to join the Rough Riders while hanging around their encampment on Montauk, where they were quarantined because of the yellow fever epidemic on their return from Cuba in 1898, when Dan was sixteen. Huntting Senior had thwarted the desired enlistment in some fashion that humiliated the son, and as a result Dan had remained for the rest of his life stuck in a time warp that included books by Theodore Roosevelt and Frederic Remington, *Frank Leslie's Illustrated Newspaper,* and a complete run of *Harper's Monthly Magazine* from circa 1850 to 1910. Both unmarried, Dan and his sister Minnie shared the family house across from the Presbyterian Church on Main Street, East Hampton, over a period extending from the presidency of McKinley to that of JFK.

Uncle Dan disliked automobiles and seldom rode in one. He referred to trains as "the cars," an expression that had seen its day already when he was a boy in the 1890s. He could remember when the New York cars had their South Fork terminus in Sag Harbor, and you had to use Jerry Baker's stage to come along to East Hampton, where all the roads were dirt roads, too.

Influenced by Uncle Dan, I secretly planned a solo railway journey up and down New England in the summer of 1948, when I was twelve. My itinerary I chose from advertisements found in *Harper's* magazines dating from the 1870s. Their covers bore the names of various ancestors, scribbled in pencil: Judge Hedges, Miss Huntting. The long *s* in *Miss* was an eye-opener. I started writing letters to the railroad ticket offices listed in the advertisements, requesting new schedules but using the addresses that appeared in the old magazines. Though already a proficient typist, I wrote the letters out in longhand, in ink, using steel pens with detachable nibs, and sealing the letters with red and green sealing wax purchased from the East Hampton News Company at the corner of Main Street and Newtown Lane, where old Ben Barnes, the proprietor, lobster red, shaky and hungover, watched me dawdle through the antique paper kites and gliders, and the pre–World War One writing supplies, with mingled amusement and exasperation. I knew those railroad lines listed in the 1870s *Harper's* had for the most part vanished from the earth. Yet the action of writing to them, using old-fashioned materials and implements, archaic language, and phantom addresses, was an experiment in ceremonial magic, an attempt to raise the dead and converse with them via the power of the pen. The letters all came back, except for the one addressed to the Boston & Maine Rail Road, which had been forwarded to the company's offices in Hartford. The agent who opened my letter of "enquiry" no doubt guessed the age and disposition of the enquirer. He sent me an elaborately courteous handwritten reply, enclosing the new schedules and wishing me luck on my travels.

Turning my back on the movie house, I strode into a package store, taking a chance they wouldn't check on my ID. I got two fifths of Kinsey Silver Seal and a couple of six-packs of Ballantine Ale.

By the time the train pulled out, I was swigging the Kinsey. I had chosen that brand thanks to the recently published Kinsey

Report. The previous summer in Paris I had frequent intercourse with a certain streetwalker who did it for love a couple of times when I was broke and even led me to believe that I was giving her pleasure. I had been unwillingly celibate ever since in the air-conditioned nightmare of America, poring over my Traveller's Companion editions of Henry Miller in Room 408, Streeter Hall, at Dartmouth. I unbuttoned my shirt, put the whiskey in my suitcase, opened a bottle of ale, and, getting out my green pocket Testament, turned to the last Book. While following the extravagant magic lantern show of John's imagination, I tried to visualize the Cave of the Apocalypse on Patmos where he originally received his Revelation. I did my best to picture John himself, but his features remained veiled to the mind's eye. To reveal (it occurred to me) means both to re-veil, or put on another veil, and de-veil, or take it off. Revelation comes in a flash, a bright mist, a mystery. You see clear, then close your eyes. Each disclosure re-veils what it reveals at the instant it de-veils it. Having revealed, it veils again in blinding darkness.

Hours later, my head banged against a seat in front of me. There had been an accident. Passengers were picking themselves up off the floor. We stood in the middle of a wheat field, midday heat shimmering in the brightness between the air-conditioned car and the horizon. My arms were covered with gooseflesh. My liquor was intact in the bag between my feet. People walked forward to see what had happened. I followed.

Someone said, "What a shame for a Sunday morning."

Reaching the open door, I swung down onto the tar road that crossed the tracks. In the middle of it were some patches of fresh blood, next to the train. Nearby, a white hat with fake roses sat in the dust. A conductor said, "The worst is farther up."

A flashing red light bounced over the wheat tops. The woman lived by herself in a farmhouse a mile up the road, always walked to church this way, must have been light-headed from the heat.

A dream came back, one that had been recurring ever since childhood. It was not a proper nightmare, but a sinister daydream or reverie edged with something like what Khlebnikov calls "the giggling of mirrors." The sun could shine, and the wee folk inhabiting storybooks be ever so snug in their wee houses, but somewhere, just out of sight, there was a shrillness as though of laughing falsetto voices. It seemed as if everything around me was a mockery of what it ought to be. Caught up in this horribly tingling wave of brightness and derision, I imagined an irresistible force pulling me toward a huge machine inside of which I was going to be crushed and ripped to pieces.

As the train sped across a dry, empty plain several hours later, even with the wind on my face at the open door in the cool of sunset, I was too dizzy to stand up very long. A sandwich man sold me a dry ham sandwich. I washed it down with a beer and a couple swigs of Kinsey, then slept like a log all the way to Denver.

Max

Every morning at eight-forty-five, one of my clocks plays the *Meistersinger* Prelude theme on a set of silver chimes, and I wake up. I lie still for another fifteen minutes, staring at the pipe and the lamp on the bedside table, and at the photograph on the wall behind the lamp, of Gül, a young woman I have never been able to forget.

At nine sharp, I light the lamp's oil-sodden wick. Aching with anticipation, I wait for the clear flame to come up, sunk back on my pillow, the pipe clasped in my left hand. I often fondle it and lick the cold, hardened pill on top of the bowl.

A few minutes later, I roll over and smoke, all in one long drag. I lie back, holding my breath to a count of forty, the euphoria of the day's first indulgence illuminating my entire being.

An unmarried woman, I live just round the corner from the Royal Saint-Germain; it's my boudoir, so to speak. At exactly nine-thirty every day, the doorbell rings, and a waiter from the Royal appears, bearing a silver tray with one croissant, sweet butter, coffee, hot milk, and *Le Figaro*, which I scan for theater and book reviews over breakfast. I've declared a moratorium on the Ben Barka affair, and I don't care what Sartre says about it. I'm not interested in the doings of Che Guevara. Nor do I share Ho Chi Minh's optimism that the Yanks are going to be out of Indochina in the next three years, say by 1970.

The coffee aroma, the bakery smell and the whiff of fresh newsprint never fail me. I have no appetite in the morning. These smells bring me back to life. At all other hours, the apartment, which like the house itself was built by Dulac, an associate of Gaudi, in 1904, smells of two things only: blond Virginia tobacco and opium. Pall Malls have a honey smell that never goes stale. I can't endure the stink of Gauloises, et cetera. "I say, Max, it's like smoking the anal hairs of an Egyptian peasant," my friend Dédé, Dédale de Saint Maur, used to exclaim, until I begged him to desist. Then Dédé's wife Gismande (my mistress as of a year ago yesterday) has tried to invade my place with scents like vetiver. There again I draw the line. Gismande occupies the guest bedroom. I *sleep* with no one. I never receive her before noon, either. At twelve sharp, Gismande knocks and comes in for her first pipe of the day, after I have had time to bathe, dress, and smoke three or four myself. Then I am ready to make one for her.

This morning while awaiting the stroke of nine, I tried to imagine the contents of my police file. One day a few years ago, during an interview with an inspector in a fourth-floor office at the Préfecture, I saw the outside of my folder. Peach-colored and tied with a pale green ribbon, it was surprisingly slim. I had rather expected it to bulge like a telephone book.

I had been summoned to appear because of an anonymous crank letter that denounced me (a) as an opium smoker, (b) as the notorious "Max," a lesbian with a special foible for pubescent girls, and (c) as a UFO zombie reporting to my alien handlers in their flying saucer via a transmitter secreted in my wisdom tooth.

The inspector handed me the letter. Its writing was childish, with carefully formed loops and the i's dotted with tiny circles. My thoughts flashed back to the pair of truants I had chanced to meet one afternoon after a matinee at the Pagode, Jacqui and Toukit. I introduced myself: "Maxine's the name, Max for short." I was intrigued when after five minutes the girls offered to boost recent jazz from the new record shop at Saint Germain des Prés where a manager had insulted me the week before. "They have to be catalogued," I objected, "one doesn't just collect at random." "We can do shorthand," Jacqui boasted, "and we type more than a hundred words a minute." I hired both of them. Within a week, they were coaxing me to teach them how to smoke. Then I noticed that a tube of codeine tablets was missing. I fired Jacqui and Toukit. I knew where they were going, I told them. I was in the street myself at their age.

To the inspector I only observed that the letter had to be the work of a very sick individual. "That goes without saying," he replied and showed me out with a handshake and a wink.

I could only speculate as to what other information might be included in my dossier. It must have contained the fact that I was an orphan. That my mother had died having me. That she had been the youngest of three daughters of Etienne Bernard, whose Trotsky book had raised a hoo-ha at the Sorbonne in 1929. That my father Colonel Duhautier had earned the Croix de Guerre in the war of 1914, and that, as a still-young, childless widower in 1930, he had become the black sheep of his Catholic Royalist family by marrying the Jewish professor's daughter in a love match unprecedented in three hundred years of an illustrious family history. That as a result of his clandestine pro-Allied activities he had been tortured to death by the Gestapo in 1943. That I had lived in the streets throughout the winter and spring of forty-three/forty-four, only to be rescued just before the Liberation of Paris by the notorious Dédale Aristide de Saint Maur—who throughout the German occupation had led a double life, that of a gilded youth often seen with the likes of Charles Trénet and Jean Cocteau while at the same time rendering important services to the Gaullist branch of the Résistance—twenty-five when he first picked me up, having mistaken me for a boy. That at age fifteen I had hired the Salle des Plantes and delivered a lecture in a zoot suit, "Defense and Illustration of Pedophilia," for which I was arrested and fined, having been put up to it by Saint Maur. That I had subsequently used Saint Maur's lawyer to represent my claim on the Bonn government for damages in the deaths of my father and the two aunts whom he had designated as my legal guardians. That I had won a favorable settlement of my claim and had been living on a sizable tax-free pension ever since. That I was seen almost daily at the Royal Saint-Germain and, since the publication of my radio play, chez Lipp, as well as at the Petit Pavé, often with Saint Maur, though we were not generally reputed to be lovers. The outside of my folder read (Mlle) DUHAUTIER, Edouarde Maxine; 43, rue du Bac; Profession: Writer; Born 3 August 1931, Hôpital de la Pitié, Paris.

In my opinion, a year and a day is long enough for anything to continue. This will be Gismande's last day here. Dédé will be coming with his car at eleven, for a couple of pipes with me and a bonjour madame to his wife when she appears. Gismande will also have a pipe or two, then go for her soak. She is regular as clockwork. At twenty-three she has a good body, enjoys looking at herself in my ceiling mirror, often falls asleep in the tub, and is never ready to go out before three.

The bathroom is where I began to discern fatal flaws in Gismande the same day she moved in. We had just taken what was to be our first and last shared bath. While toweling her down afterwards, I discovered that Gismande was heavily infested with crablice. I had to ring the pharmacy. We spent another suffocating hour in the bathroom. Hadn't she realized? I asked. Gismande replied that she had never even heard of *morpions*, save as a peculiar term of abuse. She had certainly never laid eyes on one.

"Never heard of crabs!" I shouted.

Gismande cocked her head to one side in a pout. "I don't suppose there is any need to warn your husband," I continued. She shook her head.

For a few seconds, we stood there without saying anything. Then I asked her to join me in my room for a smoke as soon as she was dressed. People are under the impression that I am easy-going, because I would rather smoke than deal with conflict. Given my bent, I was unprepared for what followed.

I had put on my dressing gown and the Moroccan slippers I wear around the house, and was pacing back and forth between the bedside tray containing my smoking gear and the glass cabinet in the next room, where I keep my collection of seventy-odd pipes, trying to make up my mind which I ought to offer to Gismande as a gift. I settled on a double-jointed one that could be unscrewed in two segments, which if dismantled with its bowl could ride unnoticed in a pocket, a model commonly known as a traveling pipe. Taking its plum red stem in both hands, I dismantled the pipe, noting, with a satisfaction that had never diminished over the years, the shininess of its silver fittings and the elegance of its tightly threaded joints. I dropped the segments in my pocket, intending to reassemble them in front of Gismande as soon as we had smoked.

Gismande had already entered the room. Wearing a white sailor suit, she sat cross-legged at the head of my bed, staring at the photograph of Gül. "Max, the day I saw this," Gismande said, "I knew I turned you on."

No one likely to make such comments had ever been admitted to this room. Never mind the fact that Gül and I had never done anything but kiss, even on the few occasions when I slept with her at the hotel. She had been preparing to leave for Germany with her Turkish friend, a black marketeer. The Germans were still in Paris. I was fourteen and had just met Dédé de Saint Maur. I had been coughing a lot. He arranged for me to enter a clinic where all the patients had flower names. Mine was *Bouton d'Or* (Buttercup). They removed half of one lung. The very next day, Dédé taught me to smoke in my hospital bed. He brought opium daily thereafter. The doctor did a paper on me. It seems the medicated smoke not only anesthetized the surgically wounded tissues, but other, as-yet-unknown alkaloids present in the opium worked to accelerate healing, at least that is what the doctor, also a smoker, theorized.

Two days before the operation I said goodbye to Gül at the hotel. She was packing her things in a cardboard suitcase and a carpetbag that had to be strapped shut with a belt. Twice she thanked me for my friendship and the second time choked on the word. She fished out a handpainted necktie that could have belonged to a pimp, together with an old prewar edition of *Le puits de la solitude* (*The Well of Loneliness*) by Radclyffe Hall, which had fallen to pieces. Tears filled her eyes as she knotted the book's two halves with the tie. I never saw Gül again. The Turk died in Hamburg during an air raid, but of Gül there was no record whatever.

Opening the book, I found Gül's photo. I told Dédé Gül had saved my life; he had the picture framed.

I could think of no suitable reply to Gismande, who had by now shifted her attention to my lacquered smoking tray. Behind her fair head loomed a black-framed screen forming the back of the bed, which was painted with a Tibetan hell scene, in which grimacing demons subjected still-unliberated souls to yet another turn of the karmic screw, a scene I always miss when smoking because turned the other way, my pipe aimed at the lamp and Gül's photo in its silver frame behind it. Gismande was right. She had indeed reminded me of Gül.

In spite of myself, I remembered the glimpse I had had a half hour before of Gismande retreating naked from the bathroom.

"Now I want you to pay close attention," I said, "to the precise amounts I use." I opened the jar and reached for the needles.

"I want to learn," Gismande murmured. Just then a detail I had never noticed in the curve of her hip drew my hand up into the flat of her belly, under the sailor shirt. Extending my thumb downward, I felt the beginning of her hair, a bit past the waistband of the trousers. With a slight quiver, she took a deep breath and leaned back, her legs spreading, her face in three-quarters profile with a cigarette dangling from the corner of her mouth. I opened her pants and was immediately put in mind of an erotic description by Verlaine at his most perverse, in which he has a lesbian marveling at the skin inside her friend's thighs:

> Smoothly white as a milkwhite rose, and pink
> As a lily under a purple sky . . .

A few minutes later, she whispered, "I like your finger better than most people's mouths."

We had not taken time to strip but only opened our clothes; now Gismande reciprocated. I was incredibly wet. "You never guessed what a cunt lapper I am," she said. I found it impossible not to surrender to the pleasure flooding me to the marrow of my bones. I made believe it was Gül's tongue instead of Gismande's. I found myself staring at the photograph. I imagined Gül's image expanding, breaking through the frame, entering the room to pick me up in an embrace I would never come back from.

I woke up with my face in Gismande's lap. The lingering odor of insecticide aroused me. I began licking her organ. Then, separating its labia between my forefingers, I looked inside. The exterior parts were of an almost translucent smoky lavender like the stems of certain mysterious plants I had seen in the woods the day I turned thirteen. I had been all alone in the country house where my father had raised me as a son, dressing me in boy's clothes. The Germans had arrested him in Marseille the day before. A friend telephoned the family lawyer, and he in turn instructed the housekeeper to pack me off to my mother's two older sisters in Paris. My father had provided for this; it had been the best he could think of.

For weeks I had been riding Banzai every day. That morning I galloped him down a cart track through the southeast corner of our property and was unexpectedly swept out of the saddle by an inconvenient branch and knocked unconscious to the ground.

I awakened to the dank smell of a clump of ghostly pale, waxy, leafless plants growing on the patch of dirt into which my face had been projected by the fall. I stuck out my tongue and licked the violet-gray flute of earth-ooze nearest to my nose, had a vision of myself turning into a mushroom, and passed out.

I revived, only to discover that my wrist was broken, and nearly swooned again. Back at the barn, Banzai was in his stall. I smeared my wrist with blue liniment, sobbing as only a child can sob, for the irrevocably lost time of life when I could pretend that I was a boy and actually believe it.

I arrived in Paris with my arm in a sling. Before I got my wrist out of the cast, the old ladies had a dressmaker measuring me. The news reached us that my father had died. We dressed in black. My aunts smothered me in hearts and flowers. The better part of a year passed. One winter afternoon, on my way in from a bookshop that had become my second home, I was intercepted in the courtyard by the concierge who told me that my aunts had been arrested. I left immediately, and a week later met Gül. She had been living in the streets ever since summer. She took me under her wing.

That was many years ago. Gismande brings it all back. However, as I smoke increasingly, I find myself taking less and less interest in Gismande, while at the same time my reveries involving Gül grow ever more absorbing.

A warm baritone voice rumbles: "Follow thy fair sun, unhappy shadow . . . " I am looking up into Dédé's enormous round face and unfathomable eyes. Soon he and I will be driving out to the flea market to call on a man who wants me to see a Second Empire wristwatch. At four we will return here to fetch my smoking things and close the apartment. Then off to the country, to arrive before dark in plenty of time to prepare a *gras-double*, our favorite supper. The meat is already packed.

Gismande will stay at the château when Dédé accompanies me to the clinic four days hence. The patient is kept in a deep sleep for three weeks. During that time, Gismande will move her things out. We'll all be friends, a happy family.

I don't want this cure. Dédé's doctor, a withered, chain-smoking gnome in thick bifocals and a white smock, talked me into it. This son of Aesculapius addresses me as "madame." "Madame, for the next six months at the very least, abstinence will be your ticket." He thinks addiction is like malaria. One brings it home from the colonies. It's in the blood.

Just now I thought of an alternative to the cure. Dédé and I would murder Gismande. It would be simple. Gismande takes massive doses of vitamin C daily before her bath. I could refill the capsules with double-strength gardenol. Then, once she was asleep in the tub, I would turn on the bathroom water heater without lighting the gas.

That would be a switch on another possibility that has been haunting me ever since a recent afternoon when Gismande asked me if I didn't think she might be Gül's double. I asked her if she would like me to kick her to death slowly. She laughed and walked out of the room. The conversation continued in my head. I imagined Gismande saying that if Dédé were to die, she would inherit, and the two of us could look forward to a lifetime of discreet pleasures.

Time and again I harked back to this speech, until I almost believed that Gismande had actually pronounced it. I wondered if she might not in fact have murderous designs on both Dédé and me. I fancied a conversation with Dédé in which I would report Gismande's proposal. He and I would arrange for her to die in the tub, then take the body out to the country and bury it in quicklime.

But before any of this came to pass, something even crazier might happen. I might go through Gismande's papers (which, it did seem very odd when I came to think of it, I'd never once seen) only to discover that she was, in some inconceivable fashion, not a mere double or revenant or incubus, but, in very fact, Gül herself in person, metamorphosed into a monster, no, an angel of unmitigated carnality, forever well and young. Then we would rush to the bathroom, Dédé and I, to find it full of gas, but Gül would be gone. There would be a note scrawled in lipstick: "Sorry."

Treading on air, as it were, we would drive out to the château. Then, as we unpacked, Gül would suddenly walk in, and the two of them, Gül and Dédé, would turn on me.

All my life I have surrounded myself with strictly 1900-style Art Nouveau things. I cannot imagine living any other way than in silence and darkness, with clocks, books, pictures, and pleasant smells.

On the bed next to me, Dédé is working with the pipe and needles. I have always been in awe of Dédé's protean trick of mind. True to his name Dédale, he has an inventor's hands and understands flight. He is the only source of the opium I have smoked, and where he gets it I have never known. He is friends with the Prefect. He takes care of my clocks and arranges the mechanism of my life. The pipe is trained over the lamp. In the silence I can hear the opium cook. Dédé inhales it at a drag, then lies still. I picture a sea lion resting in the sun.

In the Hand of the Wind

Toward the end of the fifth day I paused for breath at the head of a slope of shingle slate. Thousands of tiny slat-like fragments had been coming loose in miniature landslides every step of the way up. Now I walked out onto a field of boulders. On the other side of a big one that blocked my view of the snowfields still pink with sunset, I saw a very large, unfinished cement building constructed along fascist architectural lines, with a sweeping façade, designed, like that of the Potala in Lhasa, to give it an appearance of jutting up in interstellar blackness.

I smelled smoke. On the far side of a front courtyard, a small fire was burning on the stone porch in front of a looming cavity where the building's main entrance would have been. The yard was full of sheep, baaing, milling, filling the air with a smell of mountain meadow shit. The noise alone made for an astonishing uproar. I marched in, as matter-of-factly as I dared, grasping my stick. The dog, busy with the sheep, merely glanced my way and took no more notice.

At the fire, wrapped in a gray woolen cloak like a horseblanket, was the first human being I had seen in a week. My initial impression was of her sun-blackened face and hands, her hair sandy blond, her eyes sea-green, a rarity in Andalusia; at least, I had never encountered that reseda verging on turquoise in a southern Spanish eye. To my greeting she gave no answer. I nevertheless got the feeling it would be all right to set my pack down near the fire.

She continued to ignore me.

After a second attempt to communicate, it crossed my mind that she might not be all there. I rolled a couple of smokes, using the crumbly French military-issue tobacco still in my gear. The operation took half a minute, but she didn't seem to be watching. I noticed the construction of her face; there was nothing moronic in that wide forehead, those high cheekbones, full lips, alert eyes. It was a beautiful face.

I offered the cigarette. She accepted it without acknowledging my presence, the way somebody one is on close terms with may take a cigarette out of one's hand as though plucking it from thin air.

She seemed to enjoy it. After a while she began putting supper together. I offered ham, bread, and cheese from my pack, which she accepted impassively, as though we were a couple of workers in a short-order kitchen, instead of a shepherd and a student, a fact of which I was being insistently reminded by the sheep's baaing as we squatted on the stoop, and by the shit smell in my nostrils, even as I inhaled the dizzyingly powerful Army smoke.

We ate in silence. She never met my glances. There was no sign of another person's things. No man. I broke out the last of my wine. We shared it without a word. I began talking to her in my mind, addressing her in the style of Theocritus or Virgil.

The upshot of this mental serenade was zero. Not a move, not a glance in my direction. She looked thoughtful. What was she thinking? At the same time, I asked myself if it was all that aberrant or criminally out of line that when I look at the lineaments— mouth, jaw, nose, above all, eyes—of someone I could desire, I am reminded of a thing that tells me I have the right to speak and tell you you are beautiful, what I mean is, you look like me.

Her eyes seemed to widen. I moved over next to her and touched her back, then her knees. There was a sound. I couldn't hear but only felt it at first. It was like a purr. She purred and I stroked. It became a very loud purr. It turned into a growl. Then a spitting roar. Lickety-split she was all over me and I was rolling ass-over-backwards on the cement floor, fighting for my life, no, we were just wrestling now, just fooling. She relaxed her grip and threw her head back laughing, several teeth missing and others half rotted out. Her laughter echoed in the bare halls behind us. The wind had gone down, the sheep more or less subsided. The dog crouched at the foot of the stoop, looking at us, whining. We started making faces at each other, hooting, squawking, screeching. She kicked me, aiming at my balls. I rolled and took the point of her hard rubber sandal in the thigh. She had nothing on underneath her skirt. I tackled her and started licking the inside of one of her legs. She yanked me off by the hair, scrambled to her feet, and led me by the wrist into a room deep inside the building, where she pulled me down with her on top of a pile of rags and we fucked.

Shivering from the cold, we went back out to the fire. She kicked it up a bit. I reached into my pack, rummaging for the blue ballpoint and notebook. *Tant pis*, an event like what had just happened would never fit the narrow-gauge type of note-taking that was the best I knew how to do.

I glanced at my hand. The left, the one I used for sex. The Arabs consider it unclean. One isn't supposed to eat or offer things with a hand used for ass-wiping and touching genitals. I stared at it. *Mano sinistra*, hand of desire and of the hellfire of lust, also of strength, justice, the knife. Focusing on the part between forefinger and thumb—the part that can bulge like a little egg—I began drawing a tattoolike figure.

I started the figure with a plus sign superimposed upon an x. Within each of the wedges formed by the four lines round their common intersection I placed a dot, making a circle of eight dots in all. Atop the centerline, surmounting the figure as a whole, I drew an inverted heart-shaped leaf.

Out of the corner of my eye I could see her at my elbow almost touching me . . .

I pointed to the two uppermost dots: nostrils. The next: eyes. Then, hands. And at the bottom, feet. At the center the spine and the leaf it impales—heart, genital, tongue. Not only could the figure be either male or female, I remarked over my shoulder, it was both at once, fucking.

I began going over the figure with the ballpoint, thickening the lines, and as I worked, a crystalline voice became audible from very near, whether singing or speaking I knew not, not daring to turn, although it felt as if she had been smiling all along, to herself, as it were, and then had looked up at me with the same smile overspreading her whole face, as our eyes now for the first time actually met. Yet this was only a feeling, because she was behind me. I found myself incapable of turning around to face her. My eyes remained fixed on the blue lines I was continuing to dig into the back of my hand. The voice sang on, like a bright, possibly poisonous fluid entering my ear:

The make-believe tattoo represents the planets and the sun, including Neptune, Uranus, and Pluto. The heavenly bodies are principles of nature. The nature of each living being is that of a sembrador, or seeding machine. It has nothing to do with sperm,

*or the erroneous theory of a split in the universe somehow joined
by an infinitely repeated confluence of male and female fluids, as
though the polarity were only sexual. The seed-engine is your skin
stretched drumlike over the frame of a lifetime. The seed is an
invisible pollen emitted through your pores, each of which represents one minute, propagating something that has no name,
although there are glib words such as joy. As each pore opens, eternity rushes through. Heaven, like the sky over your head, consists
of thin air, which, if you take a closer look, is only transparent
nothingness, yet at a distance it is the unmoving blue ether, the
source and destination of everything that moves. Get out.*

I shut my eyes, then, after a while, stood up in front of the near-
dead embers. She was gone, and with her, the animals.

That afternoon, stripped to the waist in bright sunlight a long
scramble further up, I stopped at one of many brooks on the way
and had a chunk of nearly petrified cheese and some chocolate.

Sitting there, I noticed something strange coming my way from a
quarter-mile off, round the next bend in the trail. The slope of the land
was steep, with no trees, just a few bushes here and there. Six black bulls
were running toward me. From their frolicsome way of bounding up
the slope and back onto the path, I judged they must be young. Back
at the village I had been told that choice novillos destined for the ring
were pastured in the high mountains. Suddenly I was terrified. This was
like the silent-movie situation, tied to the rails in front of a rapidly
advancing train. I could see horns gleaming in the sun. I recalled a passage from a Norse saga: "The closer the army came, the greater it grew,
and their glittering weapons sparkled like a field of broken ice . . ."

The two lead bulls kept leaping off the trail, scrambling to and
fro on the slope. What was I going to do? Creep into a bush? There

was no boulder I could scale that one of them couldn't leap onto. I pictured myself being gored. I got up on a rock and sat very still. Images of Minoan Crete crossed my mind. The palace of the bulls. The bare-breasted goddess. The teenagers with big eyes on the sides of their faces doing somersaults between the bulls' sharpened, flower-wreathed horns, the mosaics of undersea life, porpoises, seasnakes, octopi, and, in the basements underneath all this, the Labyrinth, the waiting Minotaur.

They rushed by. I never felt so much live force, such almost-winged brawn, pass so near. I watched till they reached the next downtrail bend, vanishing as suddenly as they materialized.

At sundown I reached the jumping-off place for my final climb. Next to the trail was a cave, marked on the map as a "refugio natural." The opening was just big enough to wiggle through.

Inside was a space sufficient to hold a dozen people. Straw was laid down a foot thick at one end. I set out three candles. I only had four left. I chewed on a piece of the ham I'd bought in Trevélez, washing it down with cold water and the last of the brandy. I recalled a couple of lesbians I was friends with in Paris. One night we were drinking in their room at Saint Germain des Prés. They had a tiny record player. Despite bitter cold, they stripped to the waist and danced an acrobatic dance like that of the adolescent gymnasts at Knossos. They kept grabbing each other's tits and wanted me to join in but I refused.

The next thing I knew, there was daylight at the cave entrance. Getting up to heat water for tea, I found a couple of the small black beetles local people call *curas* (priests). The school teacher exiled in Trevélez had told me why: Like priests, he explained, their habit is black, they breed without fucking, and they are useless.

I put on woolen socks inside my sandals, because the snow began only a couple of hundred feet above the cave. In the cave entrance I noticed a couple of alpine flowers, pink and blue. The weather was perfect, sunny with no wind. I stowed as much of my gear as I dared in a corner of the cave and covered it with straw, then shoved my knapsack through the opening and squirmed out after it, hitching along so as not to crush the flowers. For a second, as I emerged, my eye lit on the mark I had made on my hand, with its eight dotted segments and tonguelike spade licking out of the wrist end of the heart vein like an extra finger.

Glimpsed from above ten minutes later, the boulder next to the cave looked tiny, as though seen from an airplane. I was already climbing across snow, punctuated here and there by a stretch of bare rock. I paused for breath. The air was clear and still as the inside of a bell jar. It had taken forever to boil water. My breath seemed to be coming shorter, too. In the mountains one is always being deceived by appearances. The higher I went, the simpler the view. Mountain people, having seen it, never pause to look. For the first time now, the sea was visible. Far in the distance was the port of Málaga, with tiny ships going in and out, the coastal plain extending north and south, and to my left, smoke rising from the factory town of Mortil, and on the other side of it, the plain where the sheep I had seen wintered. Most of the shepherds were on a never-ending round trip between here and there, following the seasons and the depletion of the pastures. "Hardly any own their own flocks, or eat meat, or sleep in a bed, even for a week out of the year," one that I met had told me. "Talk about the wretched of the earth," he said, hawking up a gob of yellow spit which he wiped from his bearded lips with the back of a tanned, scrawny wrist.

I looked out over the water, straining my eyes for the promised sight, "Africa visible on clear days." I was suddenly inside a swirl of fog which passed as quickly as it had enveloped me, and sailed on, a solitary cloud in a warm blue sky.

As I continued I realized climbing was getting tougher by the minute. My heart pounding, I had to stop. I heard an airplane engine. I turned. Several hundred feet to the southeast, at about my altitude and so on a level with me, moving so slowly it seemed suspended in midair like a dragonfly hovering above a pool, was a Stuka divebomber with Spanish airforce markings. I have always admired the Stuka's lines. This airplane, only yesterday the terror of Europe, looked absolutely harmless. I stared as it floated past, a rakish dream, its hull and wings covered with an olive-green skin, its huge transparent cockpit like an aquarium in which the pilot and observer were bathed in light and noise, I could even make out their flying suits and goggles. The plane banked slowly and headed toward Málaga, diminishing to a speck in the sky over the sea, and then was gone.

I had reached the summit. I stood on a crust of snow. There was no wind. The air felt cold but the sun warm. I could see Africa, a wiggly line silhouetting mountains in Morocco, just inside the blue bowl of the sky. I fished out a crumpled cigarette, the last in a pack of Ideales purchased a week earlier.

Glancing down, I noticed a fat black and yellow bee climbing across the top of my knapsack, which I had set down atop a snow-powdered cairn. It had probably ridden up with me from the cave. The life of the bee, according to Maeterlinck, represents a mysterious spiral of light in overwhelming darkness. Like my own self-illumined trajectory, the bee's seems to have been kindled to no purpose save that of perhaps entertaining darkness. A shadow crossed the sunlit canvas where the solitary hymenopteran sat trembling as though poised for flight.

"Look up," a voice commanded.

Hovering directly overhead was a thirty-foot-long cigar-shaped balloon, with an open-frame nacelle of bamboo, mahogany and woven basketwork in which sat the speaker, an olive-skinned fellow in his forties with a salt-and-pepper beard, a bowler hat, and a faded white lab smock. A rain of pearl-gray ash from a wet cheroot alighted on the snow at my feet. It was Santos-Dumont, the South American aviation pioneer, inventor of the dirigible balloon, a boyhood admiration. He had cut the engine and glided in over the mountaintop in perfect silence.

"I'm heading for a location in the high Atlas," he told me. "Throw in your knapsack, give that propeller a yank, jump clear, and when I nose her in, just grab this rail and swing aboard alongside me."

"Mighty strange, meeting you here," I exclaimed, as we soared up and away. "I'd thought you died in 1914."

"Wrong again, my friend," the aeronaut replied. "I went back to South America and spent fifteen years tinkering with heavier-than-air, but nobody understood my concept of vertical lift, so I disappeared in 1932."

"Whereas," I interrupted, "books say that you were ordered to develop a dive bomber by the French War Department, and took an overdose of sleeping pills rather than comply. You even left a note (I read it) stating your unwillingness to dishonor Aviation by turning it into an unsporting means of killing other human beings."

"I'd heard you were saying that," the old inventor groaned, "and even, I am embarrassed to say, with tears in your eyes. You misread your sources. You got me mixed up with someone else, a fellow I never liked, whose reasons for killing himself were anything but noble." He cocked an eye at me: What does one discuss, being an older and a younger person, while perched side by side in the hand of the wind?

Neither of us spoke.

At last I ventured:

"Surely there's something important to say. Most likely it would have to do with thinking."

"*Thinking*," he echoed.

"If you understand how a word breaks and vibrates—and each word does break and vibrate like the lights of a great city seen by night from high above—then you *know* that thinking progresses stepwise from the firefly-like impulses that can be pinpointed and tracked to the more subtle layers that elude all possibility of observation: and the well-formed strings never cease generating, no matter how far back, or deep, you go. Keep going, you still capture those rising and falling thirds, the wave-motion of speech. You heard it long ago in Beethoven's *Hammerklavier*. It's the core of the *Gloria tibi Trinitas cantus firmus* on which your life has turned for the past half-dozen years. It's the wave shape of language, and that is why this stepwise progression of thought, deeper and deeper into the abyss, is accomplished solely by knowers of language."

"And yet," (I put in), "the essence on the other side of all this is no doubt the causal one, ultimately."

"Wait a minute!" he said. "Don't you think we might come down a peg? You're not the twenty-two-year-old who only a week ago started up that molehill we just left behind us. You're a middle-aged man with grey hair, cropped like a convict in my day. And there's an odd line there on your skull that looks as though they'd trepanned you in some Andean cave a thousand years ago."

"Whereas *you* . . ." I cried.

"Never mind me! By this time you must have noticed that you don't *see* me. I don't see you either. Why should I? We're not blind, none of us are, you know, but we don't need to see. We *hear* everything."

At that instant, out of nowhere, words formed: We can hear. We hear a diamond weep inside your skin: *Breath, enter immortal wind . . .*

I whispered: "We heard that."

He went on:

"Your wife's father on Staten Island in the forties had a faded jersey he played ball in, in the park Sundays, same color as a lime lollypop. A gentle, agile man. The jersey had lettering in white, with a white cow: WEISSGLAS. The Weissglas Dairy had a team that he was on. You met her thirty years ago, always her dad's favorite girl. Listen. She's reading:

July 28th

Yesterday he and I cut a huge thistle in the field below. Every year it appears, and every year I cut it down before it seeds itself into the hillside. Wearing heavy gloves, we put it in a gray stoneware jug on the kitchen table. It has four heads, one already opened into the vase or thistle shape, the other three still closed.

Its leaves were a luminous silvery green, with stickers also reflecting light.

The vase-shaped flower of long mauve quills showed at its center a white section like the stopper on a thermos bottle, or a rose shape of the type called a *gül* in Central Asian weaving.

By positioning ourselves directly above, we succeeded in inhaling a very faint fresh scent, without getting stuck, or stung.

This morning, as we watched, the whole flower became a ball of quills, at the same time releasing a fine white powder of pollen all the way around.

This evening we watched as a second bud opened, but only just sufficiently to disclose a minute portion of the whiteness.

On Spirals

As soon as a child has a consciousness, the child starts altering it. Who doesn't remember that favorite in every nursery and kindergarten, the big noisy tin top with a crank you pushed all the way down, to set it spinning, and a brightly colored spiral, red or yellow, say, painted round its outside? You watched that a few times, your head was spinning, you were stoned, so screwed up you might stagger, even fall, during the first few seconds after watching it. Lacking a top, you could become one yourself, alone or with help. Each child has at least one hour's worth of background as a whirling dervish.

The spiral is a dizzying curve. No matter where you find it, you may suffer something like the giddiness of headlong forward motion, either inward toward a point of nonentity at a center, nonexistent, or outward into a limitless void whose existence is likewise problematic. Either way, it's magic. In Alejandro Jodorowsky's film *El Topo* (1970) there is a line, "The path to the center of the desert is a spiral."

Dante patterned the *Divine Comedy* in descending and ascending spirals. The funnel of the tornado that carried Dorothy to Oz was an ascending spiral. A classic descending one is the vortex in Edgar Allan Poe's "Descent into the Maelström."

The Sanskrit dictionary gives several terms for *spiral*:

आवर्तनी = whirlpool, vortex
परिवर्तक: = turn-around, revolution
व्यावर्तन = coil (of a snake)
अलकाकार = curl shape, lock of hair
चक्रकार = chakra-shape

This leaves doubt as to whether they had a fixed geometrical term for it—or did it remain for them, to quote Mallarmé,

AS IF

> *An insinuation   merely*
> *in the silence   rolled up in irony*
> *or*
> *the mystery*
> *flung down*
> *howled out*
> *in some neighboring   whirlpool of hilarity & horror.*

Our own galaxy is a spiral, of course, but there are plenty of other galactic patterns out there—the elliptical, for instance—so a spiral is by no means universal in the cosmic-patterning sense. Spiral galaxies often come in pairs with opposite rotation relative to each other, a nearby example being M51. They all consist of mass ejected from a nucleus. Physicists speculate as to whether there are black holes at the centers of these spirals.

A classic locus for spirals is the correspondence between Descartes and Father Mersenne on the logarithmic, or infinite, spiral. This spiral has the fastest rate of increment of any spiral. Descartes gave up on it as "insoluble by the human mind." Torricelli took up the challenge and in 1645 published his results in a paper, *De Infinitis Spiralibus*, describing a curve whose main characteristic was that "if any angle formed by any two radii be bisected, then the central radius is a mean proportional between the outer radii, or the square of the central radius is equal to the product of the two extremes."

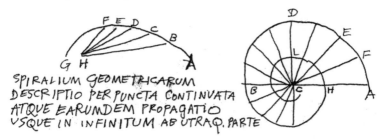

"If a line, with one of its extremities fixed revolves at a constant speed & if a point moves along this line in accordance with the law that at the same it will pass through continuously proportionate spaces, this point will describe a curve which we may call a geometrical [i.e., logarithmic, or infinite] spiral."—Letter to Michelangelo Ricci, March 17, 1646.

When René Daumal and Roger Gilbert-Lecomte launched *Le Grand Jeu* in 1929 the artist Joseph Sima created a spiral logo that appeared on the cover all *Grand Jeu* publications:

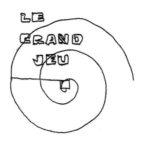

It is in fact derived from the arithmetical spiral of Archimedes, which differs from that of Torricelli as a bedspring from a snail.

In Pound's *Cantos* there is a famous passage inspired by Dante and Blake with a steel mountain and a spiral road, "like a slow screw's thread" (XVI). Eliot Weinberger writes, in *Works on Paper*, pp. 18–19: "memory is a vortex, a simultaneity. [And *vortex* is an East-West conjunction: Pound found the term in the pamphlets on Hinduism he read in his late adolescence.] . . . Our metaphor for memory is the modernist poem; and in its collages, mental shorthand, even in its incomprehensible passages, it may be the purest form of autobiography: the text closest to its inventing mind." (This is from an essay on the memory palace of Matteo Ricci published in 1984.)

The same model of memory as *vortex* was given to me verbally by John Carroll, head of the psycholinguistics lab at Chapel Hill. He says a vortex is the shape of the mind inside the brain and memory = mind = vortex. The track of our thinking is thus always in *spirals*. (Carroll was a follower and editor of the great Benjamin Lee Whorf whose name I always took for *whorl*.)

A key passage on the spiral in Jung's *Psychology and Alchemy*, pp. 207ff.:

> We can hardly help feeling that the unconscious process moves spiral-wise round a centre, gradually getting closer, while the characteristics of the centre grow more and more distinct. Or perhaps we could put it the other way round and say that the centre—itself virtually unknowable—acts like a magnet on the disparate materials and processes of the unconscious and gradually captures them as in a crystal lattice. For this reason the centre is . . . often pictured as a spider in its web, especially when the conscious attitude is still dominated by fear of

unconscious processes. But if the process is allowed to take its course . . . then the central symbol, constantly renewing itself, will steadily and consistently force its way through the apparent chaos of the personal psyche and its dramatic entanglements . . . Accordingly, we often find spiral representations of the centre, as for instance the serpent coiled round the creative point, the egg.

Indeed, it seems as if all the personal entanglements and dramatic changes of fortune that make up the intensity of life were nothing but hesitations, timid shrinkings, almost like petty complications and meticulous excuses for not facing the finality of this strange and uncanny process of crystallization. Often one has the impression that the personal psyche is running around the central point like a shy animal, at once fascinated and frightened, always in flight, and yet steadily drawing nearer.

The foregoing paragraph describes the psychic process which a musical form, the fugue, mirrors—it's called a *fugue* because it *flies* and *flees* the other voices which pursue but in fact the arrangement of subject, countersubject, and episode is like a clockwork turning on a center into which all converge, in the *stretto*; it's a centripetal implosion, as it were, out of which the coda may yet soar. The ancestor of *fugue* in Renaissance music is called a *fantasia*. The fugue has its analogue in the Garden of Eden, where Adam flees from God, which is what we all spend our lives doing, fleeing from that to which we must return. In Gnosticism (and in some Jewish mystical thinking, the Zohar for instance) we're all sparks of light that flew out of a primordial explosion and our homeward spiraling thru the void is what makes the music of the spheres. (Flight, pursuit, return are big themes in *Creation and Fall* by Dietrich Bonhoeffer and also *Gravity and Grace* by Simone Weil, both roughly contemporary and both victims of the Second World War.)

The Jung passage on the spider is borne out by Mallarmé and the Upanishads. Mallarmé: "I had found . . . the center of myself where, like a sacred spider, I hang on the main threads which I have already spun from my mind. With these—*and at their intersections*—I shall make the miraculous laces which I foresee and which already exist in Beauty's bosom."—Letter to Théodore Aubanel, July 28, 1866.

Brahma Upanishad: "The Jiva [जीव, 'mortal soul'], (identifying himself with) the Indriyas [senses], rules them like a spider. The spider throws out from a single thread out of his body a whole web, and draws it into himself by that same thread . . . 'as the spider throws out threads and draws them back,' so the Jiva goes and returns in 'the Jagrat and Swapna' [waking and sleeping states]."

The Sanskrit root *vṛt* is what many of these whirlpool and vortex words come from in Sanskrit philosophy and *vṛtti* means *change*. Thus the related Latin *vortex*, and *vertere*, to turn, to change. And the old Roman God Vertumnus, god of the changing seasons.

Three important works that I have not yet seen deal with the subject of spirals. (1) The Dover paperback titled *Mazes and Labyrinths*. (2) An essay in the late writings of Wilhelm Reich on the relation of orgasmic energy to the geometrical spiral. (3) Jill Purce, *The Mystic Spiral: Journey of the Soul*, Avon paperback, "Art and Imagination" series.

Another of the spiral-words in Sanskrit is *halika*, curl, relating to *helix*. Consider the double helix in genetic structure. Look at the caduceus with one or two snakes entwined on the rod. Also the rod on which Moses raised a metal serpent, to which Jesus compares himself as he will be on the Cross, in the Gospel of John. Also the coiled serpent of Kundalini.

According to a recent book on mystic diagrams of India, ॐ = OM, the sacred syllable, breaks down into "curves having an element of the spiral" (Madhu Khanna, *Yantra: The Tantric Symbol of Cosmic Unity*, p. 38). The same author speaks about the occult yantras appearing in the eighth-century Tantric poem the *Soundarya Lahari* (Ocean of Beauty), "in which soaring trajectories are created by the eccentric movement of linear impulses in space. Line . . . is the product of 'cosmic stress' and implies movement, flux and growth. . . . these yantras appear as a spiral around an invisible source, and are therefore to be associated with the coiled Kuṇḍalinī Śakti, the energy of the subtle body. Others form eddies or curves, tracing wandering paths, or are intersecting ovoids, dissolving into space, mapping, as it were, the cosmic secrets" (p. 154).

The Greek *helix*, spiral, curl, whirl, has other significant meanings. Homer applies it to sheep, meaning "crumple or spiral-horned." The paths of carding-wheels, Heraclitus wrote, are both twisted and straight. Is time a stream, a straight line, a trajectory like that of an arrow, a curve, a great circle like the stream of Oceanus as pictured by Homer, a tail-devouring snake, or a spiraling succession of cycles? The adjective and noun *helix*—it is both in Greek—also applied to spiral-shaped arm bands and earrings representing coiled snakes. The word also denoted tendrils, as of ivy. The related verb *helisso* meant to whirl, twirl, spin. Lightning sets the raft of Odysseus a-spinning between his departure from Calypso's island and shipwreck on the Hawaiian-sounding isle of Aiaia. The same root is present in Latin *volvo*, revolve, turn. *Vulva* might seem related by reason of its form. The thread of Ariadne, guiding Theseus from the center of the labyrinth to the outside, described a spiral. A remarkable document of the Minoan script known as Linear A is inscribed on a disc in a spiral. (The text remains undeciphered.) In the comic strips of the 1940s and '50s, a tiny free-floating spiral was one of several shapes denoting cuss words, when a character is "making the air blue." Possibly this was because the shape suggests a screw. The connection between spiral and screw is basic; the geometry of the one was first formulated by Archimedes, who was also the inventor of the other. A marine propeller, otherwise known as a screw, was invented by him as an extension of dynamic properties intuited in this curve. A question mark is a spiral (?) set above a point, the shape of the human ear, itself so formed the more efficiently to funnel the sound of every answer into the labyrinth of its Minotaurine penetralia. The Greek question mark is the same, but the point is above the spiral (;)— whereas the Spanish, last inheritors of the Minoan bullring, make an oppositely rotating pair—¿?—reminiscent of the paired spirals astronomers observe in the heavens. A corkscrew is yet another practical application of the spiral's power to uncork that which lay sealed up inside. Likewise, to screw means to fuck. The connection comes from the old terms male and female screw.

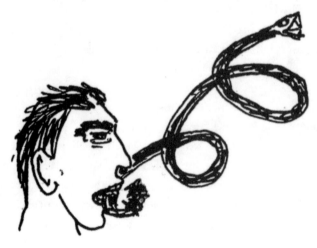

On August 22, 1945 André Breton sat in a Hopi *kiva* in New Mexico thinking of the Utopian philosopher Fourier:

> Because if the rattlesnake was one of your pet aversions . . .
>   I salute you from the bottom of the ladder which plunges into the great mystery . . . at the hour when the serpents with a last coiling show that they are ready to operate their junction with the human mouth. (*Ode to Charles Fourier*)

(Who hasn't, as a child, set off gunpowder "snakes" and watched them coil in the grass amid clouds of smoke? This leaves an oily trace on the ground, like Gerard Manley Hopkins's vision of God's grandeur, "like the ooze of oil crushed." Fireworks and the mind of God are among a child's favorite ways of screwing around.)

In Ursula K. LeGuin's future utopia *Always Coming Home* (1985), the central symbol is a pair of complementary spirals, the *heyiya*. The term is defined: "sacred, holy, or important thing, place, time, or event; connection; spiral, gyre, or helix; hinge; center; change. To be sacred, holy, significant; to connect; to move in a spiral, to gyre; to be or to be at the center; to change; to become. . . ."

Another book by a poet with the spiral as its central figure is Yeats's *A Vision* where the whole concept is developed from *gyres*. (The gyre is Yeats's version of the mystic spiral or vortex.) The spiral figures prominently in *Dawn Visions* (1964) by Daniel Moore, a book-length poem composed under the spell of Hindu philosophy, raga, and the mystique of psychedelic vision, yet with Dante's invisible presence throughout, the spirals, descending and ascending, of the *Divine Comedy*. The opening poem of *Dawn Visions* comes, via surrealism, straight from Canto I of the *Inferno*:

A hole the size of a pupil
  opens out in a spiral, O fanning out! Let us go
thru it into the wood that bares its teeth and roars silent
      down the
      narrow path of deeper insight / hold a lighted
    match our guide will try to extinguish
        and let it be extinguished!

      [. . .] our muscles will be oars
  when we reach the phosphorus river

The book closes in a vision of "SPIRAL FOOTPRINTS FROM THE PEAK."

From all of the foregoing it would appear that the spiral symbolizes the grandest motions of the human and cosmic minds, which is just what spoils it. Too easily this grand archetype degenerates into a grandiose cliché. On the negative side, I think of the phrase "turning in circles," meaning living aimlessly, foolishly. In the Mahayana classic सद्धरमपुण्डरीक (Lotus of the True Law) Chapter Five speaks of how those blind from ignorance remain in the "whirl," whereas the enlightened one, prompted by compassion, "appears in the triple world and sees with his eye of wisdom that the creatures are revolving in the circle of the mundane whirl, and are toiling without finding the right means to escape from the rotation." Likewise, the Bhagavad Gita pictures the entire cosmos as an imaginary machine turning round and round, the word for that machine being यनतुर, yantra. In Act One of Goethe's *Faust*, Satan in the shape of a poodle runs round Faust and Wagner in a tightening spiral until face to face with them in a field outside the city wall. Another negative image suggested by the spiral is in the phrase "down the drain," covering a multitude of unpleasantnesses swirling toward cesspools real or figurative.

My own earliest associations with the spiral were unpleasant. It was the shape of a toy I hated but could never escape—it was in every nursery and classroom, or so it seemed—the so-called "Slinky toy." The other association, much worse, was a film, *The Spiral Staircase*, about a woman threatened by a sex murderer in a house with a spiral staircase. The latter is I think somehow involved in the dénouement. It gave me nightmares for years; and so, long afterward, when I was translating René Crevel's *Difficult Death*, it came as no surprise that the worst of several nightmares narrated in that book also featured a spiral staircase.

As a form in nature—as a whirlpool or eddy in the surf, of the kind known on Eastern Long Island as a *seapoose* (from an old Indian word meaning a river in the ocean)—or as a shape such as that of a nautilus shell—the spiral speaks directly, without the cliché inherent in every figure of speech, even the most beautiful and apparently truthful. The edge of the ocean may be the kind of place where the spiral is more in its proper element than in books or other works of art.

The word *spiral*, by the way, does not exist in Classical Latin, but was coined by Albertus Magnus in around the year 1255.

Letter to a Young Poet

February 14, 1991

Dear R—,

You must forgive me for a hasty reply. I work a 9 to 5 job and try to keep up with my work as a writer while at the same time meeting a variety of personal commitments. This is a bit overwhelming. Your manuscript was the second unsolicited piece of writing that I have received this week with a request that I comment on it. I hope you realize that this is work for me.

I don't wish to discourage you in your endeavors, but I must say that it seems to me you are starting off wrong in a number of important ways that will obstruct your progress unless you remedy them. Because this is Valentine's Day I'm going to offer some tough love.

Your poems are full of mythological and literary references. I can't help wondering, What's Hecuba to him or he to Hecuba? Clearly you have followed Duncan's lead and swallowed Jung and his teachings whole. It seems to me that you construct from the outside (the theory of Archetypes) inward, instead of from the inside outward. You characterize your work to date as solid. That is an accurate description, in the sense of opaque. I can't begin to guess from reading the poems what manner of man is writing them. Who and what are you? How do you relate to the world we share? What dimension of this have you glimpsed that you know no one else has seen and you want to show the rest of us? None of this comes through, neither the mundane nor the transcendental. Furthermore, your choice of images and themes appears to have been dictated more by your reading than by your living. If that is true, you must do something about it. You have read all sorts of archetypal and literary background into my work which may or may not be there, but the one thing you fail to mention is life experience and fantasy, and the trick of blending the two so that the fantasy is abundant and surprising, yet the testimony of experience has the ring of absolute truth. All those archetypes and literary allusions are an involuntary background, a drone, an obligato over which I have no control. They are part of the weight of any piece of real poetry, but the poet does not have the privilege of introducing and manipulating them. I advise you to discover the events and themes and issues that mean so much to you in your own living that you cannot help putting them into poems that will get your unique vision and feeling about the situation across to an audience. Also, as you are writing, memorize short sections—especially the key sections— and say them out loud, trying to listen as if it were someone else trying to capture your attention and turn you on and around. Listen to your own voice. There are too many loose, slack, incomplete, or otherwise discombobulated sentences in your work. Go back to Duncan since he is your master. Forget about his themes and images. Forget too about his prosody and the look of his poems on the page. Go for his syntax. Look at how he plots a sentence. How he paces things between the short and incisive and the long and involved. You will find very few incomplete sentences in Duncan. You will find a marvelous wealth of grammatical tactics and strategies there. Why else would Duncan have read Pindar with such close attention? Pindar is a point of departure for Hölderlin,

Duncan, and through them for me. Also for the elliptical as against the linear progression of ideas. Listen to Duncan, listen to yourself. Anticipate your audience. On Channel 13 I once saw an unforgettable scene. A roomful of Turkish peasants deep in the Anatolian hinterland are listening to an oral epic bard. He is reciting a long poem. His audience stare at him, some of them with tears in their eyes, hanging on every word, breathless, carried away. That is what you ought to be aiming for and nothing less. I wish you well. Good luck.

Taking Risks Seriously

Interview with Ken Jordan

KEN JORDAN. Were this a *People* magazine interview, at some point you'd be asked: Just how does one become one of the invisible?

DAVID RATTRAY. "One of the invisible" really means a member of the invisible secret Utopia. It means somebody who is in this world but not really of this world. It is the antithesis of what they vulgarly call "exposure."

JORDAN. Invisible to whom?

RATTRAY. Invisible to whatever that is reflected in the glaring eye that gives you exposure, such as Channel 5, the NEA, and publications and trade publishers and a review in the *New York Times* . . .

JORDAN. They used to call this the underground.

RATTRAY. One of the first really good books that I ever read was given to me by my grandmother, who wanted to pass something good along to me: Ralph Ellison's *Invisible Man*. But that doesn't have anything directly to do with being somebody that would have been an underground artist thirty years ago.

JORDAN. Maybe it does.

RATTRAY. Maybe it does.

JORDAN. You can see where it might.

RATTRAY. If I'd never had any kind of education I probably would have ended up being some sort of an outsider artist in a jail or an insane asylum making cartoons with little texts . . .

JORDAN. If you hadn't had an education?

RATTRAY. But because I did have an education I didn't just reject the whole thing wholesale and say that every one of the professors and all the received classics was just a crock, which is what many of my respected contemporaries did. I didn't do that at all. Rather, I found in the works of many of the accepted and received classics that they had something valuable, beautiful, and real to communicate that was definitively worth listening to. So I found that my definition of the invisible could be enlarged to include figures such as John Hall Wheelock, a poet writing in a late nineteenth-century vein, who I quote in the book. A man like that is also part of the underground. Not every one of them has to be on the lam!

JORDAN. You were an undergraduate at Dartmouth?

RATTRAY. I went to the Classics Department there, and we read very intensively in Greek and Latin literature. I worked on that a lot, so it got into my blood and my bones. I read it to this day. But the one who brought it all together for me in the end was a wild man named Jack Hirschman, who is still well known as a poet.

JORDAN. He was a professor there?

RATTRAY. He was an instructor in the English department. He didn't do too well there because he wasn't just an academic, but with the students he did really well because he was a wonderful man, a fireball of energy, and he had all these great things for us to read.

JORDAN. Like what?

RATTRAY. Like John Wieners, for starters. Like Malcolm Lowry, Jean Genet, and William Burroughs. We'd never heard of these things. We got our initiation from Jack Hirschman. Artaud . . . I was sent to Artaud by Jack Hirschman. It was like living in the Book of Revelations.

JORDAN. And then where did that send you?

RATTRAY. It sent me straight to the wilds of Southern Mexico, where this poet friend, Van Buskirk, and I had a plan to smuggle vast quantities of marijuana into the United States. And we thought we would be able to live off the proceeds from selling it. It was like that movie, *The Treasure of the Sierra Madre*. It had a comically pathetic ending. We didn't get busted. We succeeded in bringing into this country something like a half a pound—some wretched amount— of rather mediocre Mexican pot. It didn't amount to a hill of beans! We brought that in at the risk of life and limb. I mean, not only did we expose ourselves to being murdered by Mexican gangsters or the police. We were friends with our landlord, the police commander where we lived. And he was a raving maniac, a very interesting man, a dope addict—I described him in great detail in the book. But if we hadn't been killed in that fashion, we had the US Immigration, the Customs Service, and the Texas Rangers to overcome.

JORDAN. Did you go straight from Dartmouth to Mexico?

RATTRAY. I first went from Dartmouth to France for two years on a Fulbright Fellowship, and I got a degree from the Sorbonne. I took it seriously and did well, I really learned a lot.

JORDAN. What were you studying?

RATTRAY. Still Latin and Greek, and we did some French studies, like Flaubert.

JORDAN. So the standard classics . . .

RATTRAY. Exactly. They were the received classics. But while I was there a poet named Harold Norse introduced me to the reading of William Burroughs. I've never met Burroughs, but I've read and admired him since 1958. Harold Norse gave me his copy of *Naked Lunch*, and I read it in one night, and it completely changed my life.

JORDAN. Why would you say that?

RATTRAY. Well, it gave me a whole perception of what is real and what is unreal, involving our culture and the things we were striving for. Burroughs had a very clear perception of that. He often used to think of how certain substances, both the standard ones like heroin and cocaine, and various mysterious other ones like yage in South America, and so on, have that specific ability to kill the editor that's in there in your optic nerves that prevents you from actually seeing things as they really are.

Burroughs was always a visually oriented guy, and so for him it's always what you see. He was literally a *visionary* and a *seer*. So he's thinking about what you see. And, obviously, 99 percent of what we see isn't really what's there. The editor that's in the optic nerve and other places in the brain that's receiving signals is sort of fudging things to help us survive, to cope better. But because it helps us cope, it also conceals from us the true nature of what we're looking at. There's a barrier between us and reality, and Burroughs was extremely keen on breaking down that barrier, and peeling away that dirty film between us and reality. And time and again he was thinking of heroin and various other things as ways to get rid of the affective garbage between us and what we really see. *The Naked Lunch* and *The Soft Machine*, these were the first ones that I gravitated towards. And I did gravitate towards them, big time. I was very, very attracted to Burroughs's vision and understanding of things.

JORDAN. Of course, so much a part of Burroughs's vision has to do with a heavily romanticized vision of life as an outsider, as a gangster . . .

RATTRAY. Well, you should have seen me in the early '60s!

JORDAN. I'm curious . . .

RATTRAY. In my black suit. I had this black suit and black wrap-around sunglasses, which I wore at all times. The breast pocket of the black suit was for my kit, which held all my drug paraphernalia . . . I was really quite a card, moving from one club to another listening to jazz, which was because of Van, who opened my ears to jazz. I embraced that romantic vision wholeheartedly.

JORDAN. It's a big leap from Dartmouth.

RATTRAY. I thought I was just jumping through a hoop that's in mid-air and coming out the other side. I remember it vividly as an experience just like that. You know, the Living Theatre had a thing towards the end of *Paradise Now*, they'd make a human pyramid, and those who dared could climb up onto the top of this pyramid and do a swan dive—it was called flying—and they would just leap off with their arms outspread like wings and fly into the waiting arms clasped together of the people in the audience who were waiting for them to come flying through the air towards the seats.

JORDAN. Did you jump?

RATTRAY. Of course. And flying was exactly what I thought I was doing when I stepped out of the academic world, out of that cocoon, to spread my wings and fly. And it included stepping into a way of living that involved the daily risk of life and limb and the systematic destruction of everything that a middle-class upbringing in East Hampton, Long Island, implied, and was supposed to lead to. I was supposed to become a professor of literature at an Ivy League college somewhere, married to a girl that'd come to East Hampton in the summertime, and it was all going to be very nice. My mother couldn't, for the life of her, understand what was wrong. She had no problem with me reading Jean Genet or the Marquis de Sade or Marcel Proust or anybody else, but . . .

JORDAN. She just didn't want you to take it seriously!

RATTRAY. Exactly. I could pursue my intellectual interest to my heart's content, but to live in a way that seemed to be implied by the things that really touched me most deeply, and made me feel that this was where I had to go—that was something that I can't blame my mother for not approving of! No one of her class and time could possibly have understood.

JORDAN. *How I Became One of the Invisible* brings together different kinds of writing—fiction, memoirs, and discursive essays—but it's wonderful the way the book coheres, because at its center are your interests and your sensibility, which is so specific and particular.

RATTRAY. I would say that this book really is a poetic autobiography. Whether it's stories of what happened in my life, as a young man and then later, or essays about books and writers that I considered or translated, the book always has to do with whatever it is that poetry is trying to find and communicate. I think that idea of finding and communicating is very important. Somebody recently asked me to define poetry, and I think it can be defined—people say that it can't, but I believe that it can. I think a simple one-phrase definition of poetry is: the invention of life or reality through language. To invent reality through words, this is what poetry does. And it isn't such a highfalutin' thing as such a definition might make it seem. I also think that if poetry isn't capable of keeping a roomful of Iraqi cab drivers enthralled for an hour, then it isn't worth a Goddamn thing. It must make people want to dance, or to make love, or to sing. It must fill them with the impulses to do something real in life; it must stimulate their imagination and their mind; it must entertain them and give them something to think about and provide them with some solid information. I believe that good poets and good poems do this.

JORDAN. The book includes essays about writers who you've translated, including Artaud, Crevel, Gilbert-Lecomte. What is it that attracted you to these figures?

RATTRAY. I *identified* with all of these people. I have a personal sense of identification with them because they shared that search to invent life through language, and it's a very dangerous and a tricky kind of search. Because you don't really know whether it's real. These guys were out on what Ken Kesey always used to call an "edge"—out on the edge—they were edge people. People who write on the edge of craziness or death or some kind of final confrontation with a recognition of the absolute emptiness and void of everything. Maybe nothing is real. Those people lived with that all the time, and so have I—all my life. And this isn't a before-and-after story. I'm living with it now. So I really identified with them. I felt a kinship with figures as different from each other as Émile Nelligan and Artaud and some of the other people that I talk about. Even ones that were spectacularly different from me, or at least the way that I conceive of myself. But those are my subjects because I feel that in a way they're my ancestors, my predecessors, my heroes.

JORDAN. What is it that brings them to the edge?

RATTRAY. Because they're stripped of the coping mechanisms that make for balanced living. In some cases this has happened to them situationally, because of the world in which we live; in other cases, maybe they willfully and perversely chose to embrace this. It happens differently to different people. But even the most well-balanced and sane people in the world can be confronted with some of these problems, and there really is not an answer to them. There really isn't any way to cope!

JORDAN. Of course, what makes these writers so fascinating to read is their commitment to write from the "edge" with such a determined honesty.

RATTRAY. To be honest in a real, absolute way is almost to be prophetic. And if you can be prophetic—though not too many people can be for very long at any time in their lives—but if at least that prophetic note is struck a few times, then it's gonna upset the applecart. And if that applecart is not upset, then conscious life just can't go on! This injection of irrationality and craziness and disorder into the ordered life is what regenerates life in general. Without it, we're going to get a hieratically ordered system, such as they had for many years in ancient Egypt, and among the Mayas, and so on. I think it could come very easily to us here, and probably will— thanks to IBM and all of these great, uniform institutions.

A very important part of what the poet is supposed to be doing is upset the applecart. Because, after all, the applecart is just an endless series of indigestible meals and social commitments that are useless and probably shouldn't even be honored, and futile, pointless conversations and gestures, and then, finally, to die abandoned and treated like a piece of garbage by people in white coats who are no more civilized or conscientious than sanitation workers. That's what the applecart means to me. And when a poet's voice, a poet's imagination, is able to touch people enough so that they will change that, of course it's upsetting the applecart. I think that poetry has a real kind of . . . I wouldn't say preachy kind of a function, but it definitely is there to support and encourage people to realize that there's a worthwhile life out there to be lived. A way of living that is there—that all you have to do is invent it. It's available to all of us.

JORDAN. When you say a "worthwhile life," and when Pat Robertson says a "worthwhile life," you're talking about two very different things. Would Artaud have been talking about a "worthwhile life"?

RATTRAY. Oh yes. He would have said, a life that is free. He would have said, without any organs. A body that didn't have any organs, meaning that all those biological imperatives, and, I suppose, social imperatives. Artaud, after he'd been sick with cancer long enough, was dreaming of a way to live that was pure and free and enlightened. And I think I can relate to that. In my book, when I was talking about cutting loose from those kinds of bonds, I quoted this poet August von Platen, whose diary of 1822 sums it up in just a rhyming quatrain:

> *To taste of nothing but the flesh of light*
> *Forever whole and sweet*
> *To drink of waters that refresh*
> *But never drive the blood to heat*

And I think that that kind of a life is really there, it just has to be invented.

JORDAN. And so the purpose of poetry . . .

RATTRAY. Is to help people invent their lives—through language!

JORDAN. And at the same time to subvert all that keeps one from living a real life.

RATTRAY. Yes, exactly. Even sometimes in a destructive way. I certainly don't think that the lessons in living that you can get from reading certain kinds of literature, including many pages by William Burroughs and Jean Genet, are all that edifying in a constructive way. But they help destroy, they help break it down. I remember the Marquis de Sade saying to someone—and of course he was always constructing these little imaginary debates—he said to this imaginary opponent: You build. You're always building. I destroy! I simplify! And many of these corrosive pages of the great or underground classics help to destroy—they're not very edifying or uplifting. They're good for people because they help to destroy something that needs to be destroyed, that needs to be subverted.

JORDAN. Would you say that there's more that needs to be destroyed today than when you started out thirty years ago?

RATTRAY. Oh, no doubt!

Excerpts from the Last Journal

Late January, 6 a.m.

Strong winds cleared the sky overnight. I got up to stars glittering
before dawn, a fingernail moon just over the line of dunes maybe two
hundred yards south of our bedroom window. A twisted pine here and
there, skirting the line formed by the dune tops silhouetted against the
moonglow, still a half hour too early for the first pale of dawn. L. and
I awoke at seven thirty, enlaced in each other's arms to cold, cloudless
sky, bright sunlight warming the luscious whiteness of the bedroom
walls which ever since I had them built and painted them in June 1988
have reminded me of the whitewashed walls of various rooms I have
occupied in the south of France, also in Andalusia, and long, long ago
in Yugoslavia and Greece: Split, Hvar, Dubrovnik, Míkonos.

I've had to turn the phone off. Persons from Porlock.
    For a long time I have desired to write a processional, pageant-like
poem that would somehow work like a cross between Hölderlin's
Friedensfeier and James Ensor's *Entry of Christ into Brussels*. This desire
of mine relates to geometry. It is a geometrical form of desire
involving horizontal and vertical axes like the ones that Simone Weil
explicates in her discursus on the Our Father (*Waiting for God*, 1942).

The Globe Theatre is too limiting a space for a *téatro del mundo*
such as the one that I keep straining to glimpse in my mind's eye.

Give me a horizontal platform between earth and heaven situated, let us say, on a flatland outside Benares. Picture a huge open space in strident sunlight and breathtaking heat beneath an absolutely empty sky in which the first detail to arrest the beholder's notice is a little room set high on stilts, a proverbial cabin in the sky, overlooking a crowd of kneeling devotees. Waving to them with an emaciated arm from a tiny window, in his white beard and turban, is their 250-year-old baba. From the window hangs an embroidered flag illustrating, diagram-like, the seven jewels of subtle reality. The crowd numbers in the ten thousands. Of holy persons there are hundreds, many of them naked and covered, Godiva-like, with the dreadlocks of decades passed in sustained yogic trance. The holy names of Vishnu and Shiva tattooed hundreds of times over their skin. Others with their tiger pelts and tridents, their hands red-stained. Devotees of Mother Kali with their skull bowls, thigh-bone flutes, and grim images of the all-consuming, all-merciful mother, their hands and faces smeared black with ashes from the cremation fires. Yet others in extravagantly gaudy peacock crowns, at once hilarious and sinister to contemplate, a thousand visions of sacred delirium on parade. An elephant slides past, its sides covered with red swastikas. On a passing float solid with marigolds, a dying swami sits propped up in half-lotus, his neck erected in samadhi, amid disciples engulfed in layered banks of cream-colored flowers in an overpowering cloud of fragrant smoke. The landing strip at the Grumman plant in Bethpage, Long Island was similarly wreathed in what for us fourteen-year-olds was sweet-smelling smoke on the day I attended the big model airplane meet there in the spring of 1950.

I hasten to add that we fourteen-year-olds of 1950 had no inkling of mind-altering chemistry, such as smoke or glue. I had seen a bit of what liquor could do and, like Stonewall Jackson, feared it more than yankee bullets. One golden morning on our side sunporch that summer as I sat over a blue Chinese bowl filled to the top with fresh peaches and cream, I read in our housekeeper Helen's *Journal-American* how the film actor Robert Mitchum had been arrested at a "Reefer Party" in Beverly Hills. What did it mean? I asked. It meant, Helen replied, that the world was full of traps that have to be avoided by hook or by crook.

Our Pusan Perimeter was rapidly shrinking. The tone, righteous and hortatory, of the North Korean, Chinese, and Soviet communiqués reminded me of that of the stirring hymns and the marches I had been playing to the other kids to sing at the East Hampton Sunday school: "Battle Hymn of the Republic," "Standing on the Promises," the "El Capitan" march. I looked at the peaches and cream and knew that the world I was growing up in was no more likely to last than the world of electric-powered buckboards, Langley Aerodromes, Moody and Sankey hymns, and John Philip Sousa marches that had long occupied my imagination.

Out on the airstrip was a bright orange biplane with stubby fuselage and wings, built for both speed and maneuverability, in, I believe I recall, 1934, by the Grumman company. This plane was to form the centerpiece of the afternoon's proceedings. A famous World War II flier (in the telling I have liked to think it was General Billy Mitchell in person) was at the controls of the orange biplane. After a few minutes of spectacular stuntflying almost directly over our heads our honored guest buzzed us and with a loud shriek hundreds of men and boys, whose voices had only just barely changed, hit the deck all at once. He buzzed us again.

The East Hampton Model Airplane Club was represented that day by maybe a dozen gasoline-powered models, set in the standard fashion, to fly round and round on a hand-held pair of wires controlling the tail and aileron flaps, to climb or dive. My brother's model was a basic silver and blue fighter, a Navy plane. And mine was a more basic high-wing monoplane, which I had painted bright red and yellow. That day my red and yellow monoplane took off fast, climbed almost vertically, then nose-dived fifty feet straight into the tartop runway where it shattered into two pieces. The force of the impact on the engine was such that the prop-shaft was bent out of alignment so that the engine could never be restarted. That afternoon I decided to abandon gas-powered flight in favor of rubberband models. The following winter my model of Blériot's monoplane took off gracefully from the basketball floor of the East Hampton High School gym and banked slowly a couple of times around the bleachers, earning me an honorable mention in the Rubberband Division.

My only regret at dropping powered flight (a Luddite from the start, I had always secretly loathed those engines) was that the old books which I preferred to any other reading on aviation almost invariably referred to airplanes as "machines." Was a rubberband model a true machine? I got out my parents' *Webster's Unabridged Dictionary*, the edition of 1909, and studied the entry for machine. This erased all doubts. My rubberband or (as I toyed with the idea of calling it, though I did not know how to pronounce the word) *caoutchouc*-powered model definitely qualified as a true machine, even though it amounted to no more than a few sticks of balsa, dovetailed using a razor blade and secured with a dab of LePage's cement, plus a thin skin of white tissue, doped and tightly stretched over the fuselage, the whole weighing no more than a couple of ounces. My monoplane flew only a few times successfully. Then one day I wound the rubber band a couple of times too many and cracked her keel. We tried stapling it with a bit of wood glue. This added too much weight and the balance became lopsided, she never flew again.

Christopher Smart states somewhere (in *Jubilate Agno*?) that the best harpsichords are strung with golden wires. This must be a figurative manner of speaking, but I have not yet deduced what he means. Napeague under wind-driven snow. Return to *The Journals of Gilbert White*. I could watch this one spot for a hundred years and never tire of it. Snowflakes chase after each other, as if alive.

Napeague.

Our friends Guy and Sarah Ouellette spent their honeymoon here three years ago and left us with a wall clock as a present. Its ticking is just the same as that which I heard for years at my grandmother's house on David's Lane, East Hampton. When they first left the clock, I failed to recognize the sound, one that I had not paid attention to in forty years. One day recently I realized that it was one of the most welcome and familiar of the small regular noises impinging on my life. We sit here, with that most inaudible ticking, and watch the dunes in the frozen sunset, consciously old-fashioned admirers of the dusk's brown air.

Just as I wrote the preceding sentence, L. drew my attention to the slider facing south from here. Barely discernable in the shadows was a fat doe, and then another, browsing in the crater of the dune touching the old Smith Meal railspur. We stood here in the dark for several minutes, watching the two animals as they passed out of sight.

It will soon be exactly thirty years since Lin and I first met. My old mentor (whom I never acknowledged as such) John Hall Wheelock described the relationship between Lin and me as one of high romance. So it is. My sister and I share a certain squint that is even there at unguarded moments, even in what for either of us would be once-in-a-blue-moon flash of delight. I oscillate between the squint and the flash.

* * *

Feb 17
My Birthday

A treat was Allen Planz who brought a group of extraordinary poems in which bioluminescences of deep-sea creatures is a main theme, but as always with Allen the poems range far. I admire the accuracy of the fishing language and idiom. Of course, Allen no longer has to aspire to that kind of "accuracy" because he *is* a fisher-man and a poet.

The bioluminescence of deep-sea creatures was not in itself a piece of news, but what I was amazed to learn from his conversation was that they have determined that *all* life is, to a degree, biolumines-cent; and that even when you get to extraordinary depths in the ocean there is still light in there, though it's very hard to detect: light is alive! That really astonished me. I think of a verse by Henry Vaughan:

> *I saw Eternity the other night,*
> *Like a great ring of pure and endless light,*
> *All calm, as it was bright.*

There is a connection between the words "calm" and "brightness" . . . "All calm, as it was bright." The connection is that "calm," from the Greek work *kaûma*, means brightness, very strong brightness, like that of an oppressively hot day at sea when there is no wind but a sizzling sun, that is the basic word from which calm derives. And yet there is the idea of brightness there. I think of the brightness of a singer's teeth, specifically Elisabeth Schwarzkopf singing a Mozart song. "*Ridente la calma, nell'alma si desti.*" Smiling calm installs itself in my soul.

Is the smile of a great opera singer necessarily comparable to that of Melville's "Maldive Shark"? I think not. But the brightness of the noonday calm over the tropical waters continues to shimmer in that one single word "calm." All the way from its oldest recorded etymons, as in a certain Western Semitic word which stands for a very white kind of linen that is shining to the eye. I think of the kind of linen that Nausicaa was washing with her friends when Odysseus arrived. All the way from that kind of image to the brightness of unmediated sunlight on the seawater, no matter how deep you go, it's still glowing in there.

There is an ancient Chinese classic that I mention in my "West from Napeague." *The Classic of Pure Calm.* For twenty years I've been putting off going to the Oriental Division of the New York Public Library to find out from Bill Paar, the librarian that I'm friends with there, in charge of Chinese antiquities, exactly what the content of *The Classic of Pure Calm* might be. It's obviously a philosophical text but I have no idea what it really is; I first found a reference to it in the Joseph Needham history of *Science and Civilisation in China.*

For years I've pondered the conclusion of Albrecht Dürer's collection of images titled *The Triumph of Maximilian*. These pictures were commissioned I think by the Emperor Maximilian in the 1520s and executed possibly by Dürer himself, possibly by his school. This work, which I have admired all my life, was published some years ago in a cheap reprint by Dover Books; it has been out of print for some time but was a boon to the public, to people like myself. The part of it that attracts me is where the procession that forms the subject of this great work trails off or thins out from a great imperial progress to, finally, a straggling group of scouts. They are no longer soldiers or knights or officials or musicians, just a group of scouts. Irregulars who are not under any visible military discipline but are simply foraging their way through the country. Somehow these final images rooted themselves very deeply in my mind. I have dreamt of creating a work that would trail off in the same way as *The Triumph of Maximilian* from something grandiose and processional into something that had lost its original character and become unrecognizable as a group that was under a special kind of discipline or formative patterning. Of course the patterning in the Dürer work is very strong and very beautiful but the ending no longer has anything to do with an imperial triumph, or with the values, I suppose, of organized culture and civilization. I should add to this that these scouts do not in any way resemble Quantrill's Rangers or other similar raiders. A very notable aspect of their appearance is that they are not threatening; they do not look like a group of dangerous evil fellows, to the contrary they look almost as if they might be harbingers of a future golden age or utopian state. They certainly do not look like cutthroats or bandits but perhaps pioneers of a new and different world. However this point is left ambiguous, happily so; the whole scene is enveloped in a mystery

that I find magical when I consider this work and the way it trails off into a kind of enigmatic shapelessness.

* * *

In the curvature of the curve

On my tenth birthday, February 17, 1946, my mother led a group of kids including myself out to a beach on Gardiners Bay, East Hampton, that was dominated by what for a child was a steep cliff. Springy Banks got its name from the fact that the first settlers used the word *bank* in the sense of "cliff," and also that these particular banks were *streaming with springs of sweet water*. It was an overcast day, bitter cold, and the bay was frozen solid. Someone had reported seeing a deer cross over to the island on the snow-encrusted ice a few days before. We ten-year-olds were eager to venture out ourselves, but to steer the proceedings away from a vision of thin ice, my mother shooed our little band up the icicle bedizened bank where soon we were scrambling along the loftiest brink, with an exhilarating view out over the bay's white surface, jagged with huge broken fragments, like an illustration from Captain Kane's Arctic expedition of 1847. I recalled my grandfather's ice saws and other tools with which he had harvested refrigerator ice, tons of it, for some years around the turn of the century. I had seen the ice houses, or roofed cellars, where it was stored, year round, so I was told. The bay and surrounding ponds had been so thickly frozen in those winters that a team and sledge could safely drive on the ice and many people went sailing on ice boats which they sailed at hair-raising speeds, just for fun. All of a sudden I lost my footing and went sliding downward.

After a terrifying moment, all was well. The incident was to repeat itself in various ways over the next half century, down to the day quite recently when a physician said that I am likely to go along nearly but not altogether okay for another few weeks or even months, and then the vital functions will give out rather suddenly, "like falling off a cliff."

The tumor presses on a nerve affecting spatial perception and relations. Yesterday I facetiously dubbed my vicissitudes within this self-distorting space ADVENTURES IN BROBDINGNAG. Though (in my mind's eye) already in free-fall, or on the verge of it, I continue to adapt rapidly, relearning how to type and play Tomkins and Frescobaldi at the keyboard every few days, so it would seem.

("It has been fascinating to be a part of this splendid evolutionary show" . . . *Harlow Shapley.*)

These adaptational skills are as inherent to the basic set-up of the central nervous system as a newborn infant's ability to swim (or even, as I recently learned, to count). The adaptations kick in so effortlessly for me in this slow-motion fall that it would come as no surprise if I were suddenly to sprout feathers and fly away, a new bird of passage. The flight in question, however, is accomplished not with a feather cloak, costumed in the plumage of one's intellect, imagination, or esthetic sense, but stark naked, without even so much as a suggestion of a single unaccompanied violin note.

("Do not choose the manner of thy dying; let God be thy chooser" . . . Jeremy Taylor, *Of Holy Dying.*)

I came to Taylor twenty years ago via the eccentric Logan Pearsall Smith, who was the son of a Camden, New Jersey bottle manufacturer, made much of as a small child by the aged and white-haired Walt Whitman. When grown, he moved to England—like Henry James, like Chips Channon, like any number of title-hunting debutantes gently spoofed in the pages of *Harper's Monthly Magazine* and *Punch.*

Logan Pearsall Smith had a mystique of perfect English prose. His *Trivia, More Trivia,* and *Unforgotten Years* show what he could do in all its curious and nectarine peachiness. In what for me was a capital episode, he had himself conveyed, a latter-day Empedocles, all the way up to the crater of the volcano surmounting Tenerife, in a sedan chair under the watchful supervision of his companion, Robert Gathorne-Hardy, a discreetly long-suffering soul whose memoirs, *Life with Logan Pearsall Smith*, gave my wife and our friend Peter Davies many hours of entertainment at some point in the late 1960s. The two of them, Bob Gathorne-Hardy and Logan Pearsall Smith, made several nearly disastrous trips together during the twenties and thirties. I seem even to remember one voyage to Iceland, presumably to get closer to the roots of Nordic narrative tradition through the works of Snorri Sturluson and the anonymous saga authors. On all of these peregrinations Gathorne-Hardy cuts the figure of a patient, loyal Mole or Ratty alongside an ebullient, often obstreperous Mr. Toad.

* * *

Lines written on the back of a map
left unfolded by design (for L.)

See along the horizon above Edmond's Col
that solitary pair of wings beating?
See the stream slipping
round that single dark brown leaf?
Iron in the water,
Sov-foto at dusk,
trout jumping for gnats
in apple-jelly air that never stays,
the crow soars, dips and oh
clears this icy rill
burning in the gaze
where my life trembles inside yours.

Alden Van Buskirk and Freddie Sherrill.

Afterword by Rachel Kushner

Tramping in the Byways

My connection to this book, which I first read at age 23, is primarily through the people who occupy its first hundred pages. These are individuals who had also occupied the first hundred pages or so of my own life, some as ghosts, others as flesh and blood people, all of whom loomed large to me, as they did to David Rattray, if in a different way. They are, principally: Johnny Sherrill, who Rattray introduces as a bit like Mezz Mezzrow (trans: a white man with a black man's soul), and a bit like a character who stepped from pages of Jean Genet's *Thief's Journal* (trans: a cool cat who'd been in prison); and Alden Van Buskirk, who was gifted in angelic looks and natural poetic talent, and cursed with a rare and fatal blood disease that killed him at 23. Rattray is the only person who has committed Johnny and Alden—or Van, as he was sometimes called—and the particular worlds both occupied, to print. He was not the person to whom either of them was closest, but he understood that they were special and rare individuals who deserved their slots in posterity. My link to this book is almost coincidental, deriving from the pure luck of being born to my parents (and aren't we all tired of those born lucky? Well, at least I wasn't born rich). Rattray himself would not have been keen on the idea of coincidence, a concept he would find too sober and positivist. He would, instead, read *meaning* into coincidence. And the truth is, so do I.

Rattray—as I always heard him called, and never David, nor Dave—was a friend of my father's from Dartmouth College. He was older than my father by a handful of years and they only overlapped briefly, in 1956, when my father and Alden, both freshmen, both on the ski team, met Rattray just before he fled to Paris, chasing European Bohemiana. My father and Alden had immediately bonded when they arrived at college, sharing a love of poetry and jazz and skiing. Dartmouth, in those years, had a poetry series run by Richard Eberhart, who invited the likes of Jack Hirschman, Kenneth Rexroth, Robert Creeley, W.D. Snodgrass, and I.A. Richards to read to a small group, which invariably included my father and Alden.

The year they were freshmen, Eberhart went out to San Francisco, heard Ginsberg read an early version of "Howl," and wrote about it in the *New York Times* (Eberhart also apparently advised Ginsberg to add something positive, to counterbalance the poem's litanies, which Ginsberg did, in the form of its famous footnote of "holy holy holys"). Rattray, meanwhile, went to St. Elizabeth hospital in St. Louis to interview Ezra Pound, who was, at the time, famously impounded there. Rattray was 21 years old, but even at that young age, he possessed the skill and wisdom to let Pound reveal himself, casually and naturally, without interference. Pound enveloped Rattray in a caul of solicitude, offering a long list of contacts on Provençal literature, rantings on the peril of hocking one's mansion to a Jew, and insane asylum cafeteria food, which, as Rattray figured out, Pound was providing as daily nourishment to his coterie of groupies, one of whom, "queen of the Beats" Sheri Martinelli, was busy sketching Pound as he expounded to Rattray. The exchange was written up as an uproariously funny and disturbing view into the mind and utterances of the grand old modernist, with his giant calves, which looked, to Rattray, like legs you'd see on an old sailor, "still spry from climbing the rigging," his by turns gallant and jagged manner, and his consistent champagne-flow of bigoted spew.

Rattray was from a quasi-aristocratic east coast lineage, an inheritance of perhaps a good deal of baggage and not a whole lot of dough. He "spoke prose," as my father put it, non-idiomatic formal English. His grandfather had been a whaler by profession off the coast of Long Island. His sister was an early bohemian who spent her time traveling the world by ocean liner and ran a vintage boutique on St. Mark's Place. She lived in a mansion in East Hampton. Once, while staying there, my father encountered the poet Delmore Schwartz, who was also staying there. At the time, my father was a graduate student in philosophy, which Delmore Schwartz had himself studied. They talked for three hours about J.L. Austin. On that visit, or another, Rattray took my father to see his grandfather's whaling boat, which was stored in an old commercial warehouse in Sag Harbor. It looked like a giant canoe, long and slim, with oars—no engine. A whale would have been harpooned from this little vessel, and then dragged behind it, for miles and miles, until, exhausted, it would finally expire.

The first thing I ever read of Rattray's was not the legendary "A Weekend with Ezra Pound," but what came to be the second chapter of this book, titled "Van," which begins with Rattray's introduction to Alden Van Buskirk. Rattray was fixated on Alden even before he'd met him, and a lot more so, once he had. Alden, who died in the winter of 1961, had that effect on people in his short life, and also after it. As Rattray narrates, he and Alden set out together for Mexico, "a journey to the edge of the world" in the Burroughs and Kerouac vein of drugs and discovery. They go to a place called Puerto Angel, which they chose for the name. As they lie in hammocks, Rattray imagines them in a late 19th-century engraving, with the title *Tramping in the Byways of Oaxaca*. Reading Rattray's account of him and Alden in Puerto Angel, a place they fled after ripping off the drug addicted constable, I was given an alternate view on someone I have been hearing about my

Johnny Sherrill. Photographs by Pinky Drosten Kushner.

whole life. My brother's middle name is Alden, in memoriam.[1] My mother and my father were each separately friends with Alden, and they met each other, and connected, and then had children, via their Alden-commonality, and so I more or less considered him the patron saint of my parents' common law "marriage," as well as mine and my brother's existences. We had no religion or traditions in our house. We had an assortment of characters who took up residence in our lives, and we had books, among them, Alden's posthumous collection of poetry, *Lami*, which Rattray had the dedicated ingenuity to collate and send to Allen Ginsberg, who was impressed by it enough to write an introduction and secure a publisher. Alden's "widow," Martha Muhs, was a friend and regular visitor. Johnny Sherrill was as well. Alden, to me, was a surviving trace among my parents and their friends, who had witnessed his beauty, energy, insights.

---

1. In "Harvest," Rattray says Johnny and Freddie will name their son Alden, in tribute, but this seems to be Rattray's mix-up with my brother. Johnny and Freddie's son is Gary William Sherrill, who has been our lifelong family friend.

In 1960, Alden had moved to St. Louis, where he had first encountered Jonny Sherrill, who, in "Van," is described by Rattray as a thirty-year-old ex-convict who makes his living "scamming, jamming, pimping and gambling, and doing time," and who "identified with everything that had soul." All true, except maybe the pimping. "He *wishes* he was a pimp," my mother says, when I ask her about Rattray's immortalizing of Johnny. If Johnny strutted like a pimp, it was more a citation of a pimp than a pimp-pimp. He was a trickster, not a salesman. Johnny Sherrill was a skilled machinist by trade, if also an itinerant carouser, joker, drinker, wordsmith, and lady's man. Johnny had robbed a train at the age of seventeen and gone to prison, where he learned machining. Rattray describes him as the son of migrant fruit pickers, and his mother as Native American. I remember Johnny's parents; his mother was probably Native American. I'm not sure if they picked fruit. His father was a leather tooler, and made folk art of Catholic themes that he and Johnny's mother sold at county fairs around rural parts of Northern California. We visited them once, when I was a child, in Oroville, where they were living. I remember his father's hands, huge and stained from leather tannins, and I can still visualize the inside of the house – my mother says it was a small trailer—which was filled with leather working tools.

Johnny, the son of these people who might be considered a certain creative underclass from the "weird, old, America," was himself deeply talented and Rattray knew it, and was drawn to him for something in Johnny that was a whole lot freer than anything in Rattray. Johnny was not escaping anything. He was into the honeypot of life as some natural disposition, whether living on the banks of a river, fishing and eating pilfered orchard peaches, or committing to no posterity whatsoever his "action poetry," which took the form, for instance, of pissing on someone's brand new Cadillac, parked on the streets of downtown

Saint Louis. (Once, just before my mother and Johnny entered a Goodwill thrift shop, Johnny placed his partly smoked joint on the hood of a car. As they left, he picked it up and continued to smoke it. In the early 1960s, this was, to say the least, brazen). In this way Alden and Johnny were kindred enjoyers of life. Alden, as Rattray describes him, saunters into a Mexican bordello "as if he owns the place." Rattray's admiration is not just that Alden can play it cool, but that for Alden, as he tells Rattray, the kingdom of heaven was "on earth" and "no place else." It was in a bordello, a gas station, at the soft serve window. On an outing to a carnival freakshow, Rattray marvels at Johnny's ability to "fall in with carny talk and point of view." He's watching people who possess a talent for life, people who were not seekers of the invisible, but embodied creatures whose life *was* the poem, not split off from, in Alden's case, the poetry he wrote.

Rattray was not only formally educated and intensely cerebral—fluent in French, German, Latin, and ancient Greek, he seems to have been someone for whom the world was full of mystery but like a book's mysteries, as if the world *was itself a book*, one that was crammed with tiny, secret writings. And the way to understand this book—the world—was to diligently decode it. Throughout *How I Became*, Rattray interprets people through lines of poetry: Swinburne, Keats, Stefan George, Beckett. When he encounters Pound, he interprets Pound through lines of Pound. In "Van," Alden tells Rattray that his "European esthetic standards" don't apply to "the reality of America." They argue, and Rattray leaves the Bay Area, where Alden had moved to seek a miracle cure to his illness. Rattray hitchhiked to St. Louis and moved in with Johnny, as if his failure to connect to one idol, or ideal, produced in him the commitment to do so with the other.

For Rattray, invisibility meant to take leave of the self in order to merge, or submerge, into life, to finally understand it. Some don't crave that kind of understanding. Don't need it. They are in the water, and not only do they resist interpretation of the water, they don't even call it "water." Johnny, in particular, was not decoding people, nor decodable, and instead taking his share, whether he had to poach it or grift it, or earn it, or whether it simply fell in his lap. When he and Rattray outrun the police and end up at the home of a drunk whose wife pours their bag of fried pig's snouts into a serving bowl, the environment, this woman, her tired resignation, the plastic on all the furniture in the place, is notable to Rattray, and recorded beautifully, but *foreign*. Johnny is his emissary into streams of American life. And the first instance of Rattray's transition to what he calls invisibility takes place while standing watch over the wild marijuana he and Johnny are attempting to harvest, along a riverbottom outside Kansas City. As if what Rattray called invisibility was pursued under Johnny's aegis.

In the years just before I was born, my mother and father lived in North St. Louis, near Johnny and Freddie, and later, after they left St. Louis in a converted school bus that Johnny convinced them to buy, to move West, we returned to St. Louis in the summers, which was how I got to know Freddie and the world of Labadie Avenue, which Rattray portrays in this book. I remember Johnny and Freddie's son Gary and my brother setting off fireworks on summer nights, and no one in that neighborhood minding. My mother tells of a fourth of July when Johnny shot his gun out the door, in a celebratory impulse, but forgot to open the screen, and put a hole in it. Freddie's father, Daddy Quinn, was a preacher whose outdoor congregation was not always visible to the rest of us. Sometimes he preached to the rows of empty automobile bench-seats that he'd arranged in the side yard of the family's house. I remember understanding that his quirks were allowed, as if his family, and the people around those parts, let him be who he was. No one said anything. It was all dealt with incredibly gently. Around the old car seats were crosses nailed to all the trees, to keep evil spirits away. Daddy Quinn had speakers mounted on the bumpers of his truck, and he drove up and down Labadie Avenue preaching the amplified word to people gathered on their stoops, to the air, to whomever. I remember hearing him from inside the house, which was always very dark—perhaps people were careful not to waste electricity, or maybe it was shut off, I'm not sure—as I sat in the parlor with Freddie's mother, Ma Dear, and a bunch of other relatives, eating White Castle hamburgers. I had been told that White Castle was racist and that we didn't eat their burgers on account of it, but there I was in a house full of black people enjoying them. These are things you remember. Lessons you draw, even if you never find out what the lesson was. Freddie's great-grandmother, who had been born, as Rattray points out, before the Civil War had ended, lived in the house. She must have been almost 110 when I knew her. Rattray identifies the women in that world as prostitutes, but like Johnny's pimping, this is another balloon my mother pricks, but differently, explaining that it wasn't a label you would use for anyone in North St. Louis, but rather, a realm in which many women, by necessity, supplemented their income on the side.

While she was still young and beautiful, Freddie Sherrill died of a heart attack. The house was burned down by a wayward grandchild who knocked wanting money from Ma Dear and was refused entry. Many of the housing lots in North St. Louis have returned to the prairie, leaving grass and traces of foundation. Johnny had long before drifted West and worked as a machinist up in Washington State. Later he worked in the ship yards in San Francisco, where he showed off to us the "pimp coat" he'd made for himself, by hand. Did Johnny know that Rattray, whom Johnny once introduced to his parole officer as an instructor at Harvard, would later immortalize him, in this book, as an *actual* pimp? Johnny was an unclassifiable character—perhaps ultimately unreadable to anyone who might be believably presented to a parole officer as a Harvard instructor. (Rattray was doing graduate studies there. Nevertheless, the officer told Johnny that Rattray looked "mighty strange.")

When Johnny catches a fish in the shallows where he and Rattray are harvesting weed, he says to the fish, "aren't you a deep goodie." This is pure Johnny and I can hear him say it. And the situations are pure Johnny—picking up, by accident, an outlaw hitchhiker who had just killed his family. Introducing Alden to the Harlem Club across the Mississippi, in East Saint Louis, where Alden is seduced by a transgender beauty. My father tells a story of a night out with Johnny at the Harlem Club, when the couple in the next booth over, a dapper and quite elderly black gentleman and a nubile teenage girl, white, obviously working as an escort, asked the club photographer to take their picture for hire. (The Harlem Club was notably a place that did not discriminate). Just before the flashbulb went off, Johnny turned around and put his head between this couple. Photobombing avant la lettre. The photo was developed on-site, and delivered to them in the booth. The girl was very pleased and proud, even despite Johnny's ghostly face between her and her date.

The Harlem Club, which was just beyond a stockyard and right up against the railroad tracks, had a giant neon sign of a waiter holding a cocktail. In 1967, my parents went back to the site of the club. It had been razed earlier that year. On the ground, my father found a piece of its famous neon sign and picked it up. He still has it somewhere. I'd like to see it, but would it tell me about the Harlem Club? Certainly not.

Sources

Grateful acknowledgment is made for portions of this book that have appeared in somewhat different form in the following:

"Lightning Over the Treasury," in *lift* 10 (1992), also in an earlier version in *Intrepid* (1971); "Van," in BOMB (Summer 1992); "The Angel," in *Now Time 3* (1992); "West From Napeague," in *Opening the Eyelid* (1991) and in *Giants Play Well in the Drizzle* 18 (1988); "Family Business," in BOMB (Winter 1985); "The Darkened Chamber," in *Just Another Asshole* 7 (1987); "French Film Friends," in *Idiolects* 9–10 (1980–81); "Difficult Life," introduction to *Difficult Death*, by René Crevel, North Point, 1986; "Roger Gilbert-Lecomte," in *Chemical Imbalance* Vol. 2, #3 (1992); "Honey-Winged Song," in *The East Hampton Star* 10/27/88; "Nelligan," in *American Letters & Commentary* 2 (1987); "A Basic Document," in *Temblor* 10 (1989); "In Nomine," in *Conjunctions* 16 (1991), and, in short version, in *Giants Play Well in the Drizzle* 25 (1990); "Translating Artaud," in Chris Kraus's video, *Foolproof Illusion*, including the Artaud poem "Workman's Hand, Monkey Hand," which appeared in *Artaud Anthology* (edited by Jack Hirschman, City Lights, 1965); "How I Became One of the Invisible," in *Conjunctions* 18 (1992).

David Rattray (1946–1993) was a poet, translator, and scholar, fluent in most Western languages, Sanskrit, Latin, and Greek. He translated the works of Antonin Artaud, René Crevel, and Roger Gilbert-Lecomte, among others.

Chris Kraus is the author of four novels, including *I Love Dick* and *Summer of Hate*; two books of art and cultural criticism; and most recently, *After Kathy Acker: A Literary Biography*. She received the College Art Association's Frank Jewett Mather Award in Art Criticism in 2008, and a Warhol Foundation Art Writing grant in 2011. She lives in Los Angeles.

Robert Dewhurst is a scholar and poet. He holds a PhD in English from the University at Buffalo (SUNY), where he participated in the Buffalo Poetics Program. With Joshua Beckman and CAConrad, he coedited *Supplication: Selected Poems of John Wieners* (Wave Books, 2015). He teaches writing at Columbia University and lives in Los Angeles, where he is currently writing a biography of Wieners.

Rachel Kushner is the bestselling author of *The Flamethrowers*, a finalist for the National Book Award and a *New York Times* Top Ten Book of 2013; *Telex from Cuba*, a finalist for the National Book Award; and *The Mars Room*, a finalist for the Man Booker Prize and the National Book Critics Award. She lives in Los Angeles.